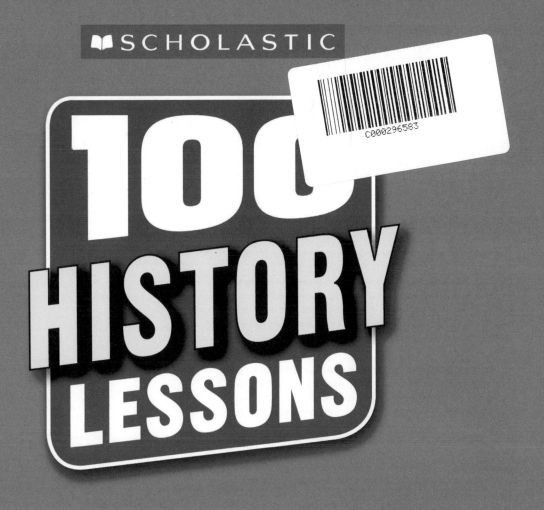

SCHOLASTIC

100 HISTORY LESSONS

C000296583

Terms and conditions

IMPORTANT – PERMITTED USE AND WARNINGS – READ CAREFULLY BEFORE USING

IF YOU ACCEPT THE ABOVE CONDITIONS YOU MAY PROCEED TO USE THE CD-ROM.

Recommended system requirements:

- Windows: XP (Service Pack 3), Vista (Service Pack 2), Windows 7 or Windows 8 with 2.33GHz processor
- Mac: OS 10.6 to 10.8 with Intel Core™ Duo processor
- GB RAM (recommended)
- 24 x 768 Screen resolution
- ROM drive (24x speed recommended)
- bit sound card
- e Reader (version 9 recommended for Mac users)
- band internet connections (for installation and updates)

nical support queries, please phone Scholastic Customer Services on 0845 6039091.

SCHOLASTIC

Book End, Range Road, Witney, Oxfordshire, OX29 0YD
www.scholastic.co.uk
© 2014, Scholastic Ltd

1 2 3 4 5 6 7 8 9   4 5 6 7 8 9 0 1 2 3

British Library Cataloguing-in-Publication Data
A catalogue record for this book is available from the
British Library.

ISBN 978-1407-12854-2
Printed by Bell & Bain Ltd, Glasgow

Due to the nature of the web we cannot guarantee the
content or links of any site mentioned. We strongly
recommend that teachers check websites before using
them in the classroom.

Extracts from *The National Curriculum in English, History
Programme of Study* © **Crown Copyright**. Reproduced
under the terms of the Open Government Licence
(OGL). http://www.nationalarchives.gov.uk/doc/open-
government-licence/open-government-licence.htm

Author
Christina You

Editorial team
Jenny Wilcox, Rachel Morgan, Kate Soar, Vicky Butt and
Margaret Eaton

Cover Design
Andrea Lewis

Design
Neil Salt

CD-ROM development
Hannah Barnett, Phil Crothers, MWA Technologies
Private Ltd

illustrations
Moreno Chiaccheira

Acknowledgements
Every effort has been made to trace copyright
holders for the works reproduced in this book,
and the publishers apologise for any inadvertent
omissions.

SCHO
www.schol

Contents

Introduction

The *100 History Lessons* series is designed to meet the requirements of the 2014 Curriculum, History Programmes of Study. There are three books in the series, Years 1–2, 3–4 and 5–6, and each book contains lesson plans, resources and ideas matched to the new curriculum. It can be a complex task to ensure that a progressive and appropriate curriculum is followed in all year groups; this series has been carefully structured to ensure that a progressive and appropriate curriculum is followed throughout.

About the new curriculum

The 2014 National Curriculum for Key Stages 1 and 2 explains the purpose and aims of history as follows: *A high-quality history education will help pupils gain a coherent knowledge and understanding of Britain's past and that of the wider world. It should inspire pupils' curiosity to know more about the past. Teaching should equip pupils to ask perceptive questions, think critically, weigh evidence, sift arguments, and develop perspective and judgement. History helps pupils to understand the complexity of people's lives, the process of change, the diversity of societies and relationships between different groups, as well as their own identity and the challenges of their time.*

The National Curriculum for History aims to ensure that all children:
- *know and understand the history of these islands as a coherent, chronological narrative, from the earliest times to the present day: how people's lives have shaped this nation and how Britain has influenced and been influenced by the wider world*
- *know and understand significant aspects of the history of the wider world: the nature of ancient civilisations; the expansion and dissolution of empires; characteristic features of past non-European societies; achievements and follies of mankind*
- *gain and deploy a historically grounded understanding of abstract terms such as 'empire', 'civilisation', 'parliament' and 'peasantry'*
- *understand historical concepts such as continuity and change, cause and consequence, similarity, difference and significance, and use them to make connections, draw contrasts, analyse trends, frame historically valid questions and create their own structured accounts, including written narratives and analyses*
- *understand the methods of historical enquiry, including how evidence is used rigorously to make historical claims, and discern how and why contrasting arguments and interpretations of the past have been constructed*
- *gain historical perspective by placing their growing knowledge into different contexts, understanding the connections between local, regional, national and international history; between cultural, economic, military, political, religious and social history; and between short- and long-term timescales.*

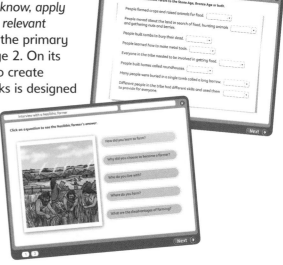

The curriculum goes on to state that *children are expected to know, apply and understand the matters, skills and processes specified in the relevant Programme of Study.* There are two Programmes of Study in the primary history curriculum: one for Key Stage 1 and one for Key Stage 2. On its own, the content of the programmes of study is insufficient to create exciting and effective learning experiences. This series of books is designed to help provide guidance and support for schools and teachers, through a coherent, challenging, engaging and enjoyable scheme of work.

Terminology
- **Curriculum objectives:** These are the statutory programme of study statements or objectives.

About the book

This book is divided into twelve chapters; six for each year group. Each chapter contains a half-term's work and is based around a topic or theme. Each chapter follows the same structure:

Chapter introduction

At the start of each chapter there is a summary of what is covered. This includes:

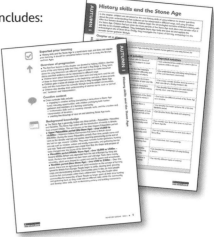

- **Introduction:** A description of what is covered in the chapter.
- **Chapter at a glance:** This is a table that summarises the content of each lesson, including: the curriculum objectives, a summary of the activities and the outcome.
- **Expected prior learning:** What the children are expected to know before starting the work in the chapter.
- **Overview of progression:** A brief explanation of how the children progress through the chapter.
- **Creative context:** How the chapter could link to other curriculum areas.
- **Background knowledge:** A section explaining grammatical terms and suchlike to enhance your subject knowledge, where required.

Lessons

Each chapter contains six weeks' of lessons, each week contains two lessons. At the start of each week there is an introduction about what is covered. The lesson plans then include the relevant combination of headings from below.

- **Lesson objectives:** Objectives that are based upon the Curriculum objectives, but are more specific broken-down steps to achieve them.
- **Expected outcomes:** What you should expect all, most and some children to know by the end of the lesson.
- **Resources:** What you require to teach the lesson.
- **Introduction:** A short and engaging activity to begin the lesson.

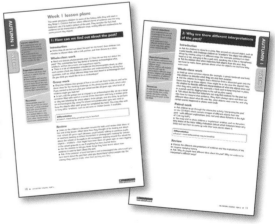

- **Whole-class work:** Working together as a class.
- **Group/Paired/Independent work:** Children working independently of the teacher in pairs, groups or alone.
- **Differentiation:** Ideas for how to support children who are struggling with a concept or how to extend those children who understand a concept without taking them onto new work.
- **Review:** A chance to review the children's learning and ensure the outcomes of the lesson have been achieved.

Assess and review

At the end of each chapter are activities for assessing and reviewing the children's understanding. These can be conducted at the end of the chapter or at a later date. They all follow the same format:

- **Curriculum objectives:** These are the areas of focus for the assess and review activity.
- **Resources:** What you require to conduct the activities.
- **Revise:** A series of short activities or one longer activity to revise and consolidate the children's learning and ensure they understand the concept(s).
- **Assess:** An assessment activity to provide a chance for the children to demonstrate their understanding and for you to check this.
- **Further practice:** Ideas for further practice on the focus, whether children are insecure in their learning or you want to provide extra practice or challenge.

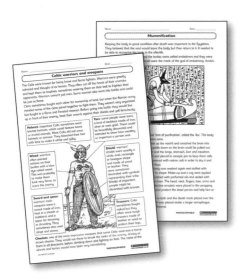

Photocopiable pages

At the end of each chapter are some photocopiable pages that will have been referred to in the lesson plans. These sheets are for the children to use. There is generally a title, an instruction, an activity and an 'I can' statement at the bottom. The children should be encouraged to complete the 'I can' statements by colouring in the traffic lights to say how they think they have done (red – not very well, amber – ok, green – very well).

These sheets are also provided on the CD-ROM alongside additional pages as referenced in the lessons (see page 7 About the CD-ROM).

About the CD-ROM

The CD-ROM contains:

- Printable versions of the photocopiable sheets from the book and additional photocopiable sheets as referenced in the lesson plans.
- Interactive activities for children to complete or to use on the whiteboard.
- Media resources to display.
- Printable versions of the lesson plans.
- Digital versions of the lesson plans with the relevant resources linked to them.

Getting started

Put the CD-ROM into your CD-ROM drive.

- For Windows users, the install wizard should autorun, if it fails to do so then navigate to your CD-ROM drive. Then follow the installation process.
- For Mac users, copy the disk image file to your hard drive. After it has finished copying double-click it to mount the disk image. Navigate to the mounted disk image and run the installer. After installation the disk image can be unmounted and the DMG can be deleted from the hard drive.
- To complete the installation of the program you need to open the program and click 'Update' in the pop-up. Please note – this CD-ROM is web-enabled and the content will be downloaded from the internet to your hard-drive to populate the CD-ROM with the relevant resources. This only needs to be done on first use, after this you will be able to use the CD-ROM without an internet connection. If at any point any content is updated you will receive another pop-up upon start up with an internet connection.

Navigating the CD-ROM

There are two options to navigate the CD-ROM either as a Child or as a Teacher.

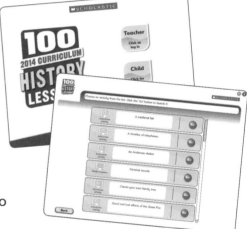

Child

- Click on the 'Child' button on the first menu screen.
- In the second menu click on the relevant class (please note only the books installed on the machine or network will be accessible. You can also rename year groups to match your school's naming conventions via the Teacher > Settings > Rename books area).
- A list of interactive activities will be displayed, children need to locate the correct one and click 'Go' to launch it.
- There is the opportunity to print or save a PDF of the activity at the end.

Teacher

- Click on the Teacher button on the first menu screen and you will be taken to a screen showing which of the 100 History books you have purchased. From here, you can also access information about getting started and the credits.
- To enter the product click 'Next' in the bottom right.
- You then need to enter a password (the password is: login).
  - On first use: Enter as a Guest by clicking on the 'Guest' button.
  - If desired, create a profile for yourself by adding your name to the list of users. Profiles allow you to save favourites and to specify which year group(s) you wish to be able to view.
  - Go to 'Settings' to create a profile for yourself – click 'Add user' and enter your name. Then choose the year groups you wish to have access to (you can return to this screen to change this at any time). Click on 'Login' at the top of the screen to re-enter the disk under your new profile.
- On subsequent uses you can choose your name from the drop-down list. The 'Guest' option will always be available if you, or a colleague, wish to use this.
- You can search the CD-ROM using the tools or save favourites.

For more information about how to use the CD-ROM, please refer to the help file which can be found in the teacher area of the CD-ROM. It is a red button with a question mark on it on the right-hand side of the screen just underneath the 'Settings' tab.

History skills and the Stone Age

In this chapter, children are introduced to the core history skills of using evidence to answer questions about the past, understanding that evidence can be interpreted in different ways, and using timelines. After four lessons devoted to these skills, children begin the chronological narrative of Britain's history with the Stone Age. Children find out when the three periods of the Stone Age took place and consider what it was like to be a hunter-gatherer. They investigate Stone Age tools and cave art and explore the archaeological site of Skara Brae. Finally, they investigate the impact of farming, comparing it to the nomadic hunter-gatherer lifestyle.

Chapter at a glance

Curriculum objectives

• Changes in Britain from the Stone Age to the Iron Age, including late Neolithic hunter-gatherers and early farmers, for example Skara Brae.

Week	Lesson	Summary of activities	Expected outcomes
1	1	• Children read about different forms of historical evidence and engage in a mock archaeological dig.	• Can understand how evidence is used to give us a picture of life in the past.
	2	• Children discuss the fact that historians interpret evidence of the past differently and write contrasting descriptions of objects.	• Can understand why contrasting interpretations of the past have been constructed.
2	1	• Children see an example of a short-term timeline and create a timeline of their own life.	• Can create a simple timeline showing events in their own life or a family member's life.
	2	• Children see an example of a long-term timeline and arrange periods of British history in order.	• Can describe how timelines are used and can identify short- and long-term timescales.
3	1	• Children read about the periods of the Stone Age and use an interactive tool to create a Stone Age timeline.	• Can locate the different periods of the Stone Age on a timeline.
	2	• Children write a story ending about a Neolithic hunter-gatherer.	• Can describe the hunter-gatherer life of the late Neolithic period.
4	1	• Children look at and sketch examples of tools and weapons from the different periods of the Stone Age.	• Can describe Stone Age tools and weaponry.
	2	• Children use websites about Skara Brae to ask, and find evidence for, a historically valid question.	• Can consider how Skara Brae gives us a picture of Stone Age life.
5	1	• Children use websites about Skara Brae to ask, and find evidence for, a historically valid question.	• Can use online information to write facts about Skara Brae.
	2	• Children look at examples of Palaeolithic cave art from Creswell Crags before creating their own artwork.	• Can create their own cave paintings.
6	1	• Children role play members of a Neolithic farming community, considering how farming allowed people to develop different skills.	• Can describe the development of early farming in Britain.
	2	• Children form 'tribes' and discuss whether a hunter-gatherer or farming lifestyle would be better.	• Can identify different types of evidence.
Assess and review		• To review the half-term's work.	

Expected prior learning

- History skills and the Stone Age is a stand-alone topic and does not require prior learning. It should be completed before moving on to study the Bronze and Iron Ages.

Overview of progression

- The first four lessons in this chapter are devoted to helping children develop some of the core history skills that they will need in Key Stage 2. They learn about the way historians use different types of evidence to make historical claims and that evidence can be interpreted in different ways.
- Children learn about timescales both short term and long term and the use of these to show important events or the beginnings and ends of time periods.
- Children gain a sense of change over time as they investigate Stone Age tools and the move from the nomadic lifestyle towards settled communities.
- Children also develop their understanding of abstract terms, such as 'period', 'era', 'evidence' and 'interpretation'.

Creative context

- Cross-curricular links include:
  - engaging in creative writing (completing a story about a Stone Age hunt); role-play opportunities, with children portraying both hunter-gatherers and members of a farming community;
  - mathematics skills such as counting, intervals, scale, and the creation and interpretation of timelines;
  - creating line drawings of cave art and sketching Stone Age tools.

Background knowledge

- The Stone Age is generally broken into three periods – Palaeolithic, Mesolithic and Neolithic. The Stone Age ended with the introduction of metals to Britain, from around 2300BC. This unit focuses on the later (Upper) Palaeolithic period.
- **Upper Palaeolithic period (Old Stone Age) – circa 45,000 to 10,000BC –** Historians believe that humans first came to Britain about 800,000BC (during the Lower Palaeolithic period). Over time, people came and went as the climate warmed and cooled, returning permanently at the end of the last ice age, around 12,000BC. They were nomadic hunter-gatherers, hunting animals such as reindeer, wolves and woolly mammoths, and gathering berries and nuts. Tools and weapons were made from flint; the shape and purpose of tools changed over the course of the Stone Age.
- **Mesolithic period (Middle Stone Age) – circa 10,000 to 4500BC –** Around 6000BC Britain was separated from the rest of Europe by rising sea levels. Hunters now stalked red deer, bears and wild pigs. Tools were mainly microliths, which were shaped to a point and used for spears and arrowheads.
- **Neolithic period (New Stone Age) – circa 4500 to 2300BC –** Over this period, there was an agricultural and social revolution as the concept of farming spread to Britain from Europe. People began to settle, clearing land, growing crops and domesticating animals. Communities grew in size, as more people could be fed, and people within them collaborated. They also fought other communities for ownership of land. People no longer spent all their time hunting and gathering food, so they could take on different roles within the community and develop other skills, such as decorating pottery and building monuments.

Week 1 lesson plans

This week introduces children to some of the history skills they will need in Key Stage 2. Children find out about different forms of evidence and the way historians use it to build a picture of the past. They consider the fact that evidence can be interpreted in different ways, writing different explanations for some present day objects.

1: How can we find out about the past?

Introduction

● Write *How do we find out about the past?* on the board. Give children two minutes to discuss ideas with a talk partner, and then discuss as a class.

Whole-class work

● Read and discuss photocopiable page 23 'How do we find out about the past?' This summarises four key forms of evidence: archaeological sites, artefacts, written documents and eyewitness reports.
● There is a lot of information included on the photocopiable sheet, so after each section check the children's attention and understanding by asking key questions, such as: *What different things have been found at archaeological sites? Do you think you would like to be an archaeologist?*

Group work

● Organise children into groups of five or six and ask them to discuss and write down ideas for the thinking challenge on the photocopiable sheet, which asks: *If you wanted to find out what your school was like 20 years ago, what kinds of evidence might you look for?*
● In turn, call the groups out to engage in an archaeological dig: set up a large container filled with sand in a corner of the classroom and bury a broken plate or clay pot (checking for sharp edges). Invite groups, one at a time, to perform an archaeological dig, using the trowel and paintbrushes (you will need to bury the objects after each group has completed the task). You may also wish to bury other 'artefacts', such as old coins or chicken bones, if available.

> **Differentiation**
> ● Support: mixed-ability groupings may be beneficial.

Review

● Listen to the children's discussion around the tasks and review their ideas at the end of the lesson. What ideas have they thought of for finding out about their school 20 years ago? (Answers could include: talking to previous pupils or teachers; looking at school newsletters or photographs; looking for articles about the school or its pupils in old newspapers; looking around the school for objects – artefacts – that might have been there 20 years ago; or even digging in the school grounds to see if anything has been buried there.
● Ask the children to tell you three things they have learnt about how evidence is used to learn about the past.
● Ask: *If the container of sand had been a real archaeological site, what could you have learnt about the past from what you found there?* (what people ate; the money they used to trade; what their pottery was like).

Lesson objectives
● To understand how our knowledge of the past is constructed from a range of sources.
● To understand that different versions of past events may exist, giving some reasons for this.

Expected outcomes
● All children will know that evidence is used to find out about the past.
● Most children will describe at least one type of evidence used to learn about the past.
● Some children will describe different types of evidence used to learn about the past.

Resources
Photocopiable page 23 'How do we find out about the past?'; a large container filled with sand; artefacts to bury in the sand, such as a broken plate or clay pot (check for sharp edges), coins, clean chicken bones; a trowel and a paintbrushes

Lesson objectives
● To understand how our knowledge of the past is constructed from a range of sources.
● To understand that different versions of past events may exist, giving some reasons for this.

Expected outcomes
● All children will know that the past can be interpreted in different ways.
● Most children will suggest why the past can be interpreted in different ways.
● Some children will consider the implications of different interpretations of the past.

Resources
A collection of objects (such as pool noodle, fork, comb, pencil); interactive activity 'Interpreting the past' on the CD-ROM

2: Why are there different interpretations of the past?

Introduction
● Ask the children to stand in a circle. Pass around an unusual object, such as a pool noodle, and challenge children to 'transform' the object into different things by miming using it in different ways (for example, putting it on their head as a hat, swinging it like a golf stick, speaking into it like a microphone).
● Tell the children that when historians find objects from the past, they too have to make clever guesses about what the objects are and how they were used.

Whole-class work
● Hold up some common objects (for example, a pencil, hairbrush and fork). Ask children to describe what they are and their purpose.
● Ask the children to imagine that a historian from a thousand years into the future has dug up these objects. How might he or she view the objects? Help the children to describe different interpretations of what the objects were and what they were used for (for example, a fork used to keep long hair in place, or a pencil used for digging holes in the soil to plant seeds).
● Talk about the fact that historians not only find evidence for the past but also have to interpret that evidence. They don't always agree and there are different ideas about what life was like, what objects were used for, and why certain events happened or places were built.

Paired work
● Ask children to go through the interactive activity 'Interpreting the past' on the CD-ROM, which contains images of different objects from the past with different explanations (one real and others fictional, in the style of 'Call my bluff').
● You may wish to show children a 'mysterious' artefact, such as the priest king statue of the Indus Valley civilisation (about which historians know very little) and ask them to come up with their own stories about it.

Differentiation
● Support: mixed-ability pairings may be beneficial.

Review
● Discuss the different interpretations of evidence and the implications of this for anyone studying history.
● Ask: *Why do people have different ideas about the past? Why can evidence be interpreted in different ways?*

Week 2 lesson plans

This week children are introduced to timelines. They look at examples of short- and long-term timelines and create a timeline of their own life. They then arrange periods of British history in chronological order.

1: How are timelines used? (1)

Introduction

- Write or print five events from your life and corresponding dates in large lettering on separate sheets of A4 paper (for example, birth, going to primary school, going to secondary school, leaving home, first year of teaching, getting married).
- Give a sheet each to five children and ask them to come to the front and hold up the events. As a class, discuss the events and arrange them in chronological order.

Whole-class work

- Read and discuss the introduction to timelines on photocopiable page 24 'Timelines (1)'.
- As a class, talk through some events that children see as important in their own lives (for example, birth, birth of a sibling, going to school, starting dance lessons, winning a trophy).
- Create a list of milestones on the board.

Independent work

- Ask the children to create a basic timeline of their own lives (see differentiation below).
- Some children might need help remembering when certain events occurred. Children could be briefed in advance to clarify events and years/dates with their parent or guardian, or even bring in photographs of the events to include on their timeline.
- The children could draw neat copies of their timelines on sheets of paper, and include illustrations, for a class display.

Differentiation
- Timeline complexity can be differentiated according to the child's ability.
- Support: children can write or draw three events and place them in order.
- Challenge: children might include up to ten events from either their own or a relative's life and should aim to show an idea of scale along the timeline.

Review
- Check the accuracy of the children's timelines in terms of ordering of events and scale.
- Some children could present their timeline to the rest of the class.

Lesson objectives
- To develop the appropriate use of historical terms.
- To construct informed responses that involve thoughtful selection and organisation of relevant historical information.
- To gain historical perspective by placing their growing knowledge into different contexts, understanding the connections between short- and long-term timescales.

Expected outcomes
- All children will order events from their life on a timeline.
- Most children will create a basic timeline of their own life.
- Some children will create a detailed timeline of their own or a relative's life.

Resources
Photocopiable page 24 'Timelines (1)'; A4 paper; photographs of important life events (optional)

Lesson objectives
● To develop the appropriate use of historical terms.
● To construct informed responses that involve thoughtful selection and organisation of relevant historical information.
● To gain historical perspective by placing their growing knowledge into different contexts, understanding the connections between short- and long-term timescales.

Expected outcomes
● All children will put at least three periods from British history in order.
● Most children will put several periods from British history in order.
● Some children will create a timeline showing several periods from British history that includes a scale.

Resources
Photocopiable page 25 'Timelines (2)'; scissors

2. How are timelines used? (2)

Introduction
● Recap the different types of evidence used to find out about the past. Ask: *If we wanted to find out about the history of this community/area what would we do?* (Suggestions might include: read old newspapers; talk to elderly residents; look at the registers of births, deaths and marriages; carry out an archaeological dig.)

Whole-class work
● Read and discuss photocopiable page 25 'Timelines (2)', which includes a timeline of some events in prehistory, as well as an activity for sequencing later events in history.
● Optionally, ask children to choose a favourite event from the past and create a timeline for it. This could be an event from their personal lives (for example, a week's holiday with family) or they could research an event from history and the events that led up to it (for example, a favourite football team's performance in the FA Cup).

Paired work or Independent work
● Organise children into groups and ask them to cut out the date cards on the photocopiable sheet and arrange them in chronological order.
● Ask the children to research a specific aspect of each of the time periods, such as costume, food, music or leisure activities (optional).

Differentiation
● Organising children into groups of similar ability may be beneficial as the task could then be differentiated (provide more or fewer cards to order according to the children's confidence).
● Support: less confident learners could work with adult support to place three or four periods in order; children of middle ability could work in pairs to order the time periods.
● Challenge: more confident learners could work in a group to create a large timeline on one of the classroom walls, creating an appropriate scale and marking in where each period began and ended.

Review
● Check the accuracy of the children's timelines or ordering of events.
● Ask some children to present their timeline to the rest of the class or group.

Week 3 lesson plans

This week, children are introduced to the topic of the Stone Age, reading about when the three periods of the Stone Age occurred and using an interactive tool to create a Stone Age timeline. They then consider what it was like to be a Neolithic hunter-gatherer, reading a story starter and continuing the narrative to reveal what happened during the narrator's first hunt.

1: When was the Stone Age?

Introduction

● Tell the children that they are going to be finding out what life was like for very early humans in Britain. Explain that hunter-gatherer people would have moved from place to place, depending on the season and the food available.
● Resources can be found online to introduce the Stone Age way of life, such as a short cartoon on the BBC's 'Hands on history/ancient Britain' web page, which shows a hunter-gatherer family moving to its winter camp.

Whole-class work

● Read and discuss the photocopiable page 'The Stone Age' from the CD-ROM, which gives an overview of the dates and events of the three stages of the Stone Age (Old, Middle and New).
● Show the children how to use the interactive activity 'Timeline maker' on the CD-ROM, by referring to the photocopiable sheet and adding the start and end dates of the Neolithic period.

Group work or Paired work

● Organise children into small groups or pairs. Ask the children to use the timeline tool to create their own Stone Age timelines, using the information on the photocopiable sheet.
● The timelines can be printed out for display.

Differentiation
● Support: less confident learners could work with an adult to add the Neolithic period to the timeline.
● Challenge: more confident learners could add all three periods and discuss their relative lengths and characteristics. Ask: *Why might the length of time during the Stone Age make it difficult to create one timeline to show all three of its periods?* (There wouldn't be room on the paper, or it would have to be written so small it would not be legible.)

Review

● Ask children to swap their completed timelines with a partner and to check each other's work.
● Look at a completed timeline as a class and ask children to correct their work if necessary.

Lesson objectives

● To understand the changes in Britain from the Stone Age to the Iron Age, including late Neolithic hunter-gatherers and early farmers.
● To develop a chronologically secure knowledge and understanding of British, local and world history, establishing clear narratives within and across the periods they study.
● To develop the appropriate use of historical terms.

Expected outcomes

● All children will place the Neolithic age on a timeline.
● Most children will place the periods of the Stone Age on a timeline.
● Some children will compare the periods of the Stone Age on a timeline.

Resources

Internet access; photocopiable page 'The Stone Age' from the CD-ROM; interactive activity 'Timeline maker' on the CD-ROM

Lesson objectives
● To understand the changes in Britain from the Stone Age to the Iron Age, including late Neolithic hunter-gatherers and early farmers.
● To develop a chronologically secure knowledge and understanding of British, local and world history, establishing clear narratives within and across the periods they study.
● To develop the appropriate use of historical terms.

Expected outcomes
● All children will describe one aspect of life as a Stone Age hunter-gatherer.
● Most children will continue a story about the life of a hunter-gatherer.
● Some children will continue and reflect on a story about the life of a hunter-aatherer.

Resources
Photocopiable page 'Hunter-gatherer' from the CD-ROM; media resource 'Hunter-gatherer audio' on the CD-ROM

2: What was it like to be a Neolithic hunter-gatherer?

Introduction
● Ask children to look out the window, or take them outside. Ask: *What is here that would not have been here in the Stone Age? What would have been here at that time?*

Whole-class work
● Read and discuss photocopiable page 'Hunter-gatherer' from the CD-ROM, which contains the opening of a fictional account of a Stone Age girl.
● If the weather is warm enough, find an outside location to read the story starter on the photocopiable sheet, so that children feel more in tune with the natural world of the people in the story.
● In the media resource 'Hunter-gatherer audio' on the CD-ROM, a narrator reads the story starter; this could be used instead of it being teacher-read.

Independent work
● Ask children to complete the activity challenge, imagining that they are the narrator in the story, on her first hunt.
● Explain to the children that they should continue the story, writing about what happens during the hunt. They should think about what they hear, see and smell in the natural world around them.
● Ask the children the following additional questions to stimulate their writing: *How do you think the narrator feels about the hunt?* (Possible answers could include: scared, excited, nervous, and so on.) *What kinds of animals might they hope to catch?* (Deer, wild boar, wild cattle, elk.) *What might happen next – to the narrator and the other hunters? Is their hunt successful or do they run into more danger?*

Differentiation
● Support: less confident learners may wish to draw a picture and write a caption to illustrate the end of the story.
● Challenge: more confident children should produce an exciting narrative, reflecting the feelings of the main character and an appropriate Stone Age setting.

Review
● Ask some children to share their stories.
● Check that the children's narratives are appropriate for the Stone Age setting, for example in terms of tools, clothing and lifestyle.

Week 4 lesson plans

This week children look at pictures of Stone Age tools and discuss how they and their purposes changed over the three Stone Age periods. They sketch a Neolithic tool and think about how it might have been used by hunter-gatherers and farmers. Children then find out about the archaeological site of Skara Brae on the Orkney Islands, using websites to explore the area and its artefacts. They use evidence to answer their own historically valid questions about life in the Stone Age village.

Lesson objectives
● To understand the changes in Britain from the Stone Age to the Iron Age, including late Neolithic hunter-gatherers and early farmers.
● To develop a chronologically secure knowledge and understanding of British, local and world history, establishing clear narratives within and across the periods they study.
● To develop the appropriate use of historical terms.
● To understand how our knowledge of the past is constructed from a range of sources.
● To understand that different versions of past events may exist, giving some reasons for this.

Expected outcomes
● All children will describe at least one Stone Age tool.
● Most children will describe several Stone Age tools.
● Some children will describe how tools changed over the different periods of the Stone Age.

Resources
Internet access; a piece of flint (optional); drawing materials

1: What tools and weapons were used in the Stone Age?

Introduction
● Ask: *Why might people in the Stone Age have needed tools and weapons? What would they be used for?*
● Discuss the children's ideas, including both hunter-gatherers and farmers in the Neolithic period.

Whole-class work
● Show children some pictures of Stone Age tools; for example the website: www.stonehengetools.co.uk includes examples of tools from each period in the Stone Age.
● Ask: *What are the tools made from? Why was this material chosen? How did the tools used change over time?* (Tools moved from hand axes to throwing weapons, such as spears and arrows, and then became increasingly culturally diverse.) *Why did they change?* (People became more skilled at making tools, and different types of tool were needed with the move from hunting to farming.) *Why were different tools needed – what types of tool might a hunter need compared with a farmer?*
● If available, hand around a piece of flint and ask children to describe it. Write a list of suitable adjectives on the board.

Independent work
● Ask the children to sketch a tool from the Neolithic period and write bullet points to describe it and show how it might have been used.

Differentiation
● Drawings and bullet points can be basic or more detailed.
● Challenge: more confident learners could draw a labelled tool from each period of the Stone Age and include notes to compare them.

Review
● Organise children to work in groups of four to six.
● They should present their labelled drawings to each other.
● Ask some children to present their work to the class. The rest of the class should listen to see if there is any information they could add.
● Check that they include information on the material used to make the tool and its purpose.

Lesson objectives
- To understand the changes in Britain from the Stone Age to the Iron Age, including late Neolithic hunter-gatherers and early farmers, such as Skara Brae.
- To develop a chronologically secure knowledge and understanding of British, local and world history, establishing clear narratives within and across the periods they study.
- To develop the appropriate use of historical terms.
- To understand how our knowledge of the past is constructed from a range of sources.
- To understand that different versions of past events may exist, giving some reasons for this.

Expected outcomes
- All children will describe at least one fact about Skara Brae.
- Most children will describe life in Skara Brae.
- Some children will describe how Skara Brae has been used to learn about the past.

Resources
Internet access; atlas or map

2: What does Skara Brae tell us about Stone Age life? (1)

Introduction
- Use an atlas or online map to locate the Orkney Islands and Skara Brae in comparison with the rest of the United Kingdom. Ask: *Why might people have chosen this location for a settlement?*
- There are many introductory interactive resources are available online: for example, the BBC Scotland's website includes several videos and interactive activities about Skara Brae.

Whole-class work
- Tell the class that Skara Brae is famous because archaeologists have discovered the remains of a Stone Age settlement there. The buildings, structures and artefacts have provided a lot of primary evidence for what life was like in the Stone Age.
- Ask the children to imagine that they are discovering Skara Brae for the first time. Create a thought shower of historically valid questions, such as: *What were homes like? What furniture did they have? What did people eat? How was food cooked? What games did children play?*
- Discuss the sorts of evidence that might be used to answer the questions.

Group work
- Tell the children that they are going to use several websites to explore Skara Brae and consider what it reveals about Stone Age life.
- Organise children into pairs and ask them to select two questions about Skara Brae, such as *What kinds of things did people have inside their homes?* or *Where did they get food?* (You may give them a list to choose from or ask them to come up with their own.)
- In this lesson the children will research their questions and look for evidence using websites. During the next lesson they will create neat copies showing their question, the answer and the evidence.

Differentiation
- Support: mixed-ability pairings may be beneficial; children could focus on the images on the websites (and what can be deduced from them).
- Challenge: more confident learners could read the website text for information.

Review
- Elicit what the children have learnt by asking: *What did you find out? How did you find evidence to answer your question? Did you use primary or secondary evidence to answer your question?*

Week 5 lesson plans

This week children continue to work on finding evidence to answer their historically valid questions about Stone Age life in Skara Brae, contributing to a class book of their findings. They also learn about cave art in the Stone Age, viewing examples from the Creswell Caves in Nottinghamshire and creating their own line drawings of British animals in the same style.

I: What does Skara Brae tell us about Stone Age life? (2)

Lesson objectives
● To understand the changes in Britain from the Stone Age to the Iron Age, including late Neolithic hunter-gatherers and early farmers, for example, Skara Brae.
● To develop a chronologically secure knowledge and understanding of British, local and world history, establishing clear narratives within and across the periods they study.
● To develop the appropriate use of historical terms.
● To understand how our knowledge of the past is constructed from a range of sources.
● To understand that different versions of past events may exist, giving some reasons for this.

Expected outcomes
● All children will describe at least one fact about Skara Brae.
● Most children will describe life in Skara Brae.
● Some children will describe how Skara Brae has been used to learn about the past.

Resources
Images of carved stone artefacts; internet access; A4 paper or card

Introduction
● Ask: *What kinds of material have lasted through the ages and what might have rotted away?* (Materials like stone and metal can last, whereas organic materials like leather and wood decompose.) *How might this affect our understanding of the past?* (We only see part of the evidence and have to piece together the rest of the picture, imagining how organic materials might have been used.)
● Show images of some of the carved stone artefacts found at Skara Brae (for example, on the BBC history website) and ask children for ideas about how they were used.

Whole-class work
● Ask several pairs of children to talk about how they looked for evidence to answer the historically valid questions they set themselves in the previous lesson.

Group work or Independent work
● Ask children to finish their research and then select one of their questions to write up neatly. They should create an A4 page with the following subtitles: 'Question', 'Answer' and 'Evidence'. Under these headings they should write down their findings, using text and drawings or printed images. (For example: Question – What kinds of furniture did people in Skara Brae have inside their homes?; Answer – People living in Skara Brae had stone cupboards, shelves, beds and a dresser, which might have been used to display precious possessions. Evidence – These items of furniture can still be seen in the Skara Brae remains today. The dresser is opposite the door and so the people living in the house might have wanted to show it off.)
● The A4 pages can be collected together to create a class book about Stone Age life in Skara Brae.

> **Differentiation**
> ● Support: mixed-ability pairings may be beneficial; children could focus on the images on the websites (and what can be deduced from them).
> ● Challenge: more confident learners could read online text for information.

Review
● Children's progress can be assessed through their ability to ask a historically valid question and then find evidence to support their answer.
● At the end of the lesson ask the children to share the most interesting thing they have learnt with the rest of the class.

Lesson objectives
● To understand the changes in Britain from the Stone Age to the Iron Age, including late Neolithic hunter-gatherers and early farmers.
● To develop a chronologically secure knowledge and understanding of British, local and world history, establishing clear narratives within and across the periods they study.
● To develop the appropriate use of historical terms.
● To understand how our knowledge of the past is constructed from a range of sources.
● To understand that different versions of past events may exist, giving some reasons for this.

Expected outcomes
● All children will create their own Stone Age art.
● Most children will describe Stone Age art and create their own.
● Some children will consider the reasons why art in the Stone Age might have been created.

Resources
Internet access; atlas or map; clay or Plasticine®; chalk or oil pastels and brown art paper (optional)

2. What was Stone Age art like?

Introduction
● Ask: *Why do people make art? What kind of art do you think people in the early Stone Age created?* Discuss children's ideas.
● Talk about what Stone Age people might have seen on a daily basis and what artists' tools they would have had to work with.

Whole-class work
● Use atlases or online maps to find the Palaeolithic site of Creswell Crags in Nottinghamshire, and look at a satellite image.
● Show the children examples of Stone Age cave art from Creswell Crags (source online). Ask: *What do the artworks show? How have they been created? What tools might have been used to make them?* (They could have used sharp tools to etch pictures into the rock, colours from charcoal or berries as paint, and straw, leaves and hollow reeds or bones to spread or blow the 'paint'.)
● Show children a different form of cave art from the Palaeolithic period in France, for example from the Lascaux Caves (source online).

Independent work
● Ask children to create their own versions of the cave art. They could look at images of animals that are native to Britain, such as wild boar, red deer, hares, red squirrels, and create basic line drawings in side view.
● Children could then either carve their drawings using pencils in clay or Plasticine® or you could stick a large sheet of brown paper across one wall of the classroom, onto which children can draw their cave art using brown and black pastels.

Differentiation
● Support: less confident learners can create simple drawings or could draw around their hand.
● Challenge: more confident learners could research Stone Age art in other areas of the world, such as the cave and bark paintings of the Australian aboriginals, considering similarities and differences.

Review
● Check that the children's artworks imitate the style of the cave art.
● Show some of the best examples to the class and ask the children to explain how they imitate cave art.

Week 6 lesson plans

This week children learn about the early development of farming during the Neolithic period and how this led to human settlement and population expansion, as food could be produced for the whole community and stored. They engage in role-play activities, considering the viewpoints of members of a farming community and a nomadic hunter-gatherer tribe, comparing the two lifestyles and considering the advantages and disadvantages of each.

1: How did farming develop in Britain?

Introduction
● Ask children to describe what they think happens on a farm. Elicit responses that include seeds being planted, crops being grown and harvested, animals being raised, and so on.

Whole-class work
● Complete interactive activity 'Interview with a Neolithic farmer' on the CD-ROM as a class. This gives an insight into what it was like to be a Neolithic farmer. Children click on questions around an illustration of a Neolithic farmer to reveal the answers. Questions include: *How did you learn to farm? Who do you live with? Where do you farm?*

Group work or Paired work
● Organise children into groups of six. Tell them that each group is a farming community and give each person a role-play card from photocopiable pages 'Neolithic farming communities' from the CD-ROM. Members of each group should take turns to read their cards, discovering what they can contribute to, and gain from, the community. Ask the children to discuss whether they can manage as a community, or if there are needs that can't be met by any of its members.
● When groups are finished, hold a wider discussion with the whole class (as different groups have will have different skills). Find out what each community is lacking and how the communities could join together to better meet their needs.
● Discuss how farming produced enough food for the community (and sometimes extra to trade) and allowed each member of the community to contribute a different skill.

> **Differentiation**
> ● Support: mixed-ability groupings may be beneficial.

Review
● Children's progress can be assessed through their discussion around why and how Neolithic farming took place.
● Ask some questions to aid the discussion: *How did the farm provide food? Why did the farmer store food? How did the farm help the farmer's community stay in one place? How did the farm help the community grow? How did farming allow people to do different jobs?*

Lesson objectives
● To understand the changes in Britain from the Stone Age to the Iron Age, including late Neolithic hunter-gatherers and early farmers.
● To develop a chronologically secure knowledge and understanding of British, local and world history, establishing clear narratives within and across the periods they study.
● To note connections, contrasts and trends over time.
● To develop the appropriate use of historical terms.
● To regularly address and sometimes devise historically valid questions about change, cause, similarity and difference, and significance.
● To construct informed responses that involve thoughtful selection and organisation of relevant historical information.

Expected outcomes
● All children will describe at least one aspect of Neolithic farming.
● Most children will describe several aspects of Neolithic farming.
● Some children will describe how farming helped Neolithic communities grow in number.

Resources
Interactive activity 'Interview with a Neolithic farmer' on the CD-ROM; photocopiable pages 'Neolithic farming communities' from the CD-ROM

Lesson objectives
● To understand the changes in Britain from the Stone Age to the Iron Age, including late Neolithic hunter-gatherers and early farmers.
● To develop a chronologically secure knowledge and understanding of British, local and world history, establishing clear narratives within and across the periods they study.
● To note connections, contrasts and trends over time.
● To develop the appropriate use of historical terms.
● To regularly address and sometimes devise historically valid questions about change, cause, similarity and difference, and significance.
● To construct informed responses that involve thoughtful selection and organisation of relevant historical information.

Expected outcomes
● All children will identify at least one difference between hunter-gatherers and farmers.
● Most children will identify similarities and differences between hunter-gatherers and farmers.
● Some children will consider the benefits and disadvantages of the hunter-gather life over farming.

Resources
Large sheets of paper; coloured marker pens

2: How did farming compare to hunting and gathering?

Introduction
● Give children two minutes to share with a talk partner what they remember about the nomadic hunter-gatherer lifestyle.
● Discuss what they remember, and fill in any gaps.

Whole-class work
● Draw two columns on the board with the titles 'Hunter-gatherer' and 'Farmer'. As a class, discuss and record some of the ways that these two lifestyles were similar (both needed food and shelter for survival, had families and lived in community groups) and different (hunter-gathers had to move with the seasons and food sources and had to devote all their time to searching for food; farmers could live in permanent shelters, had more control over their food supply and could store it, and could divide the work so that people fulfilled different roles).

Group work
● Organise children into groups and tell them to imagine that they are Neolithic tribes. They have met together to decide whether they are going to continue as nomadic hunter-gatherers or settle down and farm.
● Give each group a large sheet of paper and marker pens, so that they can write down the benefits of their choice.
● Ask each 'tribe' to share what they decided and why.
● Tell the children that eventually farming became the main method of food production and led to the population expanding and new technologies developing (in turn leading to more efficient food production and further expansion).

Differentiation
● Support: mixed-ability pairings may be beneficial.

Review
● Children's progress can be assessed through their discussion around the benefits and disadvantages of the two lifestyles.
● Ask: *What risks would there be to the food supply for each lifestyle?* (Hunter-gatherers were dependent on wild herds and hunting could be dangerous. For farmers, much depended on the weather and having a good harvest that was not stolen or destroyed by insects or animals.) *What are the benefits of staying in one place?* (Farmers could build more solid shelters and have more control over the production of food.) *Who might have more free time?* (All the members of a hunter-gatherer tribe would need to be involved in obtaining food. Fewer people were needed to farm and so people could develop specialist skills.) *How would they make sure there was food throughout the year?* (Hunter-gatherers would need to move with the herd, whereas farmers could store food for the winter.)

Lesson objective
● To understand how our knowledge of the past is constructed from a range of sources.

Resources
Interactive activity 'Y3 Autumn I quiz' on the CD-ROM

History skills

Revise
● Write on the board the four types of evidence about which children have been learning: archaeological sites, artefacts, written documents, eyewitness reports.
● As a class, devise a glossary definition for each of these.

Assess
● Ask the children to complete interactive activity 'Y3 Autumn I quiz' on the CD-ROM, in which they have to match different examples of evidence to the type of evidence it is.
● Give children a set length of time (for example, 15 minutes) to answer the questions. This can be used as part of a formal assessment or as a fun challenge activity, giving children the opportunity to show what they have learned about the topic.
● Less confident readers may need adult support to read the questions aloud.
● More confident learners could be asked to write an advantage and a disadvantage of each type of evidence.

Further practice
● Ask the children to select five items that could be put into a time capsule to give future historians a picture of their life in Britain today. What does each piece of 'evidence' reveal about them or modern life?

Lesson objective
● To know about changes in Britain from the Stone Age to the Iron Age, including late Neolithic hunter-gatherers and early farmers.

Resources
Image of a flint knife (online)

The Stone Age

Revise
● Show children an image of a flint knife, such as the one at: www.stoneagetools.co.uk.
● Hold a class discussion around how a hunter-gather might use this tool and how a farmer might use it.
● Talk about some of the daily tasks each person might carry out.

Assess
● Write on the board: *What problems would you face as a Neolithic hunter-gatherer? What problems would you face as a Neolithic farmer?*
● Ask children to write answers to the above questions. They should include at least one disadvantage for each lifestyle, but more confident learners should show deeper reflection and be able to discuss several issues for each (for example, hunter-gathers are faced with dangers of wild animals and having to move to follow the herd all the time; farmers may experience poor weather affecting crops and wild animals attacking cattle).
● Less confident writers could share their ideas verbally with adult support.

Further practice
● Ask children to write a 'To do' list for a Neolithic hunter-gatherer and a Neolithic farmer, containing some of their daily tasks.

M SCHOLASTIC
www.scholastic.co.uk

How do we find out about the past?

■ Read the text below and complete the thinking challenge.

Archaeological sites

Over time, the surface of the Earth becomes buried in layers of soil. Historians can dig down through the layers – the deeper they dig, the further back into the past they get. Archaeologists have discovered the remains of objects, people and even whole villages and cities buried in the soil.

Example: nearly 2000 years ago, a volcano erupted and buried the Roman city of Pompeii in volcanic ash. In 1748 it was rediscovered and excavated. It has told us a lot about the Roman way of life.

Artefacts

Artefacts are objects from the past. These could be pots, statues and other artworks, jewellery, weapons, tools, clothes, coins, furniture – anything that people in the past made or used.

Example: Stone Age weapons, made of flint, have been found in Britain. This has shown that humans lived and hunted here many thousands of years ago.

Written documents

Many past civilisations have written about their lives. The writing was sometimes carved into stone walls or written down on tablets or paper.

Example: in a Roman fort called Vindolanda in northern England, historians have found many wooden tablets with writing on them. The writing has shown what life was like for Roman soldiers at the fort. One tablet even contains an invitation to a birthday party!

Eyewitness reports

An eyewitness is someone who was actually there when a historical event happened. Historians read or listen to the eyewitness's stories about what they saw, heard or felt.

Example: an archaeologist called Howard Carter discovered the tomb of the ancient Egyptian pharaoh Tutankhamun in 1922. He wrote a book about this amazing experience.

■ **Thinking challenge:** if you wanted to find out what your school was like 20 years ago, what kinds of evidence might you look for?

I can think of different ways to find out about our school in the past.

How did you do?

Timelines (1)

Timelines are used to show when important events happened. They may cover a few days or thousands of years. Timelines can show the history of a country or civilisation, or the history of the world. Timelines can also show the history of a single person.

■ Look at this timeline showing some important events in the life of Prince William, then complete the activity challenge.

Timeline of Prince William's life

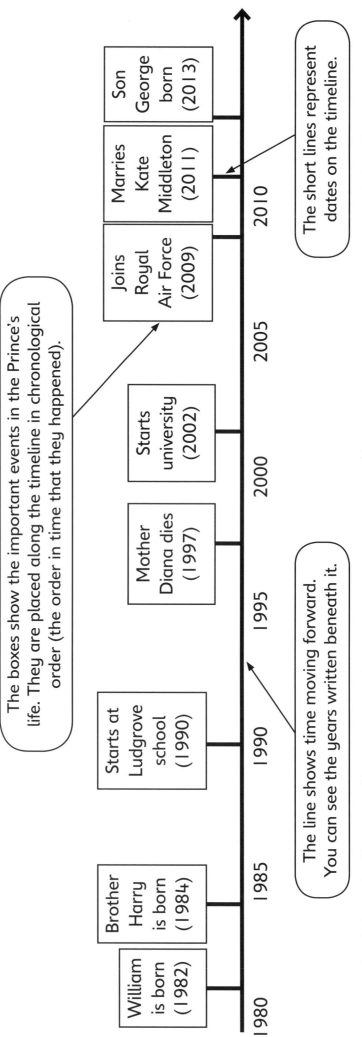

William is born (1982)

Brother Harry is born (1984)

Starts at Ludgrove school (1990)

Mother Diana dies (1997)

Starts university (2002)

Joins Royal Air Force (2009)

Marries Kate Middleton (2011)

Son George born (2013)

1980   1985   1990   1995   2000   2005   2010

The boxes show the important events in the Prince's life. They are placed along the timeline in chronological order (the order in time that they happened).

The line shows time moving forward. You can see the years written beneath it.

The short lines represent dates on the timeline.

■ **Activity challenge:** Choose some important events in your life and create your own personal timeline.

I can create a timeline.

How did you do?

Name: _____   Date: _____

Timelines (2)

History is sometimes grouped into different periods or eras of time. Timelines can show when these periods began and ended.

Dates are divided into BC (Before Christ) and AD (Anno Domini, which means 'in the year of our Lord'). Year 0 is seen as the year that Jesus Christ was born.

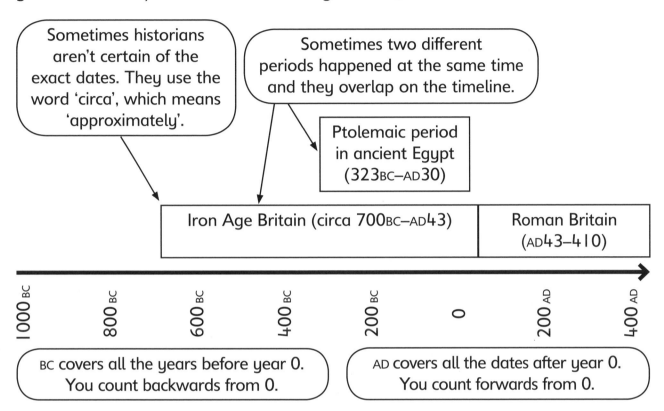

Sometimes historians aren't certain of the exact dates. They use the word 'circa', which means 'approximately'.

Sometimes two different periods happened at the same time and they overlap on the timeline.

Ptolemaic period in ancient Egypt (323BC–AD30)

Iron Age Britain (circa 700BC–AD43)

Roman Britain (AD43–410)

1000 BC 800 BC 600 BC 400 BC 200 BC 0 200 AD 400 AD

BC covers all the years before year 0. You count backwards from 0.

AD covers all the dates after year 0. You count forwards from 0.

■ **Activity challenge:** here are some important periods in British History but the order is all mixed up. Can you cut them out and put them in the right order? (All of the dates here are AD.)

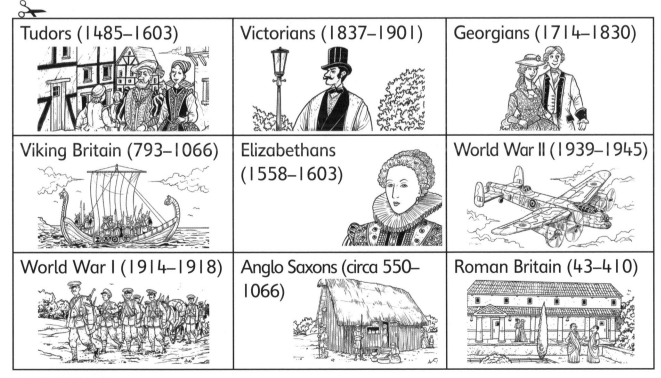

Tudors (1485–1603)

Victorians (1837–1901)

Georgians (1714–1830)

Viking Britain (793–1066)

Elizabethans (1558–1603)

World War II (1939–1945)

World War I (1914–1918)

Anglo Saxons (circa 550–1066)

Roman Britain (43–410)

The Bronze Age

This chapter continues the chronological narrative of Britain's history, moving from the Stone Age to the Bronze Age. Children find out about the immigration to Britain of the Beaker people and the impact of the metalworking technology that they brought with them. They learn about Bronze Age structures, such as roundhouses and round barrows. They begin to draw basic comparisons between the Stone Age and the Bronze Age, considering differences in tools and burial traditions. Finally, they explore the monument of Stonehenge.

Chapter at a glance

Curriculum objectives

• Changes in Britain from the Stone Age to the Iron Age, including Bronze Age religion, technology and travel, for example Stonehenge.

Week	Lesson	Summary of activities	Expected outcomes
1	1	• Children use an interactive tool to create a timeline of the Stone, Bronze and Iron Ages.	• Can show the relationship between the Stone, Bronze and Iron Ages on a timeline.
	2	• Children look at aerial photographs and consider how these can help us to study the past.	• Can describe how technology helps historians to study the past.
2	1	• Children learn about the Amesbury Archer and consider what can be inferred about the Bronze Age from his burial.	• Can use evidence to make inferences about the Bronze Age.
	2	• Children read about the introduction of metal technology to Britain and order the steps involved in making bronze objects.	• Can describe how the immigration of the Beaker people started the Bronze Age in Britain.
3	1	• Children compare Bronze Age roundhouses with their own homes today.	• Can describe a Bronze Age roundhouse.
	2	• Children look at examples of the Bell-Beaker pottery before creating their own versions.	• Can describe what Beaker pottery was like.
4	1	• Children list similarities and differences between Stone Age and Bronze Age burials through investigating archaeological sites.	• Can understand how burial rituals changed from the Stone Age (long barrows) to the Bronze Age (round barrows).
	2	• Children write a diary entry reflecting a day in the life of a Bronze Age person living in a roundhouse.	• Can write about a day in the life of a Bronze Age person.
5	1	• Children read about Stonehenge, discussing theories about its purpose. They consider the kinds of evidence needed to support the theories.	• Can describe why opinions about the origins of Stonehenge differ.
	2	• Children create a model of Stonehenge.	• Can use diagrams to create their own model of Stonehenge.
6	1	• Children create a brochure persuading tourists to visit Stonehenge.	• Can describe why Stonehenge is a significant landmark.
	2	• Children complete an interactive activity, choosing sentences as being applicable to either the Stone Age or Bronze Age or both.	• Can describe the main changes in Britain from the Stone Age to the Bronze Age.
Assess and review		• To review the half-term's work.	

Expected prior learning

● The previous topic, History skills and the Stone Age, should be completed before studying the Bronze Age, as comparisons will be drawn between the two time periods.

Overview of progression

● In this chapter, children continue to develop the core history skills that they will need in Key Stage 2. They learn about the way historians use technology to find out about the past, including radiocarbon dating, experimental archaeology and aerial photographs.

● Children revisit the creation of timelines and practise constructing the past from evidence as they explore the contents of the Amesbury Archer's grave.

● They build on their understanding of change over time, as they consider the development of tools and weapons from flint to bronze, and the change in burial traditions and lifestyle from the Stone Age to the Bronze Age.

● Children also develop their understanding of abstract terms, such as 'period', 'era', 'technology', 'revolution', 'evidence' and 'interpretation'.

Creative context

● Cross-curricular links include:
  ● engaging in creative writing, with a diary entry exploring daily life in the Bronze Age, and in persuasive writing, by creating a tourist brochure for Stonehenge;
  ● mathematical skills: counting, intervals, scale and creating timelines;
  ● creating Bell-Beaker pottery and making a model of Stonehenge.

Background knowledge

● The Bronze Age is thought to have begun around 2500BC and lasted until around 800BC. During this time there was a large immigration to Britain from Europe, bringing with it new knowledge and technologies. The Beaker or Bell-Beaker people (so called because of their use of bell-shaped pottery beakers for drinking) knew how to extract copper and tin from rocks and smelt them to create bronze objects.

● There was a social revolution during this time. Although farming had begun in the Neolithic period, it became far more widespread, with the hunter-gatherer lifestyle disappearing. People began to settle and live together in small hamlets, farming the land around them. They began to seek control of the land, raising territorial disputes with nearby communities. There was a shift from a largely equal social structure to one based on wealth and status, with bronze objects kept as prized commodities and even buried with their owners.

● Little is known about religion during this time but there was a shift in burial customs from Stone Age communal tombs (long barrows), to circular mounds designed for only one person (round barrows).

● Stonehenge was built in stages, beginning around 3000BC with a circular ditch and bank of earth, and being completed around 1500BC. During the Bronze Age, 'bluestones' were brought from over 150 miles away (around 240 miles, according to some historians) and arranged in a circle. Huge sarsen stones were then arranged around them in a larger circle. The largest sarsens were arranged in a semicircle in the middle, with one stone balanced on two others (over seven metres tall). There are many theories about how and why Stonehenge was built but it remains a mystery. There are other prehistoric constructions in the same region, such as Silbury Hill and Avebury Circle, and tombs, such as the burial place of the Amesbury Archer.

Week 1 lesson plans

This week children consolidate their understanding of timelines by exploring the relationship between the Stone Age, Bronze Age and Iron Age. They then learn about the different ways that historians use technology to investigate the past, through radiocarbon dating, experimental archaeology and aerial photographs.

1: When were the Stone, Bronze and Iron Ages?

Introduction

● Recap what children already know about timelines and their features, as well as the use of BC and AD: create a spider diagram or list of bullet points on the whiteboard, as a class, or ask quick-fire questions for the children to answer as quickly as possible, such as: *What is a timeline used to show? What does BC mean? Which comes before the year 0 – BC or AD? Why is it helpful to have a scale on a timeline?*

Whole-class work

● Tell the children that the Stone Age, Bronze Age and Iron Age are collectively called 'prehistory', as they happened before historical events were written down. The ages are so called because of the tools and weapons that were used – in the Stone Age, tools were made of stone, and so on.
● Remind the children that they have already learned about the Stone Age and explain that this topic will focus on the Bronze Age and that next term they will learn about the Iron Age.
● Refresh children's memory regarding the use of the interactive activity 'Timeline maker' on the CD-ROM, for example by creating a timeline of recent school events, or annual festivals, as a class.

Paired work or Independent work

● Write the following dates on the board and ask children to use the software to create a timeline showing the three ages of prehistoric Britain (the Neolithic Age only has been included for the Stone Age, due to the impracticalities of covering a longer period of time): New Stone Age – 4500 to 2500BC; Bronze Age – 2500 to 700BC; Iron Age – 700BC to AD43.

Differentiation
● Support: mixed-ability pairings may be beneficial.
● Challenge: children could create a more detailed timeline with images for each age. Alternatively, they could help less confident learners.

Review

● Draw a timeline on the whiteboard and ask different children to add some information, such as the name of one of the ages, or dates.
● Alternatively, create an incorrect version and ask children to correct it.

Lesson objectives

● To understand the changes in Britain from the Stone Age to the Iron Age, including Bronze Age religion, technology and travel, for example, Stonehenge.
● To develop a chronologically secure knowledge and understanding of British, local and world history, establishing clear narratives within and across the periods they study.
● To note connections, contrasts and trends over time.
● To develop the appropriate use of historical terms.
● To regularly address and sometimes devise historically valid questions about change, cause, similarity and difference, and significance.
● To construct informed responses that involve thoughtful selection and organisation of relevant historical information.

Expected outcomes

● All children will know the order in which the Stone, Bronze and Iron Ages occurred.
● Most children will create a basic timeline showing the Stone, Bronze and Iron Ages.
● Some children will create a more detailed timeline showing the Stone, Bronze and Iron Ages.

Resources

Interactive activity 'Timeline maker' on the CD-ROM

Lesson objectives

● To understand the changes in Britain from the Stone Age to the Iron Age, including Bronze Age religion, technology and travel, for example, Stonehenge.
● To develop a chronologically secure knowledge and understanding of British, local and world history, establishing clear narratives within and across the periods they study.
● To note connections, contrasts and trends over time.
● To develop the appropriate use of historical terms.
● To regularly address and sometimes devise historically valid questions about change, cause, similarity and difference, and significance.
● To construct informed responses that involve thoughtful selection and organisation of relevant historical information.
● To understand how our knowledge of the past is constructed from a range of sources.
● To understand that different versions of past events may exist, giving some reasons for this.

Expected outcomes

● All children will describe at least one method used to study the past.
● Most children will study aerial photographs and explain what they tell us about the past.
● Some children will describe in detail several methods used to study the past.

Resources

Photocopiable page 'Technology for historians' from the CD-ROM; internet access

2: How can technology help us learn about the past?

Introduction

● Recap the different types of evidence used by historians to learn about the past – archaeology, artefacts, written documents and eyewitness accounts (as described on photocopiable page 23 'How do we find out about the past?' in the previous chapter).

Whole-class work

● Tell the children that they are going to be learning about some other methods that help historians construct the past.
● Read and discuss photocopiable page 'Technology for historians' from the CD-ROM, which provides some information about radiocarbon dating, aerial and satellite images and experimental archaeology (such as finding out how roundhouses might have been built, by trying to build one using only the materials that would have been available at the time). Ask: *How reliable do you think these methods are in helping us learn about the past?*
● Using a website such as www.britainfromabove.org.uk, look at aerial photographs of an area local to you or that the children will know. Talk about what the photograph shows about the way the area used to look (considering both human-made and natural features). Ask: *What has changed? What has remained the same? What can't the photograph tell us about the past?*

Group work or Paired work

● Organise children into groups or pairs. Ask them to investigate other local areas from satellite images (direct them to specific websites, or provide printed photographs) considering what the photographs reveal about the way they used to be.
● Alternatively, ask children look at aerial photographs of different prehistoric sites (source online, or direct children to websites where aerial photographs can be found). The children should consider how the photographs could help historians know where to study the past (for example, the best places to dig for artefacts). They could search and look at the aerial photographs for Priddy Circles, Silbury Hill, Nosehill Round Barrow or Avebury Henge.

> **Differentiation**
> ● Support: mixed-ability pairings may be beneficial.

Review

● Discuss the children's findings as a whole class. Ask: *Which do you think is the most useful technology to study the past? Which is the most/least reliable? Do you think as many archaeological sites, or artefacts, would have been found without these technologies – what would people have had to do instead in order to make the same discoveries?*

Week 2 lesson plans

This week children continue the chronological narrative of British history, moving from the Stone Age to the Bronze Age. They make inferences about Bronze Age life from evidence found in the tomb of the Amesbury Archer. They then read about the beginning of the British Bronze Age with the immigration of the Beaker People and introduction of metalworking skills.

1: What can evidence tell us about the Bronze Age?

Introduction
● Write the names of various objects on the board, or have the physical objects in clear bags for children to inspect. For example: a tin of dog food, bottle of cough mixture, pair of bifocal glasses, travel brochure, receipt for a toy, empty can of sugar-free drink.
● Tell the children that these 'artefacts' are from a family's rubbish bin. Ask: *What does this evidence tell us about the family?*

Whole-class work
● Read and discuss photocopiable page 41 'The Amesbury Archer', which provides information about the Bronze Age burial. Show children the images of finds (source online) – or refer to the photocopiable page.
● Ask children to imagine that nothing is yet known about the Bronze Age. They are archaeologists and have just discovered the Amesbury Archer's tomb. Ask: *What information about the Bronze Age can we work out from this evidence?* (Answers could include: people wore jewellery; they used tools made of flint and copper; they created pottery; they travelled long distances; they probably hunted wild boar.) *What questions would we need to ask?*

Group work or Paired work
● Organise children into groups or pairs. Ask them to discuss the information on the photocopiable sheet and the images of the artefacts buried with the archer.
● They should use this evidence to make as many inferences as they can about Bronze Age life, listing these on a large piece of paper. They should also note the evidence used make such inferences.

> **Differentiation**
> ● Support: mixed-ability pairings may be beneficial.

Review
● Ask groups to share their ideas with the class. Did any groups have different interpretations of the evidence? Discuss how historians sometimes disagree as sometimes there just isn't enough evidence to be certain of events in the past.
● Ask questions to clarify their understanding, or clear up any misconceptions.

Lesson objectives

● To understand the changes in Britain from the Stone Age to the Iron Age, including Bronze Age religion, technology and travel, for example, Stonehenge.
● To develop a chronologically secure knowledge and understanding of British, local and world history, establishing clear narratives within and across the periods they study.
● To note connections, contrasts and trends over time.
● To develop the appropriate use of historical terms.
● To regularly address and sometimes devise historically valid questions about change, cause, similarity and difference, and significance.
● To construct informed responses that involve thoughtful selection and organisation of relevant historical information.
● To understand how our knowledge of the past is constructed from a range of sources.
● To understand that different versions of past events may exist, giving some reasons for this.

Expected outcomes

● All children will describe Bronze Age tools and weapons.
● Most children will describe how bronze was introduced to Britain.
● Some children will describe how the introduction of bronze impacted on Britain.

Resources

Photocopiable page 42 'Britain's Bronze Age'; photocopiable page 43 'Making bronze'; internet access or pictures of Bronze Age weapons

2: How did the Bronze Age begin in Britain?

Introduction

● Show some pictures of Bronze Age weapons (source online).
● Ask: *How are these similar to and different from weapons used in the Stone Age? Why might these be more effective?*
● Talk about the fact that bronze was harder than stone and could be shaped more easily and quickly, making weapons like swords or flanged axes possible.

Whole-class work

● Read and discuss photocopiable page 42 'Britain's Bronze Age', which includes information about the Beaker people, and how bronze was made.
● Depending on the time available, children could research, or even plan a visit to, the Bronze Age mines at Great Orme, investigating the tools and techniques used to extract Copper ore. Information about the site can be found at: www.greatormemines.info.
● Alternatively, ask the children to convert the description of the making of Bronze objects into an instructional text.

Paired work or Independent work

● Ask children to complete the activity on photocopiable page 43 'Making bronze', in which they cut out and order the steps involved in making metal objects.

Differentiation
● Support: children could work with adult support to place the pictures in order.
● Challenge: children should consider the impact of Bronze technology on Britain.

Review

● Check that the children have ordered the bronze-making steps correctly.
● Ask: *Which two metals are used to make bronze? Who were the Beaker People? How did life in Britain change with the introduction of bronze?*

Week 3 lesson plans

This week children explore Bronze Age roundhouses, considering their structure and how they were used, as they compare the different parts with their own homes. They then look at examples of Beaker pottery, before creating their own.

Lesson objectives
- To understand the changes in Britain from the Stone Age to the Iron Age, including Bronze Age religion, technology and travel, for example, Stonehenge.
- To develop a chronologically secure knowledge and understanding of British, local and world history, establishing clear narratives within and across the periods they study.
- To note connections, contrasts and trends over time.
- To develop the appropriate use of historical terms.
- To regularly address and sometimes devise historically valid questions about change, cause, similarity and difference, and significance.
- To construct informed responses that involve thoughtful selection and organisation of relevant historical information.

Expected outcomes
- All children will give a basic description of a roundhouse.
- Most children will give a more detailed description of a roundhouse.
- Some children will describe how Bronze Age people might have lived in a roundhouse.

Resources
Photocopiable page 'Roundhouses' from the CD-ROM; internet access (optional)

1: What were houses like in the Bronze Age?

Introduction
- Ask: *What do you like best about your home?*
- Discuss children's answers.

Whole-class work
- Read and discuss photocopiable page 'Roundhouses' from the CD-ROM, which explains what roundhouses were (Bronze Age homes) and what they would have been made of.
- Ask: *What would it have been like to live in a roundhouse with your family? What would be the good and bad points?*

Paired work or Independent work
- Tell the children that they are going to be comparing Bronze Age roundhouses with their own homes.
- Ask them to divide their page into two columns, with the titles 'Roundhouse' and 'My home'.
- It might be helpful to give the children the following prompts to consider as they compare the two homes: light, cooking, furniture, entertainment, heat.

> **Differentiation**
> - Support: children could discuss ideas rather than write them down.
> - Challenge: children may wish to build models of roundhouses.

Review
- Hold a class vote on whether or not they would like to live in a roundhouse. Ask children to explain their vote.
- Their progress can be assessed through their discussion around roundhouse features.

2: What was Beaker pottery like?

Lesson objectives
● To understand the changes in Britain from the Stone Age to the Iron Age, including Bronze Age religion, technology and travel, for example, Stonehenge.
● To develop a chronologically secure knowledge and understanding of British, local and world history, establishing clear narratives within and across the periods they study.
● To note connections, contrasts and trends over time.
● To develop the appropriate use of historical terms.
● To regularly address and sometimes devise historically valid questions about change, cause, similarity and difference, and significance.
● To construct informed responses that involve thoughtful selection and organisation of relevant historical information.

Expected outcomes
● All children will make a Beaker pot.
● Most children will describe Beaker pottery.
● Some children will copy the style of Bronze Age Beaker pottery.

Resources
Pictures of Beaker pottery; clay; materials for making indentations

Introduction
● Look at some examples of Beaker pottery (source online).
● Tell children that it was very important to the Beaker people and was sometimes buried in their graves with them.
● Ask: *What shape is it? What patterns have been used? What might the pottery have been used for?* Explain that Beaker people are also known as Bell-Beaker people because their pots are shaped like upside-down bells.

Whole-class work
● Tell the class that they are going to be making their own Beaker pottery. Challenge them to copy the style of the Bronze Age versions they have seen, or create their own designs.
● Talk through and demonstrate ways to shape the clay to make the Bell-Beaker shape and how to add patterns.

Independent work
● Give children some clay and ask them to create their own version of the Beaker pottery.
● They should mould the shape and then create patterns around the outside using various objects, such as a fork or pencil.

> ### Differentiation
> ● Support: some children may need help to mould the pottery into the bell shape.
> ● Challenge: children should try to copy the types of pattern found on the original artefacts.

Review
● Create a display of the pottery created by the children.
● Ask them to comment (positively) on each other's work, drawing comparisons between the class pottery and Beaker pottery. Ensure they refer to the bell shape and Beaker-style patterns.

Week 4 lesson plans

This week, children investigate Bronze Age tombs (round barrows) and compare them with the long barrows used during the Stone Age. Children then incorporate their learning about the Bronze Age into a diary entry covering a day in the life of a Bronze Age Beaker person.

1: How did Bronze Age burials compare with the Stone Age burials?

Introduction

● Look at aerial images of West Kennet or Belas Knap long barrows and Grims Mound round barrow (source online).
● Ask children to describe what they see from the air. They should be able to see the elongated shapes of the long barrows, in contrast with the circular shape of the round barrow.

Whole-class work

● Read and discuss photocopiable pages 'Prehistoric graves: long barrows' and 'Prehistoric graves: round barrows' from the CD-ROM. Look at the pictures, and relate these back to the aerial photographs just discussed; identify the walls around the burial sites, the entrances, and the mounds of earth beneath which are the burial chambers.
● Talk about some of the similarities and differences between burials in the two time periods.

Group work or Paired work

● Ask children to write bullet points to show some similarities and differences between Stone Age and Bronze Age burials, using the information on the photocopiable sheets.
● If necessary, give children suggestions to guide their answers (for example, tell them to consider the number of people buried in the tomb, the shape of the barrow, any possessions buried and the materials used).

Differentiation
● Support: mixed-ability pairings may be beneficial.

Review

● Check that the children are clear on the differences between burials in the two time periods by creating a class chart of similarities and differences, or spider diagrams to show the features of the different burials.
● Alternatively, ask the children to work in groups to create lists or diagrams on large pieces of paper. These should then be passed around from group to group, and the children should add ideas to each other's diagrams until they are all the same – and hopefully contain all the information covered in the lesson.

Lesson objectives

● To understand the changes in Britain from the Stone Age to the Iron Age, including Bronze Age religion, technology and travel, for example, Stonehenge.
● To develop a chronologically secure knowledge and understanding of British, local and world history, establishing clear narratives within and across the periods they study.
● To note connections, contrasts and trends over time and develop the appropriate use of historical terms.
● To regularly address and sometimes devise historically valid questions about change, cause, similarity and difference, and significance.
● To understand how our knowledge of the past is constructed from a range of sources.

Expected outcomes

● All children will describe at least one difference between Stone Age and Bronze Age burials.
● Most children will describe several differences between Stone Age and Bronze Age burials.
● Some children will describe similarities and differences between Stone Age and Bronze Age burials.

Resources

Aerial images of West Kennet or Belas Knap long barrows (source online); photocopiable pages 'Prehistoric graves: long barrows' and 'Prehistoric graves: round barrows' from the CD-ROM

■SCHOLASTIC
www.scholastic.co.uk

Lesson objectives

Lesson objectives
- To understand the changes in Britain from the Stone Age to the Iron Age, including Bronze Age religion, technology and travel, for example, Stonehenge.
- To develop a chronologically secure knowledge and understanding of British, local and world history, establishing clear narratives within and across the periods they study.
- To note connections, contrasts and trends over time and develop the appropriate use of historical terms.
- To regularly address and sometimes devise historically valid questions about change, cause, similarity and difference, and significance.
- To understand how our knowledge of the past is constructed from a range of sources.

Expected outcomes
- All children will describe an aspect of life in the Bronze Age.
- Most children will write a short diary from a Bronze Age person's viewpoint.
- Some children will write a detailed diary from a Bronze Age person's viewpoint.

Resources
Photocopiable page 'Roundhouses' from the CD-ROM; internet access

2: What was daily life like in the Bronze Age?

Introduction
- Give children one minute to try to remember as many artefacts from the Amesbury Archer's tomb as they can. Answers should include: flint and copper tools, wild boar tusks, fragments of pots, a pin made from bone, wrist guards, gold bands, a cushion stone and, of course, a skeleton.
- Check their answers, and look again at pictures of the Bronze Age artefacts found in the tomb (source online, for example at www.wessexarch.co.uk and www.finds.org.uk/bronzeage).

Whole-class work
- Ask children to look again at the picture of a roundhouse on photocopiable page 'Roundhouses' from the CD-ROM.
- Tell them to imagine a family living there. Ask: *What might each member of the family do throughout the day? What jobs might they do?* (Men might plough, clear land, repair the roundhouse or make tools. Women might grind grain, bake bread or make clothing. Children might feed the animals.)

Independent work
- Ask children to choose a Bronze Age family member living in a roundhouse and to write a diary entry covering a day in their life.
- Challenge them to include one or more of the Bronze Age artefacts in their writing, describing how it is used.

Differentiation
- Support: children may wish to write a few sentences about one or two of the Bronze Age artefacts.
- Challenge: children should present a detailed vision of Bronze Age life, including the feelings of their character.

Review
- Ask some children to share their diary entries.
- Check that the diaries reflect Bronze Age life. Ask other children to identify different aspects of the diary entries read out that clearly show Bronze Age life.

Week 5 lesson plans

This week children are introduced to the mysteries of Stonehenge. They read about where and when it was built, as well as the speculation surrounding its purpose. They use websites to investigate Stonehenge, create a model of the monument and write poems inspired by it.

1: Why was Stonehenge built?

Introduction

● Show the media resource 'Stonehenge slideshow' on the CD-ROM and ask the children to make comments about what they see, why it may have been built and how it makes them feel.
● The slideshow includes pictures of Stonehenge from different angles to give a full impression of the site as a whole.

Whole-class work

● Read and discuss the photocopiable page 'Stonehenge' from the CD-ROM, which gives some background information on Stonehenge, as well as a diagram to show the layout and different stones used to create it. The sheet also includes some of the theories historians have suggested for it being built.
● Ask children to talk about the different theories as to why Stonehenge was built and suggest which they agree with and why (they may even have their own ideas as to its purpose).
● Some children may have been to Stonehenge; ask them to describe their experiences there.

Group work

● Allocate a section of the classroom for each theory and ask children to stand in the area allocated to the one they feel is most plausible.
● In these groups, ask children to come up with suggestions for the kinds of evidence that would need to be found to support the theory. (For example, if Stonehenge was built as a religious temple and used for burials, one might expect to find bodies and possibly objects used in rituals buried near the site.)
● Alternatively, ask them to research extra information about Stonehenge online and write down their own facts. Direct the children to specific websites, or provide reference books.

> **Differentiation**
> ● Support: some children/groups may need help to think of the different kinds of evidence that would support their theory.

Review

● Ask children to write down the most interesting thing they have learnt about Stonehenge.
● Some children could share what they have learnt with the rest of the class.

Lesson objectives

● To understand the changes in Britain from the Stone Age to the Iron Age, including Bronze Age religion, technology and travel, for example, Stonehenge.
● To develop a chronologically secure knowledge and understanding of British, local and world history, establishing clear narratives within and across the periods they study.
● To understand how our knowledge of the past is constructed from a range of sources.
● To understand that different versions of past events may exist, giving some reasons for this.

Expected outcomes

● All children will describe at least one fact about Stonehenge.
● Most children will describe several facts about Stonehenge.
● Some children will consider why there are different opinions about why Stonehenge was built.

Resources

Photocopiable page 'Stonehenge' from the CD-ROM; media resource 'Stonehenge slideshow' on the CD-ROM; internet access

Lesson objectives
- To understand the changes in Britain from the Stone Age to the Iron Age, including Bronze Age religion, technology and travel, for example, Stonehenge.
- To develop a chronologically secure knowledge and understanding of British, local and world history, establishing clear narratives within and across the periods they study.
- To understand how our knowledge of the past is constructed from a range of sources.
- To understand that different versions of past events may exist, giving some reasons for this.

Expected outcomes
- All children will help to create a model of Stonehenge.
- Most children will describe the layout of Stonehenge.
- Some children will describe how Stonehenge has changed over time.

Resources
Photocopiable page 'Stonehenge' from the CD-ROM; internet access (optional); modelling clay or materials for model making

2: What does Stonehenge look like?

Introduction
- Look at the diagram of Stonehenge on the photocopiable page 'Stonehenge' from the CD-ROM.
- In an open space, get children to create a human model of Stonehenge, representing the larger and smaller stones and using different levels with their bodies.

Group work or Paired work
- Explain to the children that they will be using the diagram of the layout of the stones of Stonehenge to create a model of the monument. They could use modelling clay to make the stones or other model making-materials of your choice. Children could create the model as Stonehenge used to be or they could study photographs and aerial shots of Stonehenge today and replicate that.
- When the models are finished, try darkening the room and have children experimenting with shining a torch through the 'stones' to represent the sunrise, observing the effects of the shadows lengthening and shortening as the 'sun' passes overhead.

Differentiation
- Support: mixed-ability pairings may be beneficial; children could work in a group with adult help to create the finished model.
- Challenge: confident children should aim for more accurate proportion and layout.

Review
- Look at the completed models and ask: *What shapes have been used to make Stonehenge?* (Children should note the circular and semi-circular formations when the model is viewed from above. Some might mention the rectangular prisms of the stones.) *How has the monument changed over time?* (Children might comment on areas where stones are missing or have moved or fallen over.)

Week 6 lesson plans

This week children continue to explore the significance of Stonehenge, creating a brochure persuading tourists to visit the site. Children then carry out an interactive activity to demonstrate their understanding of the different changes in Britain from the Stone Age to the Bronze Age.

1: Why is Stonehenge famous?

Introduction
- Show the media resource 'Stonehenge slideshow' on the CD-ROM to the children again.
- Ask: *Why might tourists wish to visit Stonehenge? What kinds of people might most enjoy seeing it?*
- Discuss the popularity of Stonehenge at summer solstice (around 21 June), when thousands of people – practising pagans, tourists and partygoers – gather at Stonehenge to watch the sunrise. It is one of two days of the year (with the winter solstice) that the public are allowed to walk amongst the stones.

Whole-class work
- Show the children some examples of tourist brochures and ask them to identify all the reasons provided to visit Stonehenge and the features and the persuasive techniques of the brochures (such as positive adjectives, catchy headings and bullet points, enticing photographs, special offers, and so on).
- Alternatively, children could complete this task referring to the website www.stonehenge.org.uk.

Paired work or Independent work
- Explain to the children that they are going to be creating their own brochure to persuade tourists to visit Stonehenge. They may wish to use the internet to research some facts about Stonehenge to include.
- Show children how to fold an A4 sheet concertina-style and talk about the features they might include to make their brochure eye-catching and exciting.
- Ask: *Who is your brochure aimed at? What might appeal to them? What might make it eye-catching? What are the most important reasons for visiting Stonehenge?*

Differentiation
- Support: children can write simple sentences describing Stonehenge, imagining what it might be like to visit it.
- Challenge: children should produce more sophisticated brochures, including images and numerous persuasive techniques. They could research practical information, such as directions to the site and price of entry.

Review
- Organise children into groups and ask them to look at each other's brochures.
- Ask: *Did anyone in your group include information in their brochure that you hadn't thought of? How could you improve your brochure? How many reasons are there to visit Stonehenge? What are they?*

Lesson objectives
- To understand the changes in Britain from the Stone Age to the Iron Age, including Bronze Age religion, technology and travel, for example, Stonehenge.
- To develop a chronologically secure knowledge and understanding of British, local and world history, establishing clear narratives within and across the periods they study.
- To regularly address and sometimes devise historically valid questions about change, cause, similarity and difference, and significance.
- To construct informed responses that involve thoughtful selection and organisation of relevant historical information.
- To understand how our knowledge of the past is constructed from a range of sources.
- To understand that different versions of past events may exist, giving some reasons for this.

Expected outcomes
- All children will suggest reasons why tourists might visit Stonehenge.
- Most children will write at least one paragraph persuading tourists to visit Stonehenge.
- Some children will create a brochure persuading tourists to visit Stonehenge.

Resources
Media resource 'Stonehenge slideshow' on the CD-ROM; internet access or examples of Stonehenge tourist brochures

Lesson objectives

● To understand the changes in Britain from the Stone Age to the Iron Age, including Bronze Age religion, technology and travel, for example, Stonehenge.
● To develop a chronologically secure knowledge and understanding of British, local and world history, establishing clear narratives within and across the periods they study.
● To regularly address and sometimes devise historically valid questions about change, cause, similarity and difference, and significance.
● To construct informed responses that involve thoughtful selection and organisation of relevant historical information.
● To understand how our knowledge of the past is constructed from a range of sources.
● To understand that different versions of past events may exist, giving some reasons for this.

Expected outcomes

● All children will describe at least one change from the Stone Age to the Bronze Age.
● Most children will describe several changes from the Stone Age to the Bronze Age.
● Some children will consider detailed changes to aspects of life as well as overarching social changes.

Resources

Interactive activity 'Changes in Britain from the Stone Age to the Bronze Age' on the CD-ROM

2: How did Britain change from the Stone Age to the Bronze Age?

Introduction

● Ask: *What changes occurred in Britain from the Stone Age to the Bronze Age?*
● Discuss children's ideas. These could be broken down into categories, such as burials (the change from communal long barrows to round barrows designed for a single person), getting food (the move from a nomadic hunter-gatherer lifestyle towards settled farming and the growth of small hamlets and communities), houses (the change from cave dwelling and temporary shelters made from wood and animal skins towards settlements with roundhouses), tools and weapons (with the introduction of bronze and metalworking technology), lifestyle (the growth of communities and the concept of individual status, as bronze objects became prized possessions of the wealthy and important), and so on.

Paired work or Independent work

● Ask children to complete the interactive activity 'Changes in Britain from the Stone Age to the Bronze Age' on the CD-ROM, in which they need to choose the right option from a drop-down menu, based on whether the sentences apply to the Stone Age, Bronze Age or both.
● This activity could be used as an assessment tool, covering the children's learning about the Stone Age and Bronze Age.
● Alternatively, children could write their own sentences, or draw pictures, to show the progression from one period to the next.

Differentiation

● Differentiate by outcome, with more confident learners completing more of the interactive activity correctly.

Review

● In a follow-up discussion, after the interactive activity has been completed, ask: *Do you think life was easier in the Stone Age or Bronze Age? In which period would you prefer to live? In which time period was life most similar to Britain today?* Children should be able to justify their choices with historical facts about these ages.

Lesson objectives
● To understand the changes in Britain from the Stone Age to the Iron Age, including Bronze Age religion, technology and travel, for example, Stonehenge.
● To develop a chronologically secure knowledge and understanding of British, local and world history, establishing clear narratives within and across the periods they study.

Resources
Interactive activity 'Y3 Autumn 2 quiz' on the CD-ROM

The Bronze Age

Revise

● Write the following words and phrases on the board: bronze, Stonehenge, roundhouse, Amesbury Archer, round barrows, the Beaker people, aerial archaeology.
● Challenge children to talk for 30 seconds on one of the themes, without hesitation, repetition or deviation.

Assess

● Ask the children to complete the interactive activity 'Y3 Autumn 2 quiz' on the CD-ROM, in which they answer multiple-choice questions covering the chapter content.
● Give children a set length of time (for example, 15 minutes) to answer the questions. This can be used as part of a formal assessment or as a fun challenge activity, giving children the opportunity to show what they have learned about the topic.
● Some children may need adult support to read the questions aloud.

Further practice

● Show children a Bronze Age artefact, such as the Mold gold cape found at: www.britishmuseum.org. Ask: *What kind of technology might historians use to find out how old this is? Who might have owned it and why?*

Lesson objectives
● To understand the changes in Britain from the Stone Age to the Iron Age, including Bronze Age religion, technology and travel, for example, Stonehenge.
● To develop a chronologically secure knowledge and understanding of British, local and world history, establishing clear narratives within and across the periods they study.
● To note connections, contrasts and trends over time.

Resources
Internet access

Comparing the Stone Age and Bronze Age

Revise

● Recap how a roundhouse was built, for example by watching a reconstruction of a roundhouse, found online by searching for 'reconstructing a roundhouse'.

Assess

● Ask children to divide their page in two and write 'Stone Age' in one half of the page and 'Bronze Age' in the other.
● Write 'Homes', 'Burials' and 'Getting food' on the board. Ask children to choose one category and write about how it changed from the Stone Age to Bronze Age.
● Less confident writers could share their ideas verbally with adult support. Some children may wish to draw labelled diagrams rather than write their answers.

Further practice

● Ask children to write, illustrate, discuss or act out a set of simple instructions for carrying out a Bronze Age task, such as creating a roundhouse, digging a round barrow, making a piece of Bell-Beaker pottery or making bronze items from copper and tin ore.

Name: _____   Date: _____

The Amesbury Archer

■ Read the text below and complete the thinking challenge.

In 2002, archaeologists in Wiltshire made a very interesting discovery. They found the body of a man buried in the ground near Amesbury (not far from the famous stone circle, Stonehenge).

Radiocarbon dating was carried out on the skeleton and suggested that it was buried around 2300BC.

The grave contained about 100 artefacts, including objects made of gold and bronze – the oldest metal objects ever found in Britain. These helped historians to build a picture of Bronze Age life.

Here are some of the things found buried in the grave:

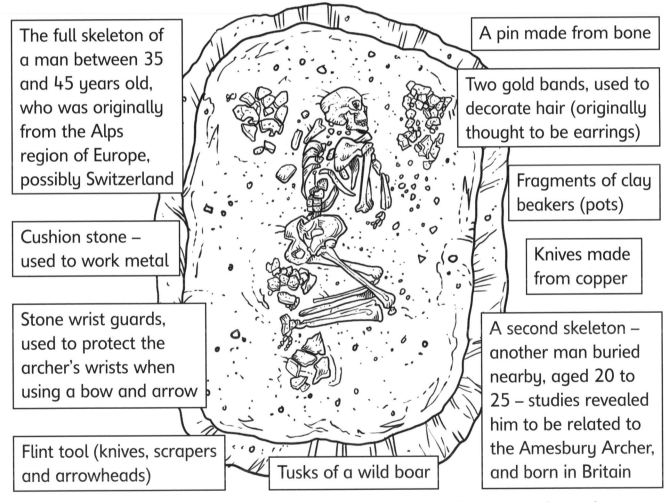

The full skeleton of a man between 35 and 45 years old, who was originally from the Alps region of Europe, possibly Switzerland

A pin made from bone

Two gold bands, used to decorate hair (originally thought to be earrings)

Fragments of clay beakers (pots)

Cushion stone – used to work metal

Knives made from copper

Stone wrist guards, used to protect the archer's wrists when using a bow and arrow

A second skeleton – another man buried nearby, aged 20 to 25 – studies revealed him to be related to the Amesbury Archer, and born in Britain

Flint tool (knives, scrapers and arrowheads)

Tusks of a wild boar

■ **Thinking challenge:** each object provides a piece of evidence about the past. What can you work out about Bronze Age life from the skeleton and his artefacts? What questions would you like to ask the archer if he were still alive?

I can use evidence to make inferences about the Bronze Age.

How did you do?

Britain's Bronze Age

■ Read the following text about the Bronze Age in Britain.

Around 2500BC a big change began in Britain. Lots of people travelled here from Europe. Historians call them the Bell-Beaker, or Beaker, people because they used pottery drinking beakers, shaped like upside-down bells.

The Beaker people brought with them new knowledge and technology. They knew how to find metal ore in rocks and create metal objects.

Britain's natural landscape contained sources of copper and tin. These two metals could be joined together to make a very hard metal called bronze. Bronze tools and weapons were much stronger than the flint ones that Stone Age people had been using for thousands of years. Metal could also be melted down and turned into different shapes.

Bronze Age people built mines, such as the one at Great Orme in Wales, to remove rocks containing metal ore. They used stone hammers and picks made from red deer antlers. The rock was crushed with a stone to separate the ore from the rock surrounding it.

People then had to create a very hot fire, using bellows, to melt the metal. Once melted, it could be poured into a mould made out of clay or stone. When it cooled, it could be shaped with hammers and then polished.

This process could be used to make anything from swords to arrowheads to jewellery. When the objects were no longer useful, they could be melted down again to make other objects.

People all over Britain began to use bronze and it was traded here and overseas. Bronze objects became valued personal possessions, used to show how important or wealthy a person was.

Making bronze

■ These pictures show how people made bronze objects, but the steps are mixed up. Cut them out and put them in the right order.

When the metal was melted, it could be poured into moulds.	The metal objects were cooled and shaped with a hammer, then polished.

During the Bronze Age, people travelled to Britain from Europe. They knew how to find metal and make metal objects.	Rocks were crushed with stones to separate the metal ore.
	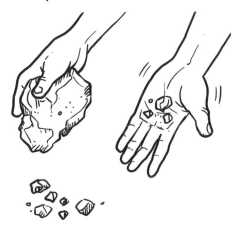
Rocks containing metal ore were mined using hammers and picks.	A very hot fire was needed to melt the metal.

The Iron Age

In this chapter, children continue the chronological narrative of Britain's history, moving on to the final stage of prehistory with the Iron Age. They further develop their understanding of the use of evidence to build a picture of the past, considering artefacts such as the Llyn Cerrig Bach hoard, archaeological sites such as hill forts, and Roman written accounts of the Celts. Children learn about the different tribes and where they settled. They study Celtic warriors and their weapons and also look at some of the advances in technology, which led to increased productivity.

Chapter at a glance

Curriculum objectives

• Changes in Britain from the Stone Age to the Iron Age, including Iron Age hill forts: tribal kingdoms, farming, art and culture.

Week	Lesson	Summary of activities	Expected outcomes
1	1	• Children learn about some of the main Celtic tribes, performing a rap of their names.	• Can describe some of the main Celtic tribes.
	2	• Children colour code a map of Britain to show some of the main tribal kingdoms of the Celts.	• Can locate the main tribal kingdoms.
2	1	• Children look at images of finds from the Llyn Cerrig Bach hoard, considering what they reveal about Iron Age life.	• Can make inferences about Iron Age life from the finds of the Llyn Cerrig Bach hoard.
	2	• Children read a Roman description of the Celts, using it to draw a picture of a Celt.	• Can describe the Celts' appearance.
3	1	• Children read about Celtic warriors and their weapons, then create sketches of Iron Age weapons from actual artefacts.	• Can describe Celtic warfare and weaponry.
	2	• Children work in groups to create a movement piece based on Celt warriors trying to scare their enemies.	• Can describe Celtic warfare and weaponry.
4	1	• Children revisit roundhouses and research two other types of Iron Age dwellings – brochs and crannogs.	• Can describe Iron Age dwellings.
	2	• Children write a letter to a friend persuading them of the benefits of living in a hill fort.	• Can describe Iron Age hill forts.
5	1	• Children work in groups or as a whole class to create a model of a hill fort.	• Can create a model of a hill fort.
	2	• Children work in groups or as a whole class to complete a model of a hill fort.	• Can create a model of a hill fort.
6	1	• Children plan and rehearse an advertisement based on an item of Iron Age technology.	• Can describe the benefits of Iron Age advances in technology.
	2	• Children film or perform an advertisement based on an item of Iron Age technology.	• Can describe the benefits of Iron Age advances in technology.
Assess and review		• To review the half-term's work.	

Expected prior learning

● The previous units on the Stone Age and Bronze Age should be completed before studying the Iron Age, in order to consolidate the chronological narrative of Britain's history. Elements of this chapter, such as the information about Celtic warriors, will be reviewed in Year 4, when children study the Roman invasion of Britain.

Overview of progression

● Children further develop their understanding of chronology, placing the ages of Britain's prehistory in order – Stone Age, Bronze Age and Iron Age.
● They continue to consolidate their understanding of different kinds of evidence to construct our understanding of the past, looking at artefacts, archaeological sites and Roman written eyewitness accounts of the Celts. They see that evidence can be interpreted in different ways.
● They gain a sense of change over time, considering how the widespread use of iron and Iron Age technology impacted on daily life. They also consider how hill forts have changed over time.
● They draw comparisons between different forms of Iron Age dwelling.
● They are given opportunities to ask and answer historically valid questions and develop their understanding of abstract terms, such as 'period', 'community', 'evidence' and 'interpretation'.

Creative context

● Cross-curricular links include:
   ● engaging in persuasive writing by creating television commercials to advertise Iron Age technology and by writing a letter to demonstrate the benefits of living in a hill fort;
   ● music, with children performing a rap featuring the names of Celtic tribes;
   ● creating a movement piece inspired by Celtic warriors trying to scare the enemy before battle;
   ● sketching Iron Age weapons, drawing a picture of a Celt from a description, and building a model of a hill fort.

Background knowledge

● During the Iron Age, iron came into increasingly widespread practical use throughout Britain. Unlike bronze, iron was available to everyone, not just the wealthy. It is much harder than bronze and can easily be reheated and reshaped when it becomes bent or dull.
● There were numerous technical innovations during this period. The first 'machines', such as the rotary quern stone (for grinding grain), iron-tipped ard (plough), pole lathe and pottery wheel meant an increase in speed, efficiency and productivity. This led to population growth and the accumulation of wealth.
● There was no sense of a unified Britain. Instead, Britain was a land inhabited by many Celtic tribes, or clans. Many historians believe that they fought each other for land, and warriors were greatly admired.
● Hill forts became common defence structures. Historians have estimated that there are over 3000 Iron Age hill forts in Britain. Tribes built settlements on the tops of hills and then dug ditches and built banks of earth in the land around making it difficult for enemies to attack. A fence was built around the community for extra protection. Hill forts were not just for defence; they were designed to mark the boundaries of the tribe's territory and to show how wealthy and powerful the tribe was.
● Roundhouses were still in use and Scotland saw the development of brochs (tall drystone towers) and crannogs (homes built on artificial wooden islands, linked to the land by a wooden causeway).

Lesson objectives
● To understand the changes in Britain from the Stone Age to the Iron Age, including Iron Age hill forts: tribal kingdoms, farming, art and culture.
● To develop a chronologically secure knowledge and understanding of British, local and world history, establishing clear narratives within and across the periods they study.
● To regularly address and sometimes devise historically valid questions about change, cause, similarity and difference, and significance.

Expected outcomes
● All children will name at least one Celtic tribe.
● Most children will perform a rap featuring the names of several Celtic tribes.
● Some children will describe several Celtic tribes.

Resources
Photocopiable page 59 'The Iron Age Celts Rap'; media resource 'The Iron Age Celts rap' on the CD-ROM

Week I lesson plans

This week children move on to the last stage of prehistory in the chronological narrative of Britain, as they learn about the Iron Age and Celtic way of life. They perform a rap featuring the names of some of the main Celtic tribes. They then use maps of Britain to find the areas in which they settled and the main tribal kingdoms.

I: What were the main Celtic tribes?

Introduction
● Look again at a timeline of Britain from the Stone Age to the Iron Age to help children identify the order of the periods.

Whole-class work
● Tell the children that the Iron Age is so called because of the use of a new metal, iron, which was cheaper and stronger than bronze, so it was more effective and could be used by everyone. People that we now call Celts lived in western Europe and many came to settle in Britain.
● Explain that different tribes took over different territories, led by a chieftain or king, and that there was a lot of competition for land.
● Read through the rap on photocopiable page 59 'The Iron Age Celts rap'. An audio version – media resource 'The Iron Age Celts rap' is also provided on the CD-ROM; refer to this for how to pronounce the different names of the tribes.
● Tell the children that they are going to rehearse and perform the rap, starting slowly and building up speed. This could be done as a whole class, with different children saying different lines or tribal names, or the children could be organised into groups to develop their own performances. The class could perform the rap to other children in the school, for example at a Celts assembly.

Differentiation
● Support: mixed-ability groupings may be beneficial.
● Challenge: children may wish to research facts about some of the tribes, or they could find out about other tribes not mentioned in the rap.

Review
● Ask the children to think of different ways to remember the tribes, such as by memorising the rap, drawing a picture or symbol for each tribe, or creating a mnemonic to help them to remember them all.
● Challenge volunteers to come to the front of the class and remember all the tribes; ask other children to help them out if they get stuck.

Lesson objectives
● To understand the changes in Britain from the Stone Age to the Iron Age, including Iron Age hill forts: tribal kingdoms, farming, art and culture.
● To develop a chronologically secure knowledge and understanding of British, local and world history, establishing clear narratives within and across the periods they study.
● To regularly address and sometimes devise historically valid questions about change, cause, similarity and difference, and significance.

Expected outcomes
● All children will match at least one Celtic tribe with its location.
● Most children will match several Celtic tribes with their locations.
● Some children will match all the main Celtic tribes with their locations.

Resources
Photocopiable page 60 'Celtic tribal kingdoms'; photocopiable page 'Celtic tribal kingdoms (answers)' from the CD-ROM; atlases or maps of Britain (showing the counties); internet access

2: Where did the Celts settle in Britain?

Introduction
● Give the children one minute to see how many Celtic tribes they can name.

Whole-class work
● Tell the children that they are going to be using atlases/maps of Britain to colour in the areas ruled by different tribes, using the map on photocopiable page 60 'Celtic tribal kingdoms'.
● If needs be, talk through the skills needed to use an atlas or map, searching for different regions within the UK.
● Discuss how to create a colour code on the photocopiable sheet, with colours relating to the different tribes.

Paired work or Independent work
● Ask children to look at the descriptions of where the main Celtic tribes lived (on the photocopiable sheet) and to colour in the appropriate area of the map, creating a colour code to link the area with the tribe name. They could check against the map on photocopiable page 'Celtic tribal kingdoms (answers), from the CD-ROM.

Differentiation
● Support: mixed-ability pairings may be beneficial.
● Challenge: children should note changes to borders in Britain from the kingdoms ruled by different tribes through to today's counties.

Review
● Check that children have colour coded their maps accurately.
● Ask: *Did you notice any changes in the way Britain is divided into different regions from the Iron Age to today?* Look at the maps again and discuss how territories have changed. For example, many of the regions have been subdivided to form the modern counties; however the territories of the Iceni (Norfolk), Parisi (East Yorkshire) and Dumnonii (Devon and Cornwall) are still largely identifiable.

Week 2 lesson plans

This week, children use two forms of evidence to build a picture of Celtic life. They investigate artefacts from the Iron Age hoard at Llyn Cerrig Bach, considering what these finds reveal about Celtic life. They then look at a Roman written eyewitness account of the Celts' appearance and manner, using the information to draw a picture of a Celt.

1: What can evidence tell us about the Iron Age?

Introduction
- Use Google Maps or satellite images to locate Llyn Cerrig Bach (a lake in Anglesey).
- Tell the children that a hoard of Iron Age artefacts was discovered in the lake during World War II. Ask: *Why might they have been in the lake?* (It is believed that water held spiritual significance for the Celts. Artefacts have often been found in lakes and rivers, thought to be religious offerings.)

Whole-class work
- Show the children one of the finds from the Llyn Cerrig Bach hoard (source online, for example at: www.museumwales.ac.uk).
- Ask: *What is it? What was it used for? Who might have owned it? What information about the Iron Age can we work out from this piece of evidence? Has anything changed since the Bronze Age? What questions would you like to ask the owner?*

Group work or Paired work
- Organise children into groups or pairs. Ask them to look through the other artefacts from the hoard, discussing the questions above for each item. Include the other Iron Age items if desired, such as a bronze cauldron, or brooch.
- The children should use this evidence to make as many inferences as they can about Iron Age life, listing these on a large piece of paper.

> **Differentiation**
> - Support: mixed-ability pairings may be beneficial.
> - Challenge: children should draw comparisons between these finds and those discovered with the Amesbury Archer, reflecting the development from Bronze Age to Iron Age.

Review
- Ask groups to share their ideas with the class. Did any groups have different interpretations of the evidence?
- Ask: *How was this hoard similar to and different from the artefacts found with the Amesbury Archer?* (For example, both were discovered in relatively recent times and included metal weapons. The Llyn Cerrig Bach hoard was found in a lake rather than buried, and it contained a much larger number and variety of artefacts. The Amesbury Archer's grave contained an individual's personal possessions, whereas the hoard's artefacts seemed to belong to different people.)

Lesson objectives
- To understand the changes in Britain from the Stone Age to the Iron Age, including Iron Age hill forts: tribal kingdoms, farming, art and culture.
- To develop a chronologically secure knowledge and understanding of British, local and world history, establishing clear narratives within and across the periods they study.
- To note connections, contrasts and trends over time.
- To regularly address and sometimes devise historically valid questions about change, cause, similarity and difference, and significance.
- To construct informed responses that involve thoughtful selection and organisation of relevant historical information.
- To understand how our knowledge of the past is constructed from a range of sources.
- To understand that different versions of past events may exist, giving some reasons for this.

Expected outcomes
- All children will describe some items found in the Llyn Cerrig Bach hoard.
- Most children will make at least one inference about the Iron Age from evidence.
- Some children will make several inferences about the Iron Age from evidence.

Resources
Pictures of the Llyn Cerrig Bach hoard (source online); large sheets of paper and marker pens

Lesson objectives

● To understand the changes in Britain from the Stone Age to the Iron Age, including Iron Age hill forts: tribal kingdoms, farming, art and culture.
● To regularly address and sometimes devise historically valid questions about change, cause, similarity and difference, and significance.
● To construct informed responses that involve thoughtful selection and organisation of relevant historical information.
● To understand how our knowledge of the past is constructed from a range of sources.
● To understand that different versions of past events may exist, giving some reasons for this.

Expected outcomes

● All children will draw a picture of a Celt.
● Most children will describe a Celt from written evidence.
● Some children will consider the limitations of relying on a Roman view of the Celts.

Resources

Photocopiable page 61 'What were the Celts like?'

2: What were the Celts like?

Introduction

● Ask the children to imagine a scenario: Oliver comes up to a teacher at lunchtime and tells her that Kyle pushed him.
● Ask: *Would it be fair if the teacher only listened to Oliver's point of view?* Discuss why or why not, and introduce the idea of bias. Ask: *How could the teacher be sure that Oliver's account was true? What if Oliver had something against Kyle and wanted to get him into trouble?*
● Tell the children that historical evidence can be similarly unfair, or biased. Explain that the Celts didn't write things down, so the only written information we have about them comes from the Romans (people from a powerful empire, who wanted to rule Britain). We therefore only have one side of the story, just like the teacher who only heard Oliver's account of being pushed by Kyle.

Whole-class work

● Read and discuss photocopiable page 61 'What were the Celts like?'. Tell the children to pick out any information it provides about the Celts. Create a class list of bullet points on the board.
● Ask: *What sort of impression does this give of the Celts? Why might Diodorus want to create this impression?* This may be a good opportunity to discuss the difference between fact and opinion, referring to the text on the photocopiable sheet. (Diodorus was a Roman, and so may have wanted to present the enemy in an unfavourable light – as uncultured savages.)

Independent work

● Ask children to draw a labelled picture of a Celt, based on the information provided on the photocopiable sheet.

Differentiation

● Support: children should incorporate one or more pieces of information about the Celts into their drawings.
● Challenge: children should consider how well the Roman eyewitness account can be relied upon; on their drawings, they could label the features that may not be accurate.

Review

● Look at some of the pictures the children have created, as a class. Check that the drawings reflect the Roman description, in terms of their dress, hair, stature and manners.
● Ask: *What are some of the problems with relying on this description?* (It may well be biased.) *What questions would you like to ask a Celt if he or she were here?*

Lesson objectives
● To understand the changes in Britain from the Stone Age to the Iron Age, including Iron Age hill forts: tribal kingdoms, farming, art and culture.
● To develop a chronologically secure knowledge and understanding of British, local and world history, establishing clear narratives within and across the periods they study.
● To develop the appropriate use of historical terms.
● To understand how our knowledge of the past is constructed from a range of sources.
● To understand that different versions of past events may exist, giving some reasons for this.

Expected outcomes
● All children will describe at least one fact about Celtic warriors and their weapons.
● Most children will describe Celtic warriors and their weapons.
● Some children will describe how evidence provides information about Celt weapons.

Resources
Photocopiable page 'Celtic warriors and weapons' from the CD-ROM; pictures of Iron Age artefacts, including the Kirkburn sword (source online)

Week 3 lesson plans

This week, children are introduced to Celtic warriors and weaponry. They read about the kinds of weapon a warrior might use and sketch examples of these from actual artefacts. In the second lesson, children work in groups on movement pieces, based on Celtic warriors scaring their enemies before battle.

1: How did the Celts fight? (1)

Introduction
● Show an image and information about the Kirkburn Sword, one of the finest Iron Age swords ever found (source online).
● Draw the children's attention to the careful engravings and different colours on the handle. Ask: *What does this artefact tell you about its owner?*
● Explain that the sword was found in a grave, buried with a man in his 20s or 30s, which was reasonably old for an Iron Age Celt! It was unusual for people to be buried with their possessions at this time. The sword was made of 37 pieces of iron, bronze and horn, and was studded with red glass. It would have been a valued possession, and shows evidence of having been repaired. The owner was therefore likely to have been an important, wealthy person.

Whole-class work
● Read and discuss the photocopiable page 'Celtic warriors and weapons' from the CD-ROM, which describes what the Celts looked like when they went into battle, and how they fought.
● Ask: *What did the Celts do to try to scare their enemies?* (They painted their bodies with woad, bleached their hair and rode noisy chariots.) *Why do you think they did these things?* (They wanted to look more intimidating so that their enemies would feel like the weaker side and be more likely to retreat.) *If you could meet a Celtic warrior, what questions would you ask him or her?*

Paired work or Independent work
● Provide the children with pictures of some Iron Age artefacts. (These can be sourced online: for example, the British Museum has an online Iron Age gallery at www.britishmuseum.org.)
● The children should select one or more of the weapons – a shield, sword, helmet, spearhead, scabbard, and so on – and complete a detailed sketch.

> **Differentiation**
> ● Challenge: children should add information about the artefacts they draw, such as the estimated date, where the object was found, the material it is made from, and so on.

Review
● Look at a range of drawings the children have created, as a class.
● Ask: *What is this? What's it made of? What would it have been used for? Who might have used it?*

Lesson objectives
● To understand the changes in Britain from the Stone Age to the Iron Age, including Iron Age hill forts: tribal kingdoms, farming, art and culture.
● To develop a chronologically secure knowledge and understanding of British, local and world history, establishing clear narratives within and across the periods they study.

Expected outcomes
● All children will participate in a movement piece based on Celtic warriors.
● Most children will help to create a movement piece based on Celtic warriors.
● Some children will critically review a movement piece based on Celtic warriors.

Resources
Open space (for example, school hall or playground)

2: How did the Celts fight? (2)

Introduction
● Take the children to an open space, such as the school hall or playground.
● Tell them that they are going to work on a movement piece based on Celtic warriors.
● Give them two minutes to share with a partner everything they can remember about Celtic warriors.
● Discuss what the children remember, as a whole class. Elicit that they were reportedly fierce, noisy, painted in woad with bleached spiky hair and brightly coloured clothing; rode in chariots and carried weapons such as sword and spear, with shields for protection.

Whole-class work
● Ask the children to move about the room in the manner of warriors returning home victorious from battle. Encourage the children to be loud, brash and gloating.
● Gather them in a circle. Begin a continuous movement, coupled with a sound, which everyone has to copy. When everyone is doing it, the focus passes to the person on the left, who comes up with the next movement and sound.

Group work
● Organise the children into groups and tell them to imagine they are Celtic clans.
● Ask them to work together to come up with five movements, each with a vocal sound, designed to scare off the enemy. These movements should be repeated to create ten movements in all.
● They should rehearse these and work on putting them together so that they flow and so that performers are in time with each other.
● Each group could have a tribal name and vocalisations could correspond with the syllables, such as Cat-u-vell-aun-i.

Differentiation
● Support: mixed-ability groups may be beneficial.

Review
● Invite groups, two at a time, to perform their pieces, facing each other.
● The rest of the children should act as audience members, responding critically to the performances.
● The audience could vote for the scariest or most effective performance, which could then be pitted against the next group until a winner is found.

Week 4 lesson plans

This week, children look at different types of Iron Age dwelling, revisiting roundhouses and investigating the brochs and crannogs that were used in Scotland and its islands. They use the internet to investigate these and consider in which they would prefer to live. Children then begin to learn about hill forts, exploring their features in preparation for making a model of a hill fort in the following lessons.

Lesson objectives
● To understand the changes in Britain from the Stone Age to the Iron Age, including Iron Age hill forts: tribal kingdoms, farming, art and culture.
● To develop a chronologically secure knowledge and understanding of British, local and world history, establishing clear narratives within and across the periods they study.
● To note connections, contrasts and trends over time.
● To regularly address and sometimes devise historically valid questions about change, cause, similarity and difference, and significance.
● To understand how our knowledge of the past is constructed from a range of sources.

Expected outcomes
● All children will describe at least one type of Iron Age dwelling.
● Most children will describe three types of Iron Age dwelling.
● Some children will compare three types of Iron Age dwelling.

Resources
Internet access; photocopiable page 'Roundhouses' from the CD-ROM (optional)

1: What were homes like in the Iron Age?

Introduction
● Ask the children to describe a roundhouse (from the previous chapter). Refresh their memory by referring to photocopiable page 'Roundhouses' from the CD-ROM, if necessary.
● Explain that the style of homes in the Iron Age was very similar, though some had stone walls instead of wattle and daub, and a metal cauldron may have been used for cooking.

Whole-class work
● Tell the children that experimental archaeology (building replicas) has been a key source of evidence about life in Iron Age homes. Look at replica Iron Age villages, if desired, for example at:
  ● www.butser.org.uk
  ● www.museumwales.ac.uk
  ● www.theroundhouse.org.
● Explain that there were two other types of house in Iron Age Britain, which were used in Scotland and some of the islands, such as Orkney and Shetland – brochs and crannogs.

Group work or Paired work
● Ask the children to read about brochs and crannogs, for example by visiting the relevant section of the BBC history website (they don't need to read about hill forts in this lesson).
● Children can either write down bullet points about each dwelling or they could answer the following questions:
  ● What is a crannog?
  ● Where can you see a reconstruction of a crannog?
  ● When were brochs built?
  ● What were broch walls made from?
  ● How tall were the brochs?
● Watch the related video clips on the BBC site or view the virtual tour of the Oakbank Crannog (optional).
● Thinking about roundhouses, brochs and crannogs, ask children to discuss with their partner or group the main features of each dwelling. Ask them to decide which they would have preferred to live in and their reasons.

Differentiation
● Support: mixed-ability groups may be beneficial.

Review
● Discuss the features of roundhouses, brochs and crannongs as a class.
● Take a class vote on which they would prefer to live in. Ask children to give reasons for their choice.

2: What was it like to live in an Iron Age hill fort?

Introduction
● Show children the aerial view of Old Oswestry hill fort, for example, by using www.pastscape.org.uk, or by searching for other satellite images online.
● Ask them to describe what they see and to offer suggestions as to what it might be.

Whole-class work
● Show some images of other hill forts (for example, Danebury and Maiden Castle).
● Read and discuss photocopiable page 'Hill forts' from the CD-ROM. This gives some background information on hill forts, and also includes aerial photographs and an illustration to show how a hill would have looked during the Iron Age.
● Ask: *Why might hill forts be good places to live?* (People were protected there, and could live in a community.) *Why might hill forts be difficult to attack?* (Any attackers could be seen from a long way off, giving the people of the hill fort time to defend themselves. It would not be easy for enemies to make their way through the ditches at the base or the climb the hill to attack.) *What resources and skills would people need in order to live here?* (People would have needed to be resilient in order to live in such exposed locations. However, they also would have worked together cooperatively, with different people taking on different roles – such as farmer, builder, tool maker, and so on.) *What disadvantages might there be?* (A major disadvantage might be the lack of a water supply within the hill fort. People would have to travel down the hill to a river or lake to obtain fresh water.) *How have they changed over time?* (Most hill forts today retain the original shape of the hill and surrounding man-made ditches. The structures on the hill itself, such as roundhouses and fence, can no longer be seen but excavations have found such artefacts as weapons, pottery, quern stones, bronze and iron artefacts, animal bones and grain storage pits.)

Group work
● Tell the children to imagine that they are an Iron Age Celt, living in a hill fort. Ask: *What kinds of daily task might people at the hill fort carry out? How would they get food and water?*
● Ask them to write a letter to a friend who lives in a small village, persuading them to come and live in the hill fort and describing the benefits of doing this.

Differentiation
● Support: children can write simple sentences or a few bullet points about the advantages of life in a hill fort.
● Challenge: children should reflect on the many benefits of life in a hill fort and use persuasive techniques in their letters.

Review
● Ask two or three children to share their letters. The rest of the class should listen to see if there's anything they could add.

Week 5 lesson plans

This week, children continue to explore Iron Age hill forts. They use photographs and artists' illustrations of hill forts to build a model. This can be completed as a whole class project or in groups.

1: What were hill forts like? (1)

Lesson objectives
- To understand the changes in Britain from the Stone Age to the Iron Age, including Iron Age hill forts: tribal kingdoms, farming, art and culture.
- To develop a chronologically secure knowledge and understanding of British, local and world history, establishing clear narratives within and across the periods they study.
- To note connections, contrasts and trends over time.
- To regularly address and sometimes devise historically valid questions about change, cause, similarity and difference, and significance.
- To understand how our knowledge of the past is constructed from a range of sources.

Expected outcomes
- All children will help to create a model of a hill fort.
- Most children will describe the features of a hill fort.
- Some children will consider proportion and scale as they help to create a model of a hill fort.

Resources
Photocopiable page 'Hill forts' from the CD-ROM; internet access; materials for model making; digital cameras (optional)

Introduction
- Ask the class to come up with a list of things that one might find inside, or as part of, a hill fort, such as a perimeter fence with a gate (perhaps hung with severed heads as a warning to potential attackers), animals, roundhouses and ploughed land for crops.

Whole-class work or Group work
- This is a two-day project in which children work together to build a model of an Iron Age hill fort. This can be organised in a number of ways, with the whole class making one large model and children allocated jobs (such as creating the hill, fence or roundhouses) or smaller models can be made by groups or individuals. It can be a child-led project, with children deciding the best way to go about the challenge, or an adult can organise the construction process.
- The model could be of an actual hill fort, such as Old Oswestry, or children could design their own, using typical features. Refer to photocopiable page 'Hill forts' from the CD-ROM as necessary.
- As a suggestion, the hill, ditches and banks could be made from papier mâché; roundhouses from card; fences from cut-down lolly sticks and animals from clay.

Differentiation
- Tasks in the model building can be differentiated.
- Support: children could complete more simple tasks, such as making posts for the fence or working with an adult to create the hill.
- Challenge: children could consider proportion and scale. If modelling a real hill fort, challenge children to research it and write facts, which can be displayed with the model.

Review
- Take stock of progress so far and check that all areas of the fort are progressing well.
- Ask questions such as: *What have you found most challenging? Do you have enough materials? Is the design working, or do we need to revisit the design at the beginning of next lesson?*

Lesson objectives
- To understand the changes in Britain from the Stone Age to the Iron Age, including Iron Age hill forts: tribal kingdoms, farming, art and culture.
- To develop a chronologically secure knowledge and understanding of British, local and world history, establishing clear narratives within and across the periods they study.
- To note connections, contrasts and trends over time.
- To regularly address and sometimes devise historically valid questions about change, cause, similarity and difference, and significance.
- To understand how our knowledge of the past is constructed from a range of sources.

Expected outcomes
- All children will help to create a model of a hill fort.
- Most children will describe the features of a hill fort.
- Some children will consider proportion and scale as they help to create a model of a hill fort.

Resources
Photocopiable page 'Hill Forts' from the CD-ROM; materials for model making; digital camera (optional)

2: What were hill forts like? (2)

Introduction
- Ask: *What have you found most challenging so far about making the model?*
- Revisit any aspects of design, or reallocate children to different tasks, as necessary, depending on the outcome of the discussion at the end of the previous lesson.

Whole-class work or Group work
- Children continue to work on their model of a hill fort.
- Ask children to take photographs of the completed model, comparing these with the images of real hill forts (optional).

Differentiation
- Support: children could complete more simple tasks, such as making posts for the fence or working with an adult to create the hill.
- Challenge: children could consider proportion and scale. If modelling a real hill fort, challenge children to research it and write facts, which can be displayed with the model.

Review
- Look at the model(s) the children have made. Ask: *How is this like a real Iron Age hill fort?*
- Use the fort(s) as a display at lunchtime or for assembly, with a small group of children talking through the features and the steps involved in putting the model together.

Week 6 lesson plans

This week children learn about three examples of Iron Age technology – the pottery wheel, the iron tip for the ard (plough) and the rotary quern stone. They discuss how these might have impacted on life and improved efficiency. In groups, children create television advertisements to 'sell' these products to Celtic chieftains.

1: How did technology change in the Iron Age? (1)

Introduction

● Write the names of three pieces of modern technology on the board (for example, mobile phone, washing machine, computer). Ask: *What do we use these for? What would we do if we didn't have them? How do these things make our lives easier? Do they have any disadvantages?*

Whole-class work

● Read and discuss photocopiable page 'Iron Age technology' from the CD-ROM.
● Talk about how each of the items on the photocopiable sheet might have made an impact on Iron Age life, considering both initial timesaving and the wider impact of increased production, generation of wealth and population growth.

Group work

● Organise children into groups. Allocate one piece of Iron Age technology for each group (or let them select their own).
● Tell the groups that they are going to be creating a short advertisement, in the style of a television commercial, for their item. The 'audience' will be Celtic chieftains in charge of hill fort communities.
● Talk about the kinds of persuasive techniques used in television commercials (for example, a summary of the product's benefits, special offers, questions, slogans, jingles, repetition, endorsements from celebrities and role models, eye-catching visuals, storylines, humour). Encourage children to incorporate some of these strategies into their adverts.
● Show some examples of television adverts if the children are unsure of how to go about creating their own.
● Provide the children with some questions to help them gather their ideas, such as: *Why might someone in a hill fort community use this item? Who is most likely to use it? How would it improve their lives? How would it benefit the community? Would it help trade?*
● Give them time to begin to plan and rehearse their adverts, ensuring that every member of the group contributes in some way

Lesson objectives
● To understand the changes in Britain from the Stone Age to the Iron Age, including Iron Age hill forts: tribal kingdoms, farming, art and culture.
● To develop a chronologically secure knowledge and understanding of British, local and world history, establishing clear narratives within and across the periods they study.
● To note connections, contrasts and trends over time.
● To regularly address and sometimes devise historically valid questions about change, cause, similarity and difference, and significance.
● To construct informed responses that involve thoughtful selection and organisation of relevant historical information.

Expected outcomes
● All children will describe at least one item of Iron Age technology.
● Most children will describe the benefits of at least one item of Iron Age technology.
● Some children will describe how Iron Age technology impacted on production.

Resources
Video clip of a quern stone in use (source online; optional); photocopiable page 'Iron Age technology' from the CD-ROM

Differentiation
● Support: mixed-ability groups may be beneficial, with children taking on different roles according to interest and confidence.
● Challenge: children should consider the wider impact that technology has on improving efficiency and generating wealth.

Review

● Have a trouble-shooting session to check children's progress. Are they stuck with anything? Are they on track to perform the adverts in the following lesson? Have they included a range of persuasive features in their adverts? Are they secure in how their object is used, and the benefits of using it?

Lesson objectives

● To understand the changes in Britain from the Stone Age to the Iron Age, including Iron Age hill forts: tribal kingdoms, farming, art and culture.
● To develop a chronologically secure knowledge and understanding of British, local and world history, establishing clear narratives within and across the periods they study.
● To note connections, contrasts and trends over time.
● To regularly address and sometimes devise historically valid questions about change, cause, similarity and difference, and significance.
● To construct informed responses that involve thoughtful selection and organisation of relevant historical information.

Expected outcomes

● All children will describe at least one item of Iron Age technology.
● Most children will describe the benefits of at least one item of Iron Age technology.
● Some children will describe how Iron Age technology impacted on production.

Resources

Photocopiable page 'Iron Age technology' from the CD-ROM; video cameras (optional)

2: How did technology change in the Iron Age? (2)

Introduction

● Ask children to talk about a television commercial that they remember or particularly like. Ask: *What features make it memorable or entertaining?*
● Recap the features of adverts discussed in the previous lesson by asking different children to name one. These could include a summary of the product's benefits, special offers, questions, slogans, jingles, repetition, endorsements from celebrities and role models, eye-catching visuals, storylines and humour. Create a list on the board for reference throughout the lesson.

Group work

● Give children time to rehearse and finalise their advertisements, bearing in mind what they've just discussed about the features of their favourite adverts.
● The groups could either perform their advertisements to a 'live' audience (the rest of the class) or they could use video cameras to record their adverts. Depending on the children's ability, these could be edited using simple software and then played to the rest of the class.

Differentiation
● Support: mixed-ability groupings may be beneficial, with children taking on different roles according to interest and confidence.
● Challenge: children should consider the wider impact that technology has on improving efficiency and generating wealth.

Review

● Ask each group to show their advert to the rest of the class, or watch the recorded versions. The children watching should act as chieftains, and consider whether they would be convinced to adopt the new technology.
● At the end of each performance, ask the 'chieftains' to comment, positively, on what they have seen. Ask: *How well has this group advertised the item? Who might the advert appeal to? What was most effective? How could it be improved?*
● Once the 'chieftains' have seen all the adverts, explain that they are only able to take on one of the items. Give the children two minutes to discuss with a talk partner which technology they think would be the most useful; then hold a class vote. Children could be asked to consider the items objectively, or they could vote according to how much they were influenced by the advert. After the vote, ask children to explain their reasons for voting as they did.

The Iron Age

Revise

● Write the following words on post-it notes or cards: Iceni tribe, Celt warrior, woad, broch, rotary quern stone, hill fort, crannog, ard, shield, torc, pottery wheel.
● Challenge children to come to the front of the class and describe one of the items without saying the word itself, while the rest of the class guess the word.

Assess

● Ask the children to complete interactive activity 'Y3 Spring I quiz' on the CD-ROM, in which they answer multiple choice questions covering the chapter content.
● Give children a set length of time (for example, 15 minutes) to answer the questions. This can be used as part of a formal assessment or as a fun challenge activity, giving children the opportunity to show what they have learned about the topic.
● Less confident readers may need adult support to read the questions aloud.

Further practice

● Ask the children to create their own Iron Age quiz to test their friends.

Iron Age mind map

Revise

● Organise the class into two quiz teams and select several children's self-devised quizzes from the previous assessment task with which to test the teams (with the children who wrote them sitting out while their quiz is used, or reading the questions aloud).

Assess

● Ask children to create a mind map (model an example if necessary) containing as much information as they can remember about the Iron Age and Celtic life.
● You may wish to write the following words on the board as prompts: tribes, warriors, weapons, Llyn Cerrig Bach, technology, hill forts, homes.
● Less confident writers could share their ideas verbally with adult support. Some children may wish to draw labelled diagrams rather than write their answers.

Further practice

● Children could incorporate what they have learned about the Iron Age into a short video presentation, which could be uploaded onto the school learning platform. Children could work in groups, each selecting a different aspect of Iron Age life on which to focus.

The Iron Age Celts rap

In prehistoric times, before history was written
People called Celts came to settle in Britain

There were many different tribes, ruled by chieftains and kings
They used the metal iron to make their weapons and things

Iron's cheaper and stronger than bronze or stone
So as 'The Iron Age' the period soon became known

The tribal names are tricky, quite a mouthful to pronounce
We'll do our best and see how many we can now announce

There's Dumnonii tribe in Cornwall and the hill-dwelling Brigantes
The Cantiaci in east Kent, below the Trinovantes

Iceni, based in Norfolk, with Boudica their queen
Up in the Scottish highlands, Caledones could be seen

Silures, based in southern Wales, just west of the Dubunni
And famous for its warriors, the great Catuvellauni

There's Novante and Carvetti, Durotreges, Votadini
Epidii, Atrebates, Ordivices and Parisi

There were many, many others but we haven't got all day
Their hill forts can still be seen across the land today

I can perform a rap about Celtic tribes.

How did you do?

Celtic tribal kingdoms

- Read the text about Celtic tribes, below.
- Create a colour code to show where some of the main Celtic tribes lived.

Each Celtic tribe had its own territory, which it defended fiercely. There was a lot of competition for land and places to farm. The names of the tribes were recorded by Roman and Greek historians long after the Iron Age was over, so it is very difficult to know for certain what the tribes were called and where the boundaries of their territories were.

Tribe	Location	Colour code
Brigantes	Yorkshire, Lancashire	
Cantiaci	Kent	
Catuvellauni	Hertfordshire, Bedfordshire	
Dumnonii	Cornwall	
Iceni	Norfolk	
Silures	South Wales	
Trinovantes	Essex, Suffolk	

I can use a map to find out where different Celtic tribes lived.

How did you do?

PHOTOCOPIABLE

What were the Celts like?

- The text below, about the Celts, was written by a Roman historian, Diodorus Sidulus, as they prepared for battle.
- Read the text then draw a picture of a Celt.

Their aspect is terrifying... They are very tall in stature, with rippling muscles under clear white skin. Their hair is blond, but not naturally so: they bleach it, to this day, artificially, washing it in lime and combing it back from their foreheads.

They look like wood-demons, their hair thick and shaggy like a horse's mane. Some of them are clean-shaven, but others – especially those of high rank, shave their cheeks but leave a moustache that covers the whole mouth and, when they eat and drink, acts like a sieve, trapping particles of food... The way they dress is astonishing: they wear brightly coloured and embroidered shirts, with trousers called bracae and cloaks fastened at the shoulder with a brooch, heavy in winter, light in summer. These cloaks are striped or checkered in design, with the separate checks close together and in various colours.

In exactly the same way as hunters do with their skulls of the animals they have slain... they preserved the heads of their most high-ranking victims in cedar oil, keeping them carefully in wooden boxes.

I can use written evidence to draw a picture of a Celt.

How did you do?

Celtic culture

In this chapter, children further explore the Iron Age, focusing on Celtic culture. They learn about the mysterious murder of Lindow Man and the elusive druids. They consider issues associated with farming and trade and learn about two Celtic festivals. They try weaving and create their own Celtic art. They investigate the legacy of the Celtic language in Britain's place names. Finally, children consolidate learning from this chapter and the previous three, considering some of the changes that occurred in Britain from the Stone Age through to the end of the Iron Age.

Chapter at a glance

Curriculum objectives

• Changes in Britain from the Stone Age to the Iron Age, including Iron Age hill forts: tribal kingdoms, farming, art and culture.

Week	Lesson	Summary of activities	Expected outcomes
1	1	• Children learn about Lindow Man and create a newspaper headline and opening paragraph about his murder.	• Can describe ways that Lindow Man provides evidence of Iron Age life.
	2	• Children read about the mystery of the druids and create a picture of what they think the druids looked like.	• Can describe Celtic religion and the role of the druids.
2	1	• Children use an artefact associated with the druids as inspiration for drama scenes.	• Can describe a druid artefact and suggest how it was used.
	2	• Children engage with a board game exploring issues for Iron Age farmers and traders.	• Can describe Iron Age farming and trade.
3	1	• Children create contrasting musical compositions, based on two of the festivals of the Celtic year.	• Can use music to represent two festivals in the Celtic calendar.
	2	• Children work in groups to create a miniature loom and have a go at weaving with wool.	• Can try weaving and can describe its importance to the Celts.
4	1	• Children look at examples of Iron Age art found on artefacts, before creating their own designs.	• Can sketch examples of Celtic art and jewellery.
	2	• Children finish their own artworks, inspired by Iron Age art.	• Can create their own Celtic-style design.
5	1	• Children look at a map of Wales and identify place names that have originated from Celtic words.	• Can identify Celtic place names in Britain today.
	2	• Children visit a local Iron Age site to make observations (option to research one online if this isn't possible).	• Can make observations about an Iron Age site.
6	1	• Children complete an interactive activity, choosing sentences as being applicable to the Stone Age, Bronze Age or Iron Age.	• Can describe changes in Britain from the Stone Age to the Iron Age.
	2	• Children draw pictures to depict a change in Britain from the Stone Age to the Iron Age.	• Can describe changes in Britain from the Stone Age to the Iron Age.
Assess and review		• To review the half-term's work.	

Expected prior learning

● The previous chapters on the Stone Age, Bronze Age and Iron Age (Celts) should be completed before studying Celtic culture, in order to consolidate the chronological narrative of Britain's history.

Overview of progression

● A major focus of this chapter is the differences between historians' interpretation of the past, through the exploration of two Iron Age mysteries – the murder of Lindow Man and the nature of the druids.

● Children continue to consolidate their understanding of archaeological evidence as a means to understanding the past, looking at the bog body, Lindow Man, artefacts, and examples of Celtic art.

● They gain historical perspective by placing their growing knowledge into cultural and religious contexts.

● They touch on the idea of the legacy of past civilisations, looking at some of the place names in Britain today that hold Celtic roots.

● They are given the opportunity to ask and answer historically valid questions as well as to develop their understanding of abstract terms.

Creative context

● Cross-curricular links include:
  ● improvising drama scenes inspired by an Iron Age artefact;
  ● creating contrasting compositions inspired by Celtic festivals;
  ● creating looms and weaving with wool;
  ● drawing imaginative portraits of druids and creating their own designs for objects, based on Celtic art.

Background knowledge

● Lindow Man is a late Iron Age bog body, found in the peat bog of Lindow Moss in Cheshire in 1984. He appeared to be the victim of a ritualistic murder and there are various theories surrounding his death.

● Water held religious significance in the Iron Age (possibly seen as a link to the spirit world) and many hoards have been found in lakes and rivers.

● Druids were the priest class of the Iron Age and they held great power. They acted as judges, doctors, academics and advisers to the king. According to Roman accounts, they engaged in human sacrifice. Historians have very little archaeological evidence about the druids.

● Farming continued to develop during the Iron Age with new technologies such as the use of grain pits – underground holes sealed with clay – which allowed grain to be stored for many months. This provided food throughout the winter and also allowed surplus for trade for foreign items like olive oil and wine. As farming developed, communities grew larger and more settled.

● Grain and land for farming became the new symbols of wealth. Villages grew and tribes or clans developed clear identities. A clearer social structure developed, with the chieftain or king ruling the tribe, and druids and warriors greatly revered.

● Burial practices changed again, with long barrows and round barrows abandoned in favour of cremation.

● The Iron Age also saw many cultural developments, such as the craftsmanship and artistry displayed on artefacts like the Kirkburn Sword and Battersea Shield.

Week 1 lesson plans

This week, children explore two great Iron Age mysteries for historians. They learn about the bog body of Lindow Man, reading different theories about his murder. They decide which they most agree with and write a newspaper article about it. Children then read about the limited information we have about the druids and use their imagination to draw a picture of a druid.

1: Why is Lindow Man important for historians?

Lesson objectives
● To understand the changes in Britain from the Stone Age to the Iron Age, including Iron Age hill forts: tribal kingdoms, farming, art and culture.
● To develop a chronologically secure knowledge and understanding of British, local and world history, establishing clear narratives within and across the periods they study.
● To understand how our knowledge of the past is constructed from a range of sources.
● To understand that different versions of past events may exist, giving some reasons for this.

Expected outcomes
● All children will describe who Lindow Man was.
● Most children will write a newspaper article describing Lindow Man's death.
● Some children will reflect on different theories about Lindow Man's death.

Resources
Photocopiable page 77 'Lindow Man'; newspapers (optional)

Introduction
● Give children two minutes to share with a partner some of the things they can remember about the Iron Age from the previous half term.
● Discuss briefly as a class.

Whole-class work
● Tell the children that they are going to be investigating a 2000-year-old murder mystery.
● Read photocopiable page 77 'Lindow Man' and discuss the different theories about his death. Ask children to think about what additional evidence might be needed to support each of the theories. Which theory do they think is most likely?

Paired work or Independent work
● Tell the children to imagine that they are a journalist for an Iron Age newspaper (clarify that such things did not exist!). They are going to be writing a headline and paragraph about Lindow Man's murder. They should select one of the theories to explain Lindow Man's death (or they may wish to come up with their own).
● Talk through some of the features and the structure of a newspaper headline (short, exciting, catchy) and introductory paragraph (stating what happened, when, where, how and why). Show some examples from real newspapers if necessary.

Differentiation
● Support: children could have a guidance sheet with the questions: What happened? When did it happen? Where did it happen? How did it happen? Why did it happen?
● Challenge: children could write a full article.

Review
● Ask some children to share their headlines and opening paragraphs. Ask: *Which headline grabs your attention the most? Has this opening paragraph included the most important information? Is there anything you could add?*
● Check that the articles include a theory to explain what happened to Lindow Man, and evidence to support this. Ask: *Why do you think this could have happened? Why did you choose to write about this theory? Why do you think this happened? Does anyone have a new theory of their own? Why do you think this could have happened? What evidence is there to support this theory?*

■SCHOLASTIC
www.scholastic.co.uk

Lesson objectives
● To understand the changes in Britain from the Stone Age to the Iron Age, including Iron Age hill forts: tribal kingdoms, farming, art and culture.
● To develop a chronologically secure knowledge and understanding of British, local and world history, establishing clear narratives within and across the periods they study.
● To understand how our knowledge of the past is constructed from a range of sources.
● To understand that different versions of past events may exist, giving some reasons for this.

Expected outcomes
● All children will discuss what druids might have looked like.
● Most children will use their imagination to draw a picture of a druid.
● Some children will reflect on historians' ideas about druids.

Resources
Photocopiable page 78 'The druids'

2: Who were the druids?

Introduction
● Allow the children two minutes to think of different types of people around the world who have power or influence.
● Discuss their ideas. They could include politicians, royalty, celebrities, religious leaders, and so on.
● Ask: *Who do you think was powerful in Iron Age society? Do you think there were any politicians/celebrities/royalty then?*

Whole-class work
● Tell the children that there was one group of people in the Iron Age which was as powerful as the chieftains or kings – the druids – but we know very little about them. Apart from accounts written by the Romans (who may well have been biased) historians have little to go on.
● Read and discuss photocopiable page 78 'The druids'. Ask: *Which description of a druid do you think was right? What do you think a druid might look like?*
● Ask: *Would you have liked to have been a druid? What are the advantages and disadvantages, according to the evidence suggested on the photocopiable sheet?* (Advantages might include: an elevated position in society; respect; power; possibly special treatment and gifts from chieftains and other people. Disadvantages might include: remoteness from everyday people; expectation from chieftains, and so on, to predict an accurate – or optimistic – future.)

Paired work or Independent work
● Ask the children to use their imagination and think about what a druid might look like.
● They should draw a picture of their druid (or they could create a collage, using magazine or newspaper images), writing labels or captions to show why they have chosen particular features or attire.

Differentiation
● Challenge: ask children to explain why they have chosen a particular look for their druid.

Review
● Look at the different pictures the children have created. Are there any similarities between the pictures? Ask: *Why did you choose to draw your druid like this? What extra evidence would you need in order to be able to draw a more accurate picture?*

Lesson objectives
● To understand the changes in Britain from the Stone Age to the Iron Age, including Iron Age hill forts: tribal kingdoms, farming, art and culture.
● To develop a chronologically secure knowledge and understanding of British, local and world history, establishing clear narratives within and across the periods they study.
● To regularly address and sometimes devise historically valid questions about change, cause, similarity and difference, and significance.
● To understand how our knowledge of the past is constructed from a range of sources.
● To understand that different versions of past events may exist, giving some reasons for this.

Expected outcomes
● All children will describe an Iron Age artefact associated with the druids.
● Most children will help to create a drama scene based on an Iron Age artefact associated with the druids.
● Some children will reflect on a drama scene, based on an Iron Age artefact associated with the druids.

Resources
Pictures of Iron Age divining spoons (source online); cardboard replicas of divining spoons (optional)

Week 2 lesson plans

This week, children continue to explore the mysterious druids. They observe an artefact that is believed to be associated with them, using it as inspiration for devising short drama scenes. They then explore some of the issues faced by farmers and traders during the Iron Age, through a board game.

1: What evidence is there for the druids?

Introduction
● Show children some pictures of bronze spoons from the Iron Age, believed to have been used by druids (source online – the British Museum website is a useful resource).
● Ask: *What might these spoons be made from? What might they be used for? Who might have used them?*

Group work
● Tell the children that some archaeologists believe that the spoons may have been used by druids for divination (telling the future). Ask: *Why might someone in the Iron Age wish to know the future?* (They might want to know whether the harvest will be a good one, when to plant crops or who to marry, and so on.)
● Organise children into groups and ask each to come up with a short drama scene inspired by these mysterious artefacts. They should decide what they are and how they were used. If you are displaying the Crosby Rowenworth spoons from the British Museum collection, draw their attention to the hole in one spoon, and the pattern on the other, which divides it into sections. (It may be helpful to provide cardboard replicas of the spoons, for children to use as props.)
● Give the children 20 minutes or so to put their scenes together.

> **Differentiation**
> ● Support: mixed-ability pairings may be beneficial.

Review
● Ask each group to perform their scene for the rest of the class.
● Discuss the different ideas. Which one do the children think is most plausible? Reiterate that we can't know for certain how the spoons were used as there is very little evidence about the druids.
● When all the groups have performed, tell the children that some historians believe that the spoons were used by holding them together and trickling blood into the hole. The pattern of the blood on the spoon with the cross would indicate the future. Of course, the druids could say whatever they liked and therefore could work events in their favour!

■SCHOLASTIC
www.scholastic.co.uk

Lesson objectives
- To understand the changes in Britain from the Stone Age to the Iron Age, including Iron Age hill forts: tribal kingdoms, farming, art and culture.
- To develop a chronologically secure knowledge and understanding of British, local and world history, establishing clear narratives within and across the periods they study.
- To regularly address and sometimes devise historically valid questions about change, cause, similarity and difference, and significance.
- To understand how our knowledge of the past is constructed from a range of sources.
- To understand that different versions of past events may exist, giving some reasons for this.

Expected outcomes
- All children will describe at least one fact about Iron Age farming or trade.
- Most children will describe several facts about Iron Age farming or trade.
- Some children will consider the main issues associated with Iron Age farming and trade.

Resources
Photocopiable page 'Iron Age farming and trade game' from the CD-ROM; counters; dice

2: Why was Iron Age farming and trade important?

Introduction
- Write the following items on the board and ask children to guess which two were items that were brought to Britain through trade with foreign countries during the Iron Age: oranges, wine, chocolates, lemonade, tomatoes, olive oil, soy sauce, rice, cheese (answers: wine and olive oil).

Whole-class work
- Tell the children that they are going to be learning about some of the issues faced by farmers and traders in the Iron Age.
- Explain that if they had a good harvest with lots of extra grain, they could store this underground in pits sealed with clay (which would keep it fresh). Ask: *What could they do with any surplus grain they didn't need?* Explain that they sold it for items the communities couldn't produce themselves – like wine and olive oil. Communities aimed to gain as much wealth as possible.
- Read and discuss photocopiable page 'Iron Age farming and trade game' from the CD-ROM. Players have to move around the board by rolling a dice and, depending on where they land, may get to move on extra places (for example, if the text on the space says that the harvest is good), or they may have to move back places (for example, if a storm means houses have to be repaired, meaning less farming can be done). By playing this game, children revise some of the features of Iron Age life learned previously in the chapter.

Paired work
- Organise children into pairs and ask them to play the game on the photocopiable sheet.

Differentiation
- Support: mixed-ability pairings may be beneficial; children could play in a small group with adult support to facilitate discussion.
- Challenge: children could further research the Iron Age technology of grain pits – vitally important for storing and preserving grain for food throughout the year and for trade.

Review
- After an allocated time, ask children what they have learned from the game about the different issues that Iron Age settlements might have faced.
- Ask: *What other issues might they have faced? Why was farming so important to the Celts? How did trade help them?*

Week 3 lesson plans

This week, children learn about two of the important festivals in the Celtic year – Lugnasad (the time of the harvest) and Samhain (the beginning of winter). They create musical compositions to represent these two contrasting festivals. Children then learn about Celtic weaving, creating their own miniature looms and weaving with wool.

1: What festivals did the Celts celebrate?

Introduction
- Select numerous instruments (for example, a guiro, triangle, maracas, rainmaker, claves and bells).
- Talk through their names, how they are played and the different sounds they make.
- Ask children to think of words to describe the sounds.

Whole-class work or Group work
- Tell the children that the Celts are thought to have celebrated different festivals throughout the year. These were linked to the changing seasons and the duties they would carry out as farmers.
- Explain that, today, the children are going to be creating short compositions to represent two particular festivals:
  - **Lugnasad (1 August)** – This was the height of summer, when the crops were ripe and could be harvested – a time of gathering together to feast and celebrate.
  - **Samhain (1 November)** – This marked the end of the year and beginning of winter. It was seen as a supernatural time when spirits were able to move from their world to the world of the living. We still have a version of this festival today, but we know it by another name – Halloween.
- This could be carried out as a whole-class activity or the children could be organised into groups. Ask them to imagine first Lugnasad and then Samhain. They should close their eyes and imagine what can be heard, smelled, seen and felt during each time.
- Talk about how these things might be represented by musical instruments, including voices (for example, shake a maraca slowly to represent a scythe cutting grain; use bells to portray a celebration on Lugnasad; use the rainmaker to represent wind in the trees or spirits flying in the air as winter approaches on Samhain).
- Choose different children to play the instruments and build up each composition. The pieces could be recorded so that the children can listen and comment on them afterwards.

> **Differentiation**
> - Challenge: children should contribute more creative ideas, helping to develop each composition.

Review
- At the end of the performance ask: *How did the two different compositions make you feel? Do you think we did a good job of representing the two different festivals? Which festival do you think you would have liked most? Why?*

Lesson objectives
- To understand the changes in Britain from the Stone Age to the Iron Age, including Iron Age hill forts: tribal kingdoms, farming, art and culture.
- To regularly address and sometimes devise historically valid questions about change, cause, similarity and difference, and significance.

Expected outcomes
- All children will describe at least one Celtic festival.
- Most children will help to create a piece of music to represent a Celtic festival.
- Some children will contribute ideas in creating contrasting pieces of music to represent Celtic festivals.

Resources
Musical instruments

Lesson objectives

● To understand the changes in Britain from the Stone Age to the Iron Age, including Iron Age hill forts: tribal kingdoms, farming, art and culture.
● To develop a chronologically secure knowledge and understanding of British, local and world history, establishing clear narratives within and across the periods they study.
● To regularly address and sometimes devise historically valid questions about change, cause, similarity and difference, and significance.
● To understand how our knowledge of the past is constructed from a range of sources.

Expected outcomes

● All children will know that the Celts wove wool to make clothing.
● Most children will make their own miniature loom and trying weaving.
● Some children will describe how the Celts spun, dyed and wove wool to make clothing.

Resources

Pictures of a modern loom and an Iron Age loom loom (source online); photocopiable page 79 'Celtic weaving'; A5 sheets of thick card; coloured wool; large needle; ruler; scissors; 3 sticks, string and weights (optional)

2: How did the Celts weave?

Introduction

● Show the children a picture of a loom (source online). Ask: *Do you know what this is? What is it used to make?*
● Explain that it's a loom, and that it is used to weave yarn to make clothes. Point out that some of the clothes that the children are wearing, such as summer dresses, or shirts, may well have been woven on some kind of loom. Can the children think of any other ways of making clothes?

Whole-class work

● Ask: *Why was weaving important to the Celts? What kinds of things would it provide? Why do you think they used different coloured wool?*
● Tell the children that they are going to make their own miniature looms and use them to weave with wool.

Independent work

● Give children a copy of the photocopiable page 79 'Celtic weaving' and the materials described for making their loom. Go through the instructions, modelling how to cut the ends of the card and then thread the wool for the loom.
● When children have completed their looms, model how to begin weaving the wool.
● More confident learners may like to change the wool colour every few rows, to create a striped effect.

Differentiation

● Support: children could work together in a small group with adult support, and may need a ready-made looms.
● Challenge: children could act as tutors for less confident learners; they could dye their own wool using natural, home-made dye.

Review

● When the children have tried weaving, and also considered how to dye the yarn and build a loom. Ask: *Did you enjoy weaving? How easy was it to create cloth in the Iron Age? Do you think the Celts would have had as many clothes as people have today?*

Week 4 lesson plans

This week, children look at examples of Celtic art, studying the patterns on an Iron Age mirror, the Wandsworth Shield and the Battersea Shield. They then create their own Celtic-style designs on circular card.

1: What was Celtic art like? (1)

Introduction

● Show a picture of the Snettisham Torc (source online). Ask: *What do you think it is? What has it been made from? How has it been made? Why might someone want to own this?* (As a status symbol, to show wealth and importance.) *What might it feel like to wear?*

● Tell the children that some Iron Age objects were made with great skill and care in the design. They are considered great works of art. Explain that over the next two lessons they will be creating their own Celtic-style artworks, based on some examples.

Whole-class work

● Show the children the Celtic designs on photocopiable page 'Celtic art' from the CD-ROM, which features drawings of Iron Age artefacts. The mirror and two ceremonial shields have been elaborately decorated.

● Ask children to comment on the features of the different designs (for example, swirling patterns, repetition, symmetry, use of curves and circles). Make a list as a class.

Independent work

● Over the next two lessons, children will work on creating their own Celtic-style designs on a piece of paper or card.

● Tell the children that they are Iron Age artists and that the tribe's chieftain has commissioned them to design a new brooch for his cloak or a new shield for a special ceremony.

● Today, give the children some rough paper, and give them time to experiment with different design elements.

● In the next lesson, they will create their final designs on card.

> **Differentiation**
> ● Support: children can create simple patterns or trace and colour the examples on the photocopiable page.
> ● Challenge: children should aim to emulate the style of Celtic design in their own artwork.

Review

● Check the children's progress.
● Tell them to choose their best design.
● Does everyone have a design they are happy with, ready for next lesson?

Lesson objectives

● To understand the changes in Britain from the Stone Age to the Iron Age, including Iron Age hill forts: tribal kingdoms, farming, art and culture.
● To develop a chronologically secure knowledge and understanding of British, local and world history, establishing clear narratives within and across the periods they study.
● To understand how our knowledge of the past is constructed from a range of sources.

Expected outcomes

● All children will create a basic piece of Celtic-style artwork.
● Most children will discuss the features of Celtic art and create a Celtic-style artwork.
● Some children will incorporate the features of Celtic art in their own artwork.

Resources

Picture of the Snettisham torc (source online); photocopiable page 'Celtic art' from the CD-ROM; circles and squares of paper

Lesson objectives
- To understand the changes in Britain from the Stone Age to the Iron Age, including Iron Age hill forts: tribal kingdoms, farming, art and culture.
- To develop a chronologically secure knowledge and understanding of British, local and world history, establishing clear narratives within and across the periods they study.
- To understand how our knowledge of the past is constructed from a range of sources.

Expected outcomes
- All children will create a basic piece of Celtic-style artwork.
- Most children will discuss the features of Celtic art and create a Celtic-style artwork.
- Some children will incorporate the features of Celtic art in their own artwork.

Resources
Photocopiable page 'Celtic art' from the CD-ROM; sheets of card, and circles of card (6cm in diameter); materials for brooch making (optional)

2: What was Celtic art like? (2)

Introduction
- Ask the children to swap their work with a partner. They should help each other to improve their designs.
- Select several children to talk through their work so far. They should explain why they have chosen certain design features and how they created them.

Independent work
- Allow the children a few minutes to look over their design and make any modifications necessary in the light of the class discussion, and feedback from a partner.
- Give the children some card, cut into a circle (around 6cm in diameter), on which to produce their final designs.
- They could draw in black only, in order to concentrate on the lines and patterns, or they could colour the designs.
- Laminate the pieces of card and add a pin to make a brooch. These can be used to pin a cloak at the shoulder in the style of the Celts (optional).
- Alternatively, allow children to choose whether their design should be used on a brooch, or on a larger item, such as a mirror or ceremonial shield. The mirror or shield designs do not necessarily need to be circular (see photocopiable sheet).

Differentiation
- Support: children can create simple patterns or colour in the examples on photocopiable page 'Celtic art' from the CD-ROM.
- Challenge: children should aim to emulate the Celtic design style in their own artwork.

Review
- Ask some children to share their designs with the rest of the class. They should explain what they designed it to be used on (a brooch, shield, mirror and so on) and explain why they chose this object for their design.
- Ask the children to identify the features of Celtic design that have been replicated. (The designs should include swirls, curves and repeated patterns; they should also be symmetrical.)
- Make a display of the different designs.

Week 5 lesson plans

This week, children consider one of the legacies of the Celts – their language, and how Celtic words can be found in modern British place names. They search a map of Wales to identify some of these. Optionally, children then visit an Iron Age site in the local area, reflecting on what it might have been like to live there at that time.

Lesson objectives
• To understand the changes in Britain from the Stone Age to the Iron Age, including Iron Age hill forts: tribal kingdoms, farming, art and culture.
• To develop a chronologically secure knowledge and understanding of British, local and world history, establishing clear narratives within and across the periods they study.
• To regularly address and sometimes devise historically valid questions about change, cause, similarity and difference, and significance.
• To understand how our knowledge of the past is constructed from a range of sources.

Expected outcomes
• All children will read some Celtic words and their meanings.
• Most children will locate at least two Celtic place names in Wales.
• Some children will locate several Celtic place names in Wales.

Resources
Audio clip of the Welsh language (source online); photocopiable page 'Celtic place names' from the CD-ROM; maps of Wales

I: Where is there evidence of Celtic culture in Britain today?

Introduction
• Play an audio clip of the Welsh language (source clips online or listen to a Welsh radio station – also available online).
• Explain that the Celtic language is no longer used in Britain today, but that there are some similarities with the Welsh language.

Whole-class work
• Read through the list of Celtic words and their meanings on photocopiable page 'Celtic place names' from the CD-ROM.
• Tell the children that we can see some of these Celtic words in British place names. Explain that, this lesson, the children are going to look for them on a map.

Paired work or Independent work
• Ask the children to look at a map of Wales (a topographical one would be ideal) and see how many place names they can identify that contain Celtic words.
• They should complete the table on the photocopiable sheet, looking out for the topographical feature within the place name, on the map of Wales. (For example: rivers meet at Abergavenny and Aberaeronis at the mouth of a river; there's a harbour at Porthmadog and a castle at Caernarfon.)

Differentiation
• Support: mixed-ability pairings may be beneficial.

Review
• After some time for searching for Celtic place names, ask: *Which places did you find? Did the Celtic word appear at the beginning, middle or end of the place name?* (All appear at the beginning.) *Was there anything in the places' local environment that linked to the words' meaning?* (Some links are more easy to spot than others – rivers are fairly clear to see on a map, and won't have changed a lot since the Iron Age; heaths or clearings are less easy to spot, and may no longer be there.)

2: What can we learn from a local Iron Age site? (optional)

Lesson objectives
● To understand the changes in Britain from the Stone Age to the Iron Age, including Iron Age hill forts: tribal kingdoms, farming, art and culture.
● To develop a chronologically secure knowledge and understanding of British, local and world history, establishing clear narratives within and across the periods they study.
● To regularly address and sometimes devise historically valid questions about change, cause, similarity and difference, and significance.
● To understand how our knowledge of the past is constructed from a range of sources.

Expected outcomes
● All children will make basic observations about a visit to an Iron Age site.
● Most children will make more complex observations about a visit to an Iron Age site.
● Some children will demonstrate in-depth reflection on a visit to an Iron Age site.

Resources
Photocopiable page 'Investigating an Iron Age site' from the CD-ROM; clipboards (optional)

Introduction
● This lesson is designed for use if there is an Iron Age site, such as a hill fort, within reach for a school trip.
● Before leaving, ask the children to think of some questions that they would like to investigate at the site (For example: *What was life here like? Have any artefacts been found buried on the site?*)

Group work
● Investigate the site before the trip, for example by looking at websites and leaflets.
● Children could simply read about the site. Alternatively, give each group a specific area to research (for example, the way it has been constructed, its location, or what it was used for).

Paired work or Independent work
● Give the children a clipboard each and a copy of photocopiable page 'Investigating an Iron Age site' from the CD-ROM, which contains guidance questions for their visit.
● Children could also draw sections of the site or artefacts found there, if viewing Iron Age artefacts in a museum.
● If it isn't possible to visit an Iron Age site, the photocopiable sheet could be completed by referring to a website or leaflets about a particular Iron Age site.

Differentiation
● Support: mixed-ability pairings are suggested.
● Challenge: children should find out about at least one artefact. As well as sketching it, they could find out what it is, what it's made of, how it's made, what it would have been used for, who would have used it, and where it was found.

Review
● Back in the classroom, talk through the children's thoughts about the trip and the things they have learned, referring to their notes on the photocopiable sheet.
● If the children have drawn any artefacts they could show these to the rest of the class, explain what the artefact is, what it's made of, and how it would have been used.

Week 6 lesson plans

In these final two lessons, before children move from examining Britain to the wider world, children are given the opportunity to reflect on what they have learned and consider the ways in which Britain changed from the Stone Age to the Iron Age; for example, in the making and use of tools and weapons, lifestyle changes from nomadic hunting and gathering to settled farming, and the shift towards living together as a community.

1: How did Britain change from the Stone Age to the Iron Age? (1)

Lesson objectives
● To understand the changes in Britain from the Stone Age to the Iron Age, including Iron Age hill forts: tribal kingdoms, farming, art and culture.
● To develop a chronologically secure knowledge and understanding of British, local and world history, establishing clear narratives within and across the periods they study.
● To note connections, contrasts and trends over time.
● To regularly address and sometimes devise historically valid questions about change, cause, similarity and difference, and significance.
● To construct informed responses that involve thoughtful selection and organisation of relevant historical information.
● To understand how our knowledge of the past is constructed from a range of sources.

Expected outcomes
● All children will describe at least one change from the Stone Age to the Iron Age.
● Most children will describe several changes from the Stone Age to the Iron Age.
● Some children will consider detailed changes to aspects of life as well as overarching social changes.

Resources
Interactive activity 'Changes in Britain from the Stone Age to the Iron Age' on the CD-ROM; large sheets of paper; marker pens

Introduction
● As a class, discuss some of the ways in which the lives of people in Britain changed from the Stone Age to the Iron Age. Examples could include: the carving of flint tools to melting and moulding bronze then iron to make better tools; the move from a nomadic lifestyle hunting and gathering food to settling in one place and farming; the growth of the population and communities living together; the building of homes and monuments; the growth of trade.

Paired work or Independent work
● Ask children to complete the interactive activity 'Changes in Britain from the Stone Age to the Iron Age' on the CD-ROM, in which they drag sentences to appropriate time periods, based on whether they apply to the Stone Age, Bronze Age or Iron Age.
● This activity could be used as an assessment tool, covering the children's learning about the Stone Age and Iron Age.
● Ask the following additional questions: *Do you think life was easier in the Stone Age, Bronze Age or Iron Age? In which period was life hardest? In which period would you prefer to live? In which time period was life most similar to Britain today?*

Review
● Organise the children into groups and allocate them one age: Stone Age or Iron Age (the Stone Age could be divided into two stages).
● The children should put everything they can think of about their age onto the large sheet of paper. They could do this in various ways: as bullet points, a mind map, quick sketches, and so on.
● Ask each group to present their notes, moving through the groups chronologically from Stone Age to Iron Age.

Lesson objectives

● To understand the changes in Britain from the Stone Age to the Iron Age, including Iron Age hill forts: tribal kingdoms, farming, art and culture.
● To develop a chronologically secure knowledge and understanding of British, local and world history, establishing clear narratives within and across the periods they study.
● To note connections, contrasts and trends over time.
● To regularly address and sometimes devise historically valid questions about change, cause, similarity and difference, and significance.
● To construct informed responses that involve thoughtful selection and organisation of relevant historical information.
● To understand how our knowledge of the past is constructed from a range of sources.

Expected outcomes

● All children will describe at least one change from the Stone Age to the Iron Age.
● Most children will describe several changes from the Stone Age to the Iron Age.
● Some children will consider detailed changes to aspects of life as well as overarching social changes.

Resources
Squares of paper

2: How did Britain change from the Stone Age to the Iron Age? (2)

Introduction

● Ask: *If you had the choice, would you most like to live in the Stone Age, Bronze Age or Iron Age? Why?*
● Ask children to share their ideas and reasons.

Group work

● Tell the children that they are going to be putting together a picture book for a younger age group, to show the way Britain changed from the Stone Age to the Bronze Age and the Iron Age. Ask children to divide their page into three (or give them ready-cut squares of paper).
● Tell them that they are going to select one aspect of life in Britain (for example, tools and weapons, getting food, homes, or communities). They should draw three pictures to depict the changes in this area through the Stone Age, Bronze Age and Iron Age. (A theme of 'tools and weapons' might show a hunter-gatherer skinning an animal with a flint knife, a wealthy Bronze Age person displaying a bronze ceremonial sword and an Iron Age farmer using an iron scythe to cut grain.)
● Alternatively, the children could work in groups to develop short sketches in which a time-travelling television journalist interviews a Stone Age family and an Iron Age family, showing the contrast in life.

Differentiation
● Support: children may choose a simple change, like the advancement of weapons from flint to bronze to iron. Some children may wish to complete just two drawings, showing the Stone Age and Iron Age.
● Challenge: children may wish to create detailed drawings featuring several changes and labels or captions.

Review

● Look at some of the children's drawings as a whole class. Ask: *What change(s) in Britain from the Stone Age to the Iron Age does this drawing show?*
● Have the children covered all aspects of life? Is there anything missing from the drawings that the children can add in discussion?

Lesson objectives
● To understand the changes in Britain from the Stone Age to the Iron Age, including Iron Age hill forts: tribal kingdoms, farming, art and culture.
● To understand how our knowledge of the past is constructed from a range of sources and that different versions of past events may exist, giving some reasons for this.

Resources
Internet access (optional)

The druids

Revise

● Ask the children to think about the contrasting views that historians have about what the druids were like. Remind children that two main sources of evidence that we have for the druids include the divination spoons and written eyewitness reports from the Romans (who wanted to invade and rule Britain and might have felt threatened by the druids' power).

● Ask: *If a druid walked into the room now, what questions would you ask him or her? What questions would help you to work out whether the druids could be seen as good or bad?*

Assess

● Ask children to write two contrasting descriptions of the druids – one agreeing with the Roman view that they were cruel people who sacrificed human beings, and the other from the point of view of a Celt with an injury, who has gone to the druids for healing.

Further practice

● Ask children to use websites to further explore the field of archaeology and the tasks carried out by archaeologists.

Lesson objectives
● To understand the changes in Britain from the Stone Age to the Iron Age, including Iron Age hill forts: tribal kingdoms, farming, art and culture.
● To develop the appropriate use of historical terms.

Resources
Sets of cards featuring the following historical terms from the Iron Age topic: crannog, rotary quern stone, loom, Trinovantes, radiocarbon dating, ard, Brigantes, roundhouse, artefact, broch, archaeology, hill fort, Iceni

Historical terms

Revise

● Organise the class into groups and give each group a set of historical term cards.

● Ask children to work together collaboratively to sort the cards into groups. You may wish to allow children to devise the categories themselves or provide them (for example, tribal names, places Celts lived, things Celts used, methods historians use to study the past).

● Discuss how the children have grouped their cards.

Assess

● Choose one of the words from the cards and model writing a glossary definition of the word and a sentence, using it in context.

● Ask children, working individually, to select three words from the cards. Each word must belong to a different group from the sorting activity. For each word they should write a definition and then use the word in context, in a sentence.

● Less confident writers could share their ideas verbally with adult support.

Further practice

● Ask children to create a glossary of terms relevant to the Iron Age or to Britain's prehistory, which can be used for a class studying this period the following year.

Lindow Man

- Read the text about Lindow Man.
- Write a newspaper headline and opening paragraph of an article based on what you think happened to Lindow Man. Remember to use evidence!

A two thousand year old murder mystery

In 1984, a body was found in a bog in Lindow Moss in Cheshire. The bog had stopped the body from rotting away to a skeleton. It still had its skin, nails, hair and some internal organs.

The body was taken to the British Museum to be carefully cleaned and examined. Here are some of the things that scientists and historians discovered:

- Radiocarbon dating showed that he died around the end of the Iron Age, about two thousand years ago.

- He had been murdered in a very nasty way. He had been hit on the head twice and also on the back, breaking one of his ribs. He was strangled with a cord and his neck was broken. His throat was cut and he was placed face-down in the bog.

- He was aged about 25 when he died.

- He might have been someone quite important. His nails were in good condition, so it was unlikely that he did a difficult job like farming. It looks as though he ate a good, healthy diet.

- Today, you can see Lindow Man in the British Museum.

Why did Lindow Man die?

Historians have many ideas about this. Here are three of the suggestions:

Lindow Man was killed as part of a religious ritual by Celtic priests (called druids). He may have been a human sacrifice.	Lindow Man was the victim of robbers. They stole his valuables, killed him and dumped him in the bog.	Lindow Man was executed as punishment because he had committed a crime.

I can use evidence to write a newspaper article about what happened to Lindow Man.

How did you do?

The druids

- Read the text about druids.
- What do you think the druids looked like? Create a picture of a druid in the box.

In the Iron Age, religion was based around things in nature – like rivers, lakes, trees, plants and the sun. There was one group of people who were very important to the Celts. They were called the druids and they were a bit like priests. They are a great mystery to historians, because we know very little about them – not even what they looked like!

Here are some of the things that historians think about druids:

Mistletoe, water and oak trees were important to the druids.	Druids gave advice to kings and tribal rulers.	Druids might have been male or female.

Druids were seen as very wise and were greatly respected.

Druids sometimes acted as judges, deciding on laws and punishments.

Iron Age people believed that the druids could tell the future.

Iron Age people sometimes went to the druids for healing, like doctors.

People had to study very hard to become a druid, memorising their ways and rituals.

The druids performed religious rituals, sacrificing animals and sometimes even human beings.

I can draw and describe what a druid might have looked like.

How did you do?

Name: _____   Date: _____

Celtic weaving

How to make your own loom

You will need: Strong card (A5 size), scissors, ruler, wool, large needle

Step 1: Rule two lines, 2cm from the top and 2cm from the bottom of the card.

Step 2: Add a mark every 1cm at the top and bottom of the card. Cut slits on these marks, up to the 2cm line.

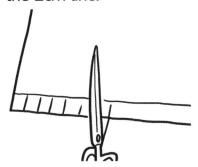

Step 3: Push the end of the wool into the first slit at the top of the card, leaving about 5cm of wool at the back.

Step 4: Pull the wool down to the opposite slit, at the bottom of the card.

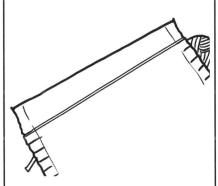

Step 5: Pull the wool through the slit, loop it round and pull it back through the next slit.

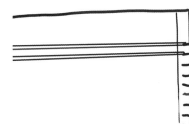

Step 6: Pull the wool back to the top of the card and keep going until you reach the slits at the other end. Cut the wool, leaving 5cm at the end. Your loom is now ready.

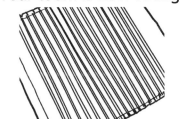

Step 7: To start weaving, thread the needle with about 100cm of wool. Weave over the first piece of stretched wool, then under the next, then over and so forth.

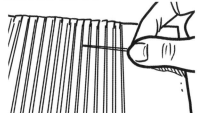

Step 8: When you reach the end, pull the wool through, loop it loosely around the last strand and weave another row, opposite to before. (Go under threads that you previously went over.)

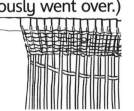

Step 9: When you have finished all your rows, take the weaving off the loom. Snip the loops and tie up all the ends.

Ancient Egypt (1)

In this chapter, children move away from the chronological narrative of Britain's history. After an overview of four of the world's earliest civilisations, they begin a depth study of the life and achievements of the ancient Egyptians. Children investigate how Egyptian society was structured and read about how the discovery of the Rosetta Stone. They explore the mysteries of the Great Pyramid and learn about the achievements of some famous ancient Egyptians. Finally, children learn about how the discovery of King Tutankhamun's tomb and its artefacts provided insight into the life of the pharaoh.

Chapter at a glance

Curriculum objectives

• The achievements of the earliest civilisations – an overview of where and when the first civilisations appeared: ancient Egypt.

Week	Lesson	Summary of activities	Expected outcomes
1	1	• Children read about four of the earliest civilisations, place them using atlases and discuss why people chose to settle there.	• Can use maps to identify where the earliest civilisations appeared.
	2	• Children work together to create physical representations of timelines showing the earliest civilisations.	• Can use timelines to identify when the earliest civilisations appeared.
2	1	• Children order the different classes of Egyptian society and investigate what their lives were like.	• Can describe ancient Egyptian social structure.
	2	• Children use historical evidence to find out about Egyptian clothing before designing and making their own Egyptian-style jewellery.	• Can create some Egyptian-style jewellery.
3	1	• Children learn how the Rosetta Stone helped people to decipher hieroglyphics. They use symbols to work out the name on a cartouche. • Children design their own cartouches, writing their name in hieroglyphics.	• Can understand how the discovery of the Rosetta Stone led to the deciphering of Egyptian hieroglyphics. • Can recreate some Egyptian hieroglyphs.
	2	• Children transfer their cartouche designs onto clay or foil.	• Can recreate some Egyptian hieroglyphs.
4	1	• Children read about the pyramids and sphinx and then write pyramid poems inspired by them.	• Can describe what is known about why and how the great pyramids were built. • Can write a poem about pyramids.
	2	• Children work in groups, using different methods to build pyramid shapes or scale models.	• Can create a model of the Great Pyramid at Giza.
5	1	• Children work in groups to research a famous Egyptian and create a mobile of facts about them and related images.	• Can describe the achievements of some famous Egyptians.
	2	• Children write a diary from the point of view of Howard Carter, as he discovers King Tutankhamun's tomb.	• Can describe the significance of Howard Carter's discovery of Tutankhamun's tomb.
6	1	• Children investigate artefacts from Tutankhamun's tomb, sketching them and writing about what they tell us about the past.	• Can describe artefacts from Tutankhamun's burial treasure and how they were used.
	2	• Children look at the details of Tutankhamun's death mask before sketching and painting it.	• Can create an artwork based on Tutankhamun's death mask.
Assess and review		• To review the half-term's work.	

Expected prior learning

● Ancient Egypt is a stand-alone topic; however it would be useful if children are familiar with timelines.

Overview of progression

● Children develop their understanding of the wider world in a historical context as they explore four different ancient civilisations, concentrating on ancient Egypt in depth. Children extend their knowledge of timelines, looking at the beginning and end of the ancient civilisations.

● The major learning focus for this chapter is the use of evidence to make historical claims and the methods of historical enquiry. Children understand the importance of evidence from Egyptian paintings, sculpture, jewellery, artefacts from Tutankhamun's tomb, the Rosetta Stone and archaeological sites in helping us to build a picture of the Egyptian civilisation.

Creative context

● Cross-curricular links include:
  ● writing poems inspired by the pyramids and a diary from the viewpoint of Howard Carter; reading information texts;
  ● exploring maps and diagrams showing the location of ancient civilisations;
  ● creating scale models of the Great Pyramid;
  ● designing and creating a cartouche featuring hieroglyphics and Egyptian-style jewellery; sketching and painting the famous death mask of Tutankhamun.

Background knowledge

● The ancient Egyptian civilisation lasted from around 3150BC with the first pharaoh until the conquest of Alexander the Great in 332BC. This was followed by the era of Greek rule – the Ptolemaic dynasty – ending with the death of Cleopatra VII and Roman conquest in 30BC.

● Egyptian society had a pyramidal structure with the pharaoh and his family at the top, followed by the nobles and priests. Next came the soldiers and scribes, followed by craftsmen, servants of the wealthy, farmers and slaves.

● Symbols were very important to the Egyptians and featured in the jewellery they wore. Jewellery was worn by both men and women and made from gold and precious stones like topaz and garnet.

● The Rosetta Stone was discovered in 1799. It is inscribed with the same text in three different languages – ancient Greek, Demotic (the ordinary language of the Egyptian people) and Hieroglyphics (the sacred writing used by scribes). Comparing the hieroglyphs with the other two known languages enabled Egyptologists to decipher them.

● No one is certain how or why the Great Pyramid was built. Many Egyptologists believe it to be the tomb of the pharaoh Khufu, but a body was never found in the sarcophagus.

● In 1922, Howard Carter discovered the tomb of Tutankhamun in the Valley of the Kings. All other tombs had been robbed of all treasures centuries before, but Tutankhamun's tomb was intact and filled with hundreds of artefacts.

Week 1 lesson plans

This week provides an overview of four of the world's earliest civilisations – ancient Sumer, the Shang Dynasty of China, the Indus Valley and ancient Egypt – in preparation for a depth study of the achievements of the ancient Egyptians. Children use atlases to locate these civilisations, considering why they developed in these areas. They then place them on a class timeline.

1: Where did the earliest civilisations live?

Lesson objectives
● To learn about the achievements of the earliest civilisations – an overview of where and when the first civilisations appeared and a depth study of ancient Egypt.
● To develop a chronologically secure knowledge and understanding of British, local and world history, establishing clear narratives within and across the periods they study.
● To regularly address and sometimes devise historically valid questions about change, cause, similarity and difference, and significance.

Expected outcomes
● All children will identify where at least one early civilisation lived.
● Most children will identify where four early civilisations lived.
● Some children will identify why the early civilisations lived where they did.

Resources
Photocopiable page 'Early civilisations' from the CD-ROM; dictionaries; atlases

Introduction
● Ask the children to share with a talk partner what they like and dislike about where they live (this could be the village, town or city, or where their house is located within the area).
● Discuss as a class.

Whole-class work
● Write the word 'civilisation' on the board. Ask children to guess at, and then use dictionaries to find, the meaning. It may be helpful for them to also define related words: 'society', 'development', 'culture', 'technology'. Use these to help write a class definition of 'civilisation', which the children can copy into their books (for example, an organised society that uses technology to advance, and has different cultural elements, such as art, writing and music).
● Tell the children that they are going to be learning about four of the earliest human civilisations, which developed in different parts of the world around 5000 years ago. These began as simple farming communities and then developed into civilisations through advances in technology, culture and social structure.
● Read through photocopiable page 'Early civilisations' from the CD-ROM. Talk about and list on the board the things a civilisation might require in order to flourish in an area (for example, fresh water, materials for building, shelter, an area that is easy to defend from attack, farmland for food, ways to transport goods for trade, a good climate).

Group work or Paired work
● Organise children into small groups or pairs and give each a copy of the photocopiable sheet and an atlas (preferably one that shows the country's terrain). Ask children to read the information on the sheet about were the civilisations took place and then find the areas on a map.
● They should discuss why these were good places for an advanced settlement to develop (for example, living by the river would provide food and fresh water).
● Alternatively, children could cut out the information and images from the sheet and glue these into their books around the world map, drawing a line from the image and text to the correct area of the world.

Differentiation
● Support: mixed-ability groupings/pairings may be useful; children could work in a small group with adult support.
● Challenge: children could research additional information about the civilisations.

Review
● Discuss the activity as a whole class. Ask: *What is a civilisation? Why could these be considered civilisations? What do their locations have in common?* (For example, they are all near land suitable for farming; three are near rivers.) *In which modern countries did the civilisations take place?* (Iraq, Pakistan, Egypt and China) *Were these good locations for settlement?* (Yes – people could live, farm and trade there.)

2: When were the earliest civilisations?

Introduction

Lesson objectives
- To learn about the achievements of the earliest civilisations – an overview of where and when the first civilisations appeared and a depth study of ancient Egypt.
- To develop a chronologically secure knowledge and understanding of British, local and world history, establishing clear narratives within and across the periods they study.
- To regularly address and sometimes devise historically valid questions about change, cause, similarity and difference, and significance.

Expected outcomes
- All children will help to identify when at least one early civilisation lived.
- Most children will help to identify when four early civilisations lived.
- Some children will compare the timescales of the early civilisations.

Resources
Photocopiable pages 'Early civilisations' from the CD-ROM; coloured ribbons or rope; open space (school hall, playground) (optional)

- Split the class into two groups. Use photocopiable page 'Early civilisations' from the CD-ROM to give the children a quick quiz about the four civilisations. For example, ask: *Which civilisation had two major cities called Harappa and Mohenjo-Daro?* (Indus Valley) *Which was near the Euphrates River?* (Ancient Sumer) *Which built pyramids?* (Ancient Egyptians) *Which made pots of bronze?* (The Shang Dynasty)

Whole-class work

- Ask the class to look at the photocopiable sheet again. Discuss the dates listed for when each civilisation took place. Help the children to put the dates in order (remind them that BC dates work backwards), for example: 3300BC ancient Sumer begins, 3150BC Egyptian civilisation begins, 2500BC Indus Valley civilisation begins.
- Draw a horizontal line on the board and model mapping one of the civilisations onto it.
- Talk about the most sensible scale to use for the dates (for example, a range of 3300 to 0BC, counting down in 500s).
- Take the children to an open space. Explain that they are going to work as a class to create a big timeline showing when each civilisation began and ended.
- Use one ribbon or rope as the timeline. Have two children hold either end and position children at intervals along it with signs (3300BC, 3150BC and so on).
- Through class discussion, arrange each of the four coloured ropes to show where each civilisation appears on the timeline, and how they overlap. The ropes can be taped to the floor as the whole class 'time travels' by walking down the length of the rope, passing each civilisation.
- Alternatively, if no open space is available, children could complete a similar task in groups.

Differentiation
- Support: mixed-ability groupings may be beneficial; children could work in a group with adult support.

Review

- Discuss the activity at the end of the lesson and recap on the key dates.
- Ask the children:
  - *Which civilisation lasted for the longest time?* (Ancient Egyptian)
  - *Which started latest?* (The Shang Dynasty)
  - *Why might the civilisations have ended?* (All four ended due to invasion/ take over from another civilisation, apart from the Indus Valley, which ended due to unknown reasons – possibly war or natural disaster.)
  - *Was there a time when all four existed at once?* (Not quite.)

Lesson objectives
● To learn about the achievements of the earliest civilisations – an overview of where and when the first civilisations appeared and a depth study of ancient Egypt.
● To develop the appropriate use of historical terms.

Expected outcomes
● All children will identify the position of pharaohs and slaves in Egyptian society.
● Most children will describe the order of importance of different classes in Egyptian society.
● Some children will describe the characteristics of different classes in Egyptian society.

Resources
Interactive activity 'Egyptian society' on the CD-ROM; materials for creating a wall poster (optional)

Week 2 lesson plans

This week introduces the depth study of ancient Egypt, as children learn about the different members of Egyptian society. They then consider how evidence – art and artefacts – has helped us to determine what the ancient Egyptians wore. Finally, children design and make their own Egyptian-style jewellery.

1: Who was most important in Egyptian society?

Introduction

● Ask the children to create a mind map of their existing knowledge of ancient Egypt or to write questions that they would like to find out about ancient Egyptian life. (They will have learned about the key features of ancient Egypt in the previous lesson – such as the dates of the civilisation, and about the pyramids at Giza, farming by the Nile, pharaohs and jewellery; they may also come to the lesson with some knowledge of Tutankhamun, modern Egypt, and so on.)

Group work or Paired work

● Tell the children that they are going to be finding out about the people who were most and least important in Egyptian society.
● Organise them into small groups or pairs and ask them to complete the interactive activity 'Egyptian society' on the CD-ROM, in which they order the different social classes of Egypt from most to least important.
● Talk about how the life of a pharaoh might have been different from the life of a slave. The children could use role play to explore their ideas about these two classes. It may be necessary to explain what a slave is first.
● If time allows, allocate each group an Egyptian social class. Ask the children to draw pictures of the members of their class and list some facts about them. This could involve additional research into their daily lives, what they wore, their occupations, and so on. These can be used to create a large wall poster in the shape of a pyramid, showing Egyptian society.

> **Differentiation**
> ● Support: mixed-ability groupings or pairings may be beneficial; children should investigate the more clear-cut social classes (pharaoh or slaves) with adult support.
> ● Challenge: children could research the classes between pharaoh and slave (viziers, nobles, priests, scribes, soldiers, craftsmen and farmers).

Review

● Give each section of the class an Egyptian social class and give them two minutes to think about the following questions:
  ● *How might you spend your day?*
  ● *What might you worry about?*
  ● *What might you wear?*
  ● *In what sort of house might you live?*
● Discuss as a class.

Lesson objectives
● To learn about the achievements of the earliest civilisations – an overview of where and when the first civilisations appeared and a depth study of ancient Egypt.
● To develop the appropriate use of historical terms.

Expected outcomes
● All children will design an item of Egyptian-style jewellery.
● Most children will describe and design an item of Egyptian-style jewellery.
● Some children will describe the meaning of symbols worn by the Egyptians.

Resources
Pictures of a pharaoh, slave, scarab beetle, Eye of Horus, Ankh (source online); paper plates; paints (including gold); tin foil, cellophane and other materials for jewellery making

2: What did the Egyptians wear?

Introduction
● Show children an image of a pharaoh and a slave. Ask them to guess which social class they belong to. Ask: *How does what they are wearing give us evidence for who they are?* (A pharaoh would have worn jewellery around his neck and arms, a headdress and colourful clothes; a slave's attire would have been much simpler.)

Whole-class work
● Ask: *How might we find evidence about what the Egyptians wore?* Talk about different forms of evidence – ancient Egyptian paintings, artefacts such as statues and jewellery – which have provided Egyptologists with clues.
● Show examples of wall paintings, statues and artefacts. (Source online, for example at: www.metmuseum.org. Explain that these give us a lot of clues about Egyptian society.)

Independent work
● Tell the children that they are going to be designing and making their own Egyptian jewellery. Designs could be based on a beaded necklace or a scarab beetle, Ankh or Eye of Horus amulet. Show the children some examples of these (source online) and explain that an amulet is an object that was thought to protect the wearer from danger.
● Children can design amulets on card and attach these to string. Alternatively, use gold-painted paper plates to create necklaces. Neck holes can be cut out and the remaining plate slit so that it can be attached around the neck. This could then be decorated to look as though it contains beads and gemstones.

> ### Differentiation
> ● Children can create simple or more complex designs according to ability.
> ● Support: children may need help with cutting out materials.
> ● Challenge: children could research the meaning behind different symbols (for example, ankh was linked to life, the scarab beetle was linked to the sun and rebirth, and the Eye of Horus was linked to health and protection).

Review
● Recap on what's been discussed during this lesson. Ask:
  ● *How can we use evidence to find out about what the Egyptians wore?* (Wall paintings, statues and artefacts)
  ● *Where might we find this evidence?* (Ancient tombs and monuments, archaeological digs – or today, in museums.)
● Look at some examples of the children's designs. Ask:
  ● *What materials and colours have been used?*
  ● *Who might have worn a piece of jewellery like this?*
  ● *Does it have a special meaning?*

Week 3 lesson plans

This week, children explore hieroglyphic writing. They learn about how the discovery of the Rosetta Stone enabled historians to finally decipher the hieroglyphs. Children use similar methods to work out the name on a cartouche, before designing and making cartouches with their own names.

I: Why was the Rosetta Stone important?

Lesson objectives
● To learn about the achievements of the earliest civilisations – an overview of where and when the first civilisations appeared and a depth study of ancient Egypt.
● To develop a chronologically secure knowledge and understanding of British, local and world history, establishing clear narratives within and across the periods they study.
● To regularly address and sometimes devise historically valid questions about change, cause, similarity and difference, and significance.
● To understand how our knowledge of the past is constructed from a range of sources.

Expected outcomes
● All children will write hieroglyphic symbols.
● Most children will write their own name in hieroglyphics.
● Some children will describe the way the Rosetta Stone was used to decipher hieroglyphics.

Resources
Picture of the Rosetta stone (source online); photocopiable pages 95 'Egyptian writing'; photocopiable page 96 'My cartouche'

Introduction
● Show the class an image of the Rosetta Stone. Make sure that the inscriptions on the stone can be seen clearly.
● Without giving any information about the artefact, let children describe it and share their ideas about why it might be important. Ask: *How old do you think this stone might be? Do you recognise any shapes inscribed on the stone – are they letters or pictures? What do you think the words/pictures say?*

Whole-class work
● Read and discuss photocopiable page 95 'Egyptian writing', which explains what the Rosetta Stone is, and why it was such an important discovery. Discuss whether any of the children's ideas brought up in the introduction were correct.
● Check the children's understanding of the text on the photocopiable sheet by asking questions, such as: *Why was the Rosetta Stone such an important discovery? Why hadn't anyone been able to decipher hieroglyphics before the Rosetta Stone was discovered?*
● The photocopiable sheet shows the cartouche of Pharaoh Ptolemy; the children need to use this to decipher the name on a second cartouche (Kliopatra – also known as Cleopatra). This could be done as a class, or children could work in groups or pairs.

Independent work
● Distribute photocopiable page 96 'My cartouche'. The children use the hieroglyphics on the sheet to design a cartouche featuring their name (those with long names may prefer to use initials).
● During the next lesson, the children will transfer their designs onto clay or tin foil.

Differentiation
● Support: children could use initials only to create a simpler design.
● Challenge: children should use their full name.

Review
● Organise children into pairs or groups to look at each other's work.
● They should comment on each other's work, offering support, or suggestions as to how the cartouche could be improved.
● In class discussion, ask children to make positive comments on each other's work, and share some of the best examples.

Lesson objectives
● To learn about the achievements of the earliest civilisations – an overview of where and when the first civilisations appeared and a depth study of ancient Egypt.
● To regularly address and sometimes devise historically valid questions about change, cause, similarity and difference, and significance.
● To understand how our knowledge of the past is constructed from a range of sources.

Expected outcomes
● All children will write letters from their name in hieroglyphics.
● Most children will create a cartouche with their name in hieroglyphics.
● Some children will research where Egyptian writing was used.

Resources
Images of Egyptian hieroglyphics (source online); photocopiable page 96 'My cartouche'; clay or tin foil

2: How did the Egyptians write?

Introduction
● Show children some images of Egyptian hieroglyphics on temples, tombs and papyrus (source online). Ask them to comment on the different characters and symbols that make up the writing and guess what the words might say.

Whole-class work
● Look at an image of a cartouche engraved on the wall of a temple (source online).
● Discuss the way the symbols have been chiselled into the stone. Ask: *How might the scribes have done this? What tools might they have used?*

Independent work
● Ask the children to recreate their cartouche designs on clay. They will need to roll out the clay and cut out an oval shape. They can then imprint their design using a pencil tip.
● As an alternative, designs can be traced onto thick tin foil. The children should put a cloth or paper towel under the foil and then lie their paper design face down on the foil. They can then trace their design. Flipping the foil over, they can press down the space around their symbols with the back of a pencil to give the symbols a raised, embossed look.

Differentiation
● Support: children may need assistance in selecting the hieroglyphs for their name. Some children will need assistance with tasks involving fine motor skills.
● Challenge: children could research the training and life of an Egyptian scribe.

Review
● Collect in all the cartouches and then distribute them around the class at random. Ask the children to decipher each other's cartouches. Ask: *Did you manage to decipher the cartouche? Have the correct hieroglyphs been used? Does the cartouche look nicely presented?*
● Create a class display of all the cartouches. Invite children from another class, or parents, to come and decipher them.

Week 4 lesson plans

This week, children explore the pyramids and the Great Sphinx at Giza, reading about how and why Egyptologists believe they were built. They imagine what it must be like to visit the pyramids and write pyramid poems. In the second lesson, children work in groups to construct simple or scale models of the Great Pyramid.

1: Why and how were the pyramids built?

Lesson objectives
● To learn about the achievements of the earliest civilisations – an overview of where and when the first civilisations appeared and a depth study of ancient Egypt.
● To understand how our knowledge of the past is constructed from a range of sources.

Expected outcomes
● All children will describe basic facts about the pyramids.
● Most children will create a poem inspired by the pyramids.
● Some children will capture the atmosphere of the pyramids in their poems.

Resources
Pictures of the pyramids and Great Sphinx (source online); photocopiable page 97 'The pyramids (1)'; photocopiable page 'The pyramids (2)' from the CD-ROM; limestone and granite tiles (optional); yellow card (optional)

Introduction
● Show numerous images of the pyramids and Great Sphinx (source online).
● Ask the children to think of anything they would like to know about these, such as what they are, where they are built.
● Make a list on the board, to be reviewed at the end of the lesson.

Whole-class work
● Read through photocopiable page 97 'The pyramids (1)' as a class, which describes the pyramids and Great Sphinx at Giza, as well as theories suggesting why and how they were built.
● Photocopiable page 'The pyramids (2)' from the CD-ROM shows and describes the inside of a pyramid.
● Show some samples of limestone and granite tiles from a local hardware store and pass these round, asking children to describe their appearance and texture. Ask: *What would it be like to visit the pyramids? What would it be like to be inside the Great Pyramid? How might you feel? What might you see, hear and smell?*
● Tell the children that although we don't know for certain why or how the pyramids were built, people have been fascinated by them and their sense of mystery for thousands of years. In this lesson, the children will use them as inspiration for writing their own pyramid poems.
● Share the following example and discuss the content and structure; or create one as a class, using the children's suggestions for words or phrases:

Sphinx

Ancient   watcher

Mysterious, mystical, majestic

Protector   of   dead   kings

You   watch   the   ages   pass

Independent work
● Children should write their own pyramid poem using the pyramids and Sphinx as inspiration.
● Provide triangles of card for children to create a copy for display. Four of these triangles could be glued together on a square base to create mini pyramids, which can be displayed on a shelf or strung up on a string across the classroom.

> **Differentiation**
> ● Support: children could work in a group with adult support to write down their ideas and form the poem.
> ● Challenge: children could write longer poems with greater use of poetic devices, such as imagery, alliteration and metaphor.

Review
● Look again at the questions listed on the board at the beginning of the lesson. Can the children answer these questions now?
● Children could research any unanswered questions at home.
● Read some of the pyramid poems as a class. Do they convey the atmosphere of the pyramids?

Lesson objectives
● To learn about the achievements of the earliest civilisations – an overview of where and when the first civilisations appeared and a depth study of ancient Egypt.
● To understand how our knowledge of the past is constructed from a range of sources.

Expected outcomes
● All children will help to build a basic pyramid.
● Most children will describe the process involved in building their pyramid.
● Some children will build a scale model of the Great Pyramid.

Resources
Satellite images of the pyramids (source online); photocopiable page 97 'The pyramids (1)'; blocks or building blocks; card; straws and other materials for pyramid building (see lesson notes)

2: How big are the pyramids?

Introduction
● Ask: *What shape are the sides of the pyramids?* (Triangles.) *If we could view the pyramids from above, what shape do you think they would be?*
● Show satellite images of the pyramids. Ask the children to comment on the shape and layout of the pyramids. (They look square from above, although half the pyramid often looks in shadow, giving the impression of two triangles next to each other, creating a square shape.)
● Some images online show the pyramids behind modern Cairo; showing one of these images will help the children to understand how enormous the pyramids are.

Group work
● Organise children into groups of similar ability. Tell the children that their challenge for the lesson is to build a pyramid. This can be done in a number of ways (using blocks or modelling materials – see below); differentiate the materials according to the ability of the children in each group.
● Groups should discuss ideas for the best way to build their pyramid before commencing; also encourage them to draw sketches of their designs.

Differentiation
● Support: children could create basic pyramids from rows of building blocks.. More confident learners could create basic square pyramid shapes with straws and blue tack, and then cover these with card.
● Challenge: children could create scale models of the Great Pyramid out of card, using the height and side width measurements on photocopiable page 97 'The pyramids (1)'. They could be challenged to work out the length of the edges by building their model.

Review
● Ask each group to present the pyramid they have made to the rest of the class.
● Ask: *What materials did you use to build your pyramid? What shapes were needed? How did you begin? What did you do next? How did you make sure the pyramid was sturdy? How did you keep your pyramid to scale?*
● Ask children who have built a scale model to explain how many times bigger than their model a real pyramid would be.

Week 5 lesson plans

This week explores some famous Egyptians, with children researching their achievements and related artefacts and working in groups to turn these into a mobile for the classroom. Children then find out about the discovery of King Tutankhamun's tomb in 1922 and explore some of the treasures found there. They write a diary from Howard Carter's point of view.

1: Who were some famous Egyptians?

Lesson objectives
● To learn about the achievements of the earliest civilisations – an overview of where and when the first civilisations appeared and a depth study of ancient Egypt.
● To develop a chronologically secure knowledge and understanding of British, local and world history, establishing clear narratives within and across the periods they study.
● To regularly address and sometimes devise historically valid questions about change, cause, similarity and difference, and significance.
● To understand that different versions of past events may exist, giving some reasons for this.

Expected outcomes
● All children will name at least one famous Egyptian.
● Most children will describe at least one famous Egyptian.
● Some children will describe several famous Egyptians.

Resources
Photocopiable page 'Famous Egyptians' from the CD-ROM; reference books about ancient Egypt, or internet access; card; paper; string; wooden sticks for mobile making

Introduction
● Ask: *Why might someone be remembered 5000 years after their death?* Allow children time to discuss this question with a talk partner.
● Ask some children to share their ideas with the class.

Whole-class work
● Read and discuss photocopiable page 'Famous Egyptians' from the CD-ROM. This sheet gives some information about some of the most famous Egyptian pharaohs – Hatshepsut, Amenhotep III, Akhenaten and his wife Nefertiti, Ramesses II and Cleopatra VII – and explains what they were renowned for.

Group work
● Organise children into groups and allocate one famous Egyptian to each. Provide the children with reference books about ancient Egypt, or access to the internet, and ask them find more information about their Egyptian and any artefacts associated with him or her. Direct children to specific websites, such as that of the British Museum or BBC.
● Give each group wooden sticks (they should be stuck in a cross shape to form the top of the mobile, which may be better done in advance of the lesson), card, paper and string. Challenge each group to create a mobile about their famous Egyptian. The objects hung from it might include interesting facts, images of the people and artefacts associated with them (either drawn or printed), their name in hieroglyphs, a map with their tomb's location, and so on. Children should back their information and images with card to make them sturdy.

> **Differentiation**
> ● Support: mixed-ability groups may be beneficial.
> ● All children in the group should participate and be involved in the research, but they may play to their own strengths regarding tasks; some may prefer to write facts, others to draw pictures.

Review
● Ask the different groups to present their mobiles to the rest of the class. Ask questions if necessary, such as: *When was the person born? How old were they when they died? Why are they remembered? What were some of their achievements? Is there any evidence for the person's personality? What objects might they have used? What might they have worn? What did they build? Were there any wars when this person was pharaoh?*
● Display the mobiles around the classroom so that children can learn from the work of other groups.

Lesson objectives
● To learn about the achievements of the earliest civilisations – an overview of where and when the first civilisations appeared and a depth study of ancient Egypt.
● To develop a chronologically secure knowledge and understanding of British, local and world history, establishing clear narratives within and across the periods they study.
● To regularly address and sometimes devise historically valid questions about change, cause, similarity and difference, and significance.
● To understand that different versions of past events may exist, giving some reasons for this.

Expected outcomes
● All children will describe the discovery of Tutankhamun's tomb.
● Most children will write a diary from the point of view of Howard Carter.
● Some children will consider the way Howard Carter felt when discovering Tutankhamun's tomb.

Resources
Photocopiable page 'Tutankhamun's tomb' from the CD-ROM

2: How was Tutankhamun's tomb discovered?

Introduction
● Tell the children that Egyptians believed that when they died they would travel to a new world. They were buried with all the possessions they would need in the afterlife.
● Ask children to share with a talk partner their five most valued possessions that they would want to take with them.
● Discuss their ideas as a whole class.

Whole-class work
● Read through photocopiable page 'Tutankhamun's tomb' from the CD-ROM, which explains the events leading up to the discovery of the tomb. Talk about how Howard Carter might have felt just before he discovered the tomb of Tutankhamun, when he first peered into the tomb, then after his discovery. Ask one or two children to be Carter in the 'hot-seat' while the rest of the class interview him. Allow children a few minutes to prepare their questions (or answers, if acting as Carter).

Independent work
● Ask the children to imagine that they are Howard Carter.
● Explain that their task is to write diary entries from Howard Carter's point of view, sharing his thoughts and feelings around the time of the tomb's discovery.
● If necessary, make a list on the whiteboard of the features of a diary for the children to refer to when writing their own diary entries (for example, first person, personal thoughts and emotions, details of what happened during the day or week).

Differentiation
● Support: children can write simple sentences about the discovery of Tutankhamun's tomb.
● Challenge: children should write more detailed and reflective diaries and describing the mix of emotions that Carter may have felt.

Review
● Ask some children to share their diaries with the rest of the class. Check that the examples reflect the events of Howard Carter's discovery of Tutankhamun's tomb.
● Tell the other children that, when they are listening, they should think of one good thing to say about the diary entry, and something they could add or change to improve it. Discuss as a class.

Week 6 lesson plans

This week, children develop their understanding of the way that evidence is used to tell us about the past, as they explore some of the treasures found inside King Tutankhamun's tomb, sketching the artefacts and discussing what they reveal about the pharaoh's life. They then create a detailed portrait of what is probably the most famous Egyptian artefact of all time – Tutankhamun's death mask.

1: What artefacts were found in Tutankhamun's tomb?

Lesson objectives
- To learn about the achievements of the earliest civilisations – an overview of where and when the first civilisations appeared and a depth study of Ancient Egypt.
- To regularly address and sometimes devise historically valid questions about change, cause, similarity and difference, and significance.
- To understand how our knowledge of the past is constructed from a range of sources.
- To understand that different versions of past events may exist, giving some reasons for this.

Expected outcomes
- All children will describe at least one artefact from Tutankhamun's tomb.
- Most children will describe several artefacts from Tutankhamun's tomb.
- Some children will describe how Tutankhamun's treasure has provided evidence of Egyptian life.

Resources
A news article relating to scientific analysis of Tutankhamum's remains; pictures of artefacts from Tutankhamun's tomb (source online); internet access or reference books

Introduction
- As a class, read a news article relating to scientific analysis of Tutankhamum's remains.
- Discuss how scientists have exhumed and examined Tutankhamun's mummified body, using technology such as X-rays to find evidence for how he died.

Whole-class work
- Show some pictures of the artefacts found in Tutankhamun's tomb (galleries of the treasures are available online).
- Select one of the treasures (other than the death mask, which they will be painting in the next lesson) and discuss what it tells us about Tutankhamun and the life of an Egyptian pharaoh.
- The treasures tell us a lot about Tutankhamun (for example, how wealthy he was, what games he liked to play, and so on) and even more about Egyptian civilisation (mummification, burial, clothing, painting and artwork, past-times, and so on).

Group work or Paired work
- Ask the children to look at Tutankhamun's treasures online or in reference books.
- They should choose four or five artefacts to look at. Try to ensure that each group considers different items.
- For each, they should imagine that they are discovering the object for the first time and share ideas with their partner or group about what they think the object is or might be used for. They should then read the information about it. Direct children to specific websites, such as the BBC or British Museum, or reference books.
- The children should select an artefact and sketch it, writing bullet points about it underneath. Ask them to consider the following questions: *What do you think the artefact is used for? What is it made from? Why might it be included in the tomb? What does it tell us about Tutankhamun?*

> **Differentiation**
> - Support: mixed-ability groups may be beneficial; children should research one or two items only; provide guidance as to where information can be found – for example, the relevant page of a book.

Review
- Ask each group to choose one item that they have researched. They should tell the rest of the class everything they have found out about this item.
- Alternatively, ask the children to choose the most unusual item they have found out about. They should give three explanations as to what the object might be, and how it is used. The rest of the class has to decide which is correct. Hold a class vote, and then ask the group to reveal and explain the correct usage.

Lesson objectives
● To learn about the achievements of the earliest civilisations – an overview of where and when the first civilisations appeared and a depth study of ancient Egypt.
● To regularly address and sometimes devise historically valid questions about change, cause, similarity and difference, and significance.
● To understand how our knowledge of the past is constructed from a range of sources.
● To understand that different versions of past events may exist, giving some reasons for this.

Expected outcomes
● All children will create an artwork based on Tutankhamun's death mask.
● Most children will also describe Tutankhamun's death mask.
● Some children will describe, and create a detailed portrait of Tutankhamun's death mask.

Resources
Internet access; an image of Tutankhamun's death mask (source online, or see photocopiable page 'Tutankhamun's tomb' from the CD-ROM); card or art paper; paints or pastels

2: What was Tutankhamun's death mask like?

Introduction
● Show the children a large image of Tutankhamun's death mask, renowned as one of the most valuable, important and beautiful Egyptian artefacts ever found.
● Ask children to come up with words to describe the mask.
● Ask: *What colours have been used?* (The headdress was made of blue glass and gold, called the 'nemes'. This was only worn by royalty.)
● Ask: *What animals appear on the headdress?* (There's a vulture and a cobra, representing Upper and Lower Egypt. The cobra was also worshipped by the Egyptians, and was used as a protective symbol; the vulture was considered to be nearer to god.)
● Ask: *What jewellery is worn?* (There is a broad collar, and the false beard adopted by pharaohs. His ears are shown to be pierced, although no earrings are in place.)
● Ask: *Do you think it is an accurate portrait of Tutankhamun?* (It's impossible to know for certain, although the shape of features such as the lips are in keeping with the mummified body, so it is thought to be a reasonable likeness – although possibly a more idealistic, younger version.)
● Ask: *Why do you think the mask is so well known? How do you feel when you look at it?*

Independent work
● The children are going to be creating their own portrait out of card, based on the death mask of Tutankhamun. Children could draw the mask themselves, or give them a template with the basic face and head shape, which they can paint in the appropriate colours.
● Alternatively, ask the children to create masks rather than portraits.
● If you wish, these could be face-sized, with eye holes cut out to create actual masks.

Differentiation
● Support: children may need help with the basic sketching and could work from a template.
● Challenge: children should aim for an accurate depiction of proportion and colours.

Review
● Make a display of the masks and ask children to create labels on paper to act as bullet points. They should aim to include as much of the information discussed in the introduction as possible.
● Stick the labels on the display and use string to link each label to the relevant part of the mask.

Lesson objectives
● To learn about the achievements of the earliest civilisations – an overview of where and when the first civilisations appeared and a depth study of ancient Egypt.
● To develop a chronologically secure knowledge and understanding of British, local and world history, establishing clear narratives within and across the periods they study.

Resources
Interactive activity 'Y3 Summer 1 quiz' on the CD-ROM

Ancient Egypt quiz (1)

Revise

● Write on the board the four types of evidence about which children have been learning: archaeological site, artefact, written document, eyewitness report.
● As a class, think of one or more examples of each of these in relation to ancient Egypt (for example, the archaeological site of King Tutankhamun's tomb, his death mask as an artefact, the Rosetta Stone as a written document, Howard Carter's eyewitness account of his discovery) and what they have told historians about ancient Egypt (or Carter's findings).

Assess

● Ask the children to complete the interactive activity 'Y3 Summer 1 quiz' on the CD-ROM, in which they answer multiple-choice questions covering the chapter content.
● Give children a set length of time (for example, 15 minutes) to answer the questions. This can be used as part of a formal assessment or as a fun challenge activity, giving children the opportunity to show what they have learned about the topic.
● Less confident readers may need adult support to read the questions aloud.

Further practice

● Ask children to create a brochure persuading tourists to visit the pyramids or the Valley of the Kings.

Lesson objectives
● To learn about the achievements of the earliest civilisations – an overview of where and when the first civilisations appeared and a depth study of ancient Egypt.
● To address and sometimes devise historically valid questions about change, cause, similarity and difference, and significance.

Tutankhamun

Revise

● Write the following words, names and phrases on the board: pyramids, hieroglyphics, King Tutankhamun, Ramesses II, Great Sphinx, Rosetta Stone, Howard Carter.
● Tell the children that these are answers to questions. Challenge them to devise one or more questions for each answer.

Assess

● Ask children to imagine that they are news reporters or TV journalists. They are to have an exclusive interview with King Tutankhamun. Ask them to create a list of questions that they (and most historians) would wish to ask him.
● Encourage children to think of questions concerning his cause of death, what his life was like (similarities to and differences from life today, or the life of other ancient Egyptians) and his treasures.
● Less confident writers could share their ideas verbally with adult support.

Further practice

● Challenge children to discuss or write similarities and differences between life in ancient Egypt and either life in Britain today or life in prehistoric Britain.

Egyptian writing

- Read the text below.
- Complete the activity at the bottom of the page.

The mystery of the Rosetta Stone

For centuries, Egyptologists looked at the mysterious pictures and symbols in Egyptian writing (hieroglyphics) but had no idea what they meant. In 1799, a French soldier found a large, ancient stone in the foundations of a fort near the Egyptian town of Rosetta. This stone held the key to working out what the hieroglyphics meant.

The stone was inscribed with the same text in three different languages – ancient Greek, Demotic (the ordinary language of the Egyptian people) and hieroglyphics (the sacred writing used by special Egyptian writers called scribes).

People could read the other two languages and use them to work out the hieroglyphic symbols. Each symbol stood for a different letter, sound or word. An English scientist, Thomas Young, noticed that some of the symbols had ovals drawn around them. These were called cartouches and they contained royal names. A French Egyptologist, Jean-Francois Champollion, was able to work out many of the hieroglyphic symbols. At last, the ancient Egyptian writing could be understood! The Rosetta Stone is now in the British Museum.

Now, it's your turn to be a code-breaker. Here is the cartouche of the pharaoh, Ptolemy (also referred to as Ptolemies):

Use Ptolemy's cartouche and the clues to work out the name on this cartouche. (It's the name of a famous Egyptian queen.)

___

I can read the name on an Egyptian cartouche.

How did you do?

Name: _____ Date: _____

My cartouche

■ Use the following Egyptian hieroglyphs to create a cartouche of your name.

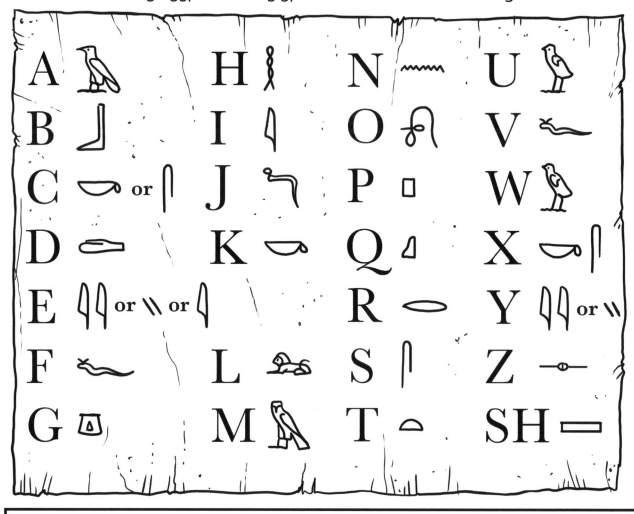

I can create an Egyptian cartouche of my own name.

How did you do?

96 ■ 100 HISTORY LESSONS   **PHOTOCOPIABLE**   ■SCHOLASTIC
www.scholastic.co.uk

The pyramids (1)

The Great Pyramid at Giza, just outside the Egyptian capital city of Cairo, was finished around 2560BC. Many Egyptologists believe that it was built as a tomb for the pharaoh, Khufu. It is made from around 2.3 million blocks of limestone and the chambers inside are made of granite.

Nobody knows how the pyramid was actually built. The workers might have been farmers whose lands were flooded by the Nile for several months each year. The limestone blocks may have been cut from local quarries and transported to the site. A ramp of mud might have been built so that the blocks could be dragged up to the next level. Once in place, the outer layer of blocks would have been cut and sanded down to make the sides smooth. Today, most of the outer layer has disappeared.

Next to the Great Pyramid are two other large pyramids, dedicated to later Egyptian kings – Khafre and Menkaure. There are also smaller pyramids for the queens, mortuary temples for worshipping the dead kings and tombs for the king's relatives and officials. Nearby is the Great Sphinx, a mysterious statue with the head of a man and a lion's body. It is around 73 metres long and 20 metres high.

Ancient Egypt (2)

In this chapter, children continue their depth study of the ancient Egyptians, focusing on their beliefs and customs. Children explore the Egyptian gods and goddesses, as well as the myths surrounding them – the story of Osiris and Seth and the ceremony of weighing the heart. They learn about the mummification process and make their own canopic jars. They study papyrus art and consider how the Nile River helped Egypt to become a wealthy and powerful civilisation. Finally, children are given the opportunity to work independently, creating a poster to answer their own historically valid question.

Chapter at a glance

Curriculum objectives

• The achievements of the earliest civilisations – an overview of where and when the first civilisations appeared and a depth study of ancient Egypt.

Week	Lesson	Summary of activities	Expected outcomes
1	1	• Children look at images of Egyptian temples and create flashcards of different Egyptian gods and goddesses.	• Can describe some of the different gods and goddesses worshipped by the Egyptians.
	2	• Children create illustrations to reflect the different stages of the Osiris and Seth myth.	• Can describe the story of Osiris and Seth.
2	1	• Children create movement and dance pieces inspired by scenes from the myth of Osiris and Seth.	• Can re-create the story of Osiris and Seth.
	2	• Children read about the practice of weighing the heart and consider deeds that might make the heart lighter or heavier.	• Can describe Egyptian beliefs about life after death.
3	1	• Children read about, and then write instructions for, the process of mummifying a body.	• Can describe the mummification process.
	2	• Children read about how canopic jars were used in the mummification process and model their own out of clay.	• Can make their own canopic jars.
4	1	• Children look at examples of papyrus art before creating their own papyrus paper.	• Can describe some of the features of Egyptian art.
	2	• Children draw their own Egyptian-style pictures on their papyrus paper.	• Can create their own examples of Egyptian pictures.
5	1	• Children answer comprehension questions about the Nile.	• Can describe why the Nile was important to ancient Egyptians.
	2	• Children select a topic and create a plan for an independent poster on the theme of ancient Egypt.	• Can create a presentation about an aspect of Egyptian life.
6	1	• Children continue to work on their poster on the theme of ancient Egypt.	• Can continue work on a presentation about an aspect of Egyptian life.
	2	• Children complete and share their poster on the theme of ancient Egypt.	• Can present their own information about an aspect of Egyptian life.
Assess and review		• To review the half-term's work.	

Expected prior learning

● It would be useful if children have completed the previous topic, Ancient Egypt (1).

Overview of progression

● Children will develop their understanding of the wider world in a historical context, as they explore ancient Egypt in depth. They continue to develop their understanding of the use of evidence to make historical claims, for example how depictions of farming in Egyptian art reveal how important it was to the Egyptians.

● They also develop their understanding of abstract terms, such as 'civilisation' and 'evidence'.

● The major learning focus is the ability to ask and answer historically valid questions. Children conclude the topic with independent research into an aspect of ancient Egyptian life.

Creative context

● Cross-curricular opportunities include:

  ● writing instructional texts showing how to make a mummy; completing a reading comprehension about the Nile River;

  ● exploring Egyptian papyrus art, creating their own paper and drawing in the style of ancient Egyptians; illustrating the myth of Osiris and Seth; modelling canopic jars out of clay;

  ● reading about the 'weighing of the heart' ceremony and considering the kinds of good and bad deeds that would make the heart lighter or heavier (PSHE).

Background knowledge

● The ancient Egyptians worshipped many deities, each of whom was responsible for a different aspect of the world.

● One of the most important gods was Osiris, who ruled the land of the dead. The story of his murder at the hands of his brother, Seth (pronounced 'Set') was the most well-known of Egyptian myths. In the myth, Osiris's dead body is embalmed and restored – the basis for the Egyptian practice of mummification.

● Another important god was Anubis, the god of embalming. He featured in the 'weighing of the heart' ceremony – the Egyptian belief that every person must have their heart weighed against the feather of Maat (goddess of justice and truth) before they can pass into the afterlife.

● It was believed that the soul left the body and then returned. People wanted to have a well preserved corpse, so that the soul would recognise it in the afterlife. Professional embalmers mummified the body, carefully preparing it over many weeks, removing the vital organs and placing them in protective canopic jars, drying the body with natron salt, rubbing it in oils and finally wrapping it in linen bandages.

● The Nile River was extremely important to the Egyptians. It provided fresh water, fish, transport, a place to wash and papyrus plants. Its annual flood and the rich soil it left behind enabled farmers to guarantee an excellent harvest every year. This provided surplus produce for trade, which helped the country to become wealthy and powerful.

Week 1 lesson plans

This week introduces children to Egyptian beliefs. They learn about the different gods and goddesses that the Egyptians worshipped, creating flashcards with their pictures, names and characteristics. Children then read and illustrate the myth of Osiris and Seth, helping to create a class display of the different sections of the story.

1: What gods and goddesses did the Egyptians worship?

Lesson objectives
● To learn about the achievements of the earliest civilisations – a depth study of ancient Egypt.
● To regularly address and sometimes devise historically valid questions about change, cause, similarity and difference, and significance.

Expected outcomes
● All children will identify at least two Egyptian gods and goddesses.
● Most children will describe several Egyptian gods and goddesses.
● Some children will describe several Egyptian gods and goddesses and their responsibilities.

Resources
Pictures of Egyptian temples (source online); photocopiable pages 'Egyptian gods and goddesses' from the CD-ROM (photocopied onto card, if possible)

Introduction
● Give the children two minutes to share with a talk partner as much as they can remember about the ancient Egyptians.
● Discuss as a class; eliciting what the children remember about hieroglyphics, the pyramids, famous Egyptians and Tutankhamun.

Whole-class work
● Tell the children that, in this topic, they are going to be learning all about the beliefs of the ancient Egyptians. Explain that they didn't have just one god, but worshipped many and that each god and goddess was responsible for a different part of life or the world.
● Tell the children that the Egyptians built big temples to honour the gods. Show some examples: Philae Temple, dedicated to Isis; Edfu Temple, dedicated to Horus; Kom Ombo, dedicated to Sobek and Horus; Dendera Temple, dedicated to Hathor. Ask: *What is similar about all of these temples?* (They are made of stone and contain columns, obelisks, wall carvings and statues.)
● Show children photocopiable pages 'Egyptian gods and goddesses from the CD-ROM, which contain templates for flashcards. The cards can be cut out and the name and information folded up at the back so that it can be read when held up. Read through two or three of the descriptions of gods and point out the features described.

Paired work or Independent work
● Give each child a copy of the photocopiable sheets. Ask the children to colour in the images of the gods and goddesses, then cut out, fold and stick the cards so that the illustrations are one side and the text the other.
● When they have finished, they could combine their cards with a partner's and play a pair matching game. They should begin with one set of cards face up and the other face down. In turns, the players choose a picture card and then try to select the matching name and description. If successful, the player keeps that pair. The winner is the player with most cards when all the cards have been paired.
● Alternatively, children can use the cards as flashcards to test their partner.

Differentiation
● Support: same-ability pairings may be beneficial.
● Challenge: research additional features of Egyptian temples.

Review
● Divide the class into four teams and use the flashcards to play a game. Show each team in turn the illustration on one of the flashcards for them to name the god or goddess. They should confer before giving their answer so that all children are involved.
● If the team gives an incorrect answer, the question is open to the other teams. The child who puts up their hand first is allowed to answer.
● If a team answers correctly, they win the card; the winning team is the one with the most cards at the end of the game.

Lesson objectives
● To learn about the achievements of the earliest civilisations – a depth study of ancient Egypt.
● To regularly address and sometimes devise historically valid questions about change, cause, similarity and difference, and significance.

Expected outcomes
● All children will illustrate an event in the myth of Osiris and Seth.
● Most children will illustrate and describe an event in the myth of Osiris and Seth.
● Some children will describe the full myth of Osiris and Seth.

Resources
Egyptian gods and goddess flashcards from the previous lesson; photocopiable page 113 'The myth of Osiris and Seth'; squares of paper

2: What was the myth of Osiris and Seth? (1)

Introduction
● Ask one child to come to the front of the room. Give him or her one of the Egyptian gods flashcards and invite the rest of the class to ask up to 20 questions (with answers 'yes' or 'no') to determine which deity it is.
● Repeat with one or two other cards and children.

Whole-class work
● Tell the children that the Egyptians believed many stories about their gods and goddesses. One of the most famous was the myth of Osiris and Seth. This myth also involved Isis, Nephthys, Thoth and Anubis.
● Read and discuss photocopiable page 113 'The myth of Osiris and Seth'. It should be noted that the myth varied considerably in different parts of Egypt and has also changed over time; the photocopiable sheet contains one of the many versions.

Group work
● Organise the children into small groups. Tell them that they are going to turn the story into a comic strip with pictures and captions.
● Allocate one of the scenes on the photocopiable sheet to each group. Give children squares of paper and ask them to illustrate the scene. If possible, they should consider the characteristics of the deities, using their flashcards for guidance.
● When the children are finished, the pictures and excerpts from the myth can be displayed in order around the room or along a wall.
● Children can then do a 'story walk', reading the scenes and looking at the related images, so they become familiar with the whole myth.

Differentiation
● Support: children may wish to trace the characters from the flashcards.
● Challenge: children can be encouraged to add speech bubbles to show what the characters might be saying.

Review
● After the story walk, check the children's understanding of the myth by asking:
   ● *Who was Osiris?* (He was an Egyptian king and god of the underworld.)
   ● *Why did Seth kill Osiris?* (He was jealous of Osiris and wanted to be king himself.)
   ● *What happened to Osiris after he died?* (The parts of his body were recovered, he was embalmed, and then briefly brought to life for one last time.)
   ● *Who helped Isis to find the body of Osiris?* (Isis's sister, Nephthys.)
   ● *Who was Horus?* (Isis's son.)

Week 2 lesson plans

This week, children continue to explore the myth of Osiris and Seth, this time through movement and dance. They then learn about Egyptian beliefs concerning the afterlife and the weighing of the heart ceremony. They consider the kinds of deeds that might make a person's heart lighter or heavier.

1: What was the myth of Osiris and Seth? (2)

Lesson objectives
- To learn about the achievements of the earliest civilisations – a depth study of ancient Egypt.
- To regularly address and sometimes devise historically valid questions about change, cause, similarity and difference, and significance.
- To understand how our knowledge of the past is constructed from a range of sources.

Expected outcomes
- All children will describe an event or character in the myth of Osiris and Seth.
- Most children will create a movement piece portraying the myth of Osiris and Seth.
- Some children will evaluate a movement piece portraying the myth of Osiris and Seth.

Resources
Photocopiable page 113 'The myth of Osiris and Seth'; open space (such as school hall, playground)

Introduction
- Take the children to an open space, such as the school hall or playground.
- Explain that they are going to use their bodies to portray some characters and scenes from the Osiris myth.

Whole-class work
- Ask the children to move about the room as different characters: Osiris, Isis and Seth. Explain that the movements should reflect what they know about them. For example, Osiris was thought to be a good, fair king, so he might move slowly and proudly, but with a kind, smiling expression; Seth was jealous and angry so he might move more aggressively or sneakily, and be sneering; Isis might move sadly, or children could choose to show her searching despairingly.
- Tell the children that they are going to be creating a movement piece or dance inspired by the following scenes from the myth:
  - Isis and Nephthys turn into falcons and search for Osiris
  - Horus grows from a boy to a man
  - Seth turns himself into a hippopotamus.
- Choose one scene and model some different movements that could be used to depict it, or have different children demonstrate some ideas.

Group work
- Organise children into small groups and ask them to work together to create their three scenes. They should think about ways to make their piece interesting for the audience, such as using different levels, or changing formation. They should also find a way to create a smooth transition between the three movements.
- Give the children music to work with (optional). Suggestions could include 'Arabian Dance' from *The Nutcracker*, 'Possente Ftha' from *Aida* or 'In the Hall of the Mountain King' from *Peer Gynt*.

> **Differentiation**
> - Support: mixed-ability groupings may be beneficial.

Review
- Ask each group to perform their movement pieces while the others act as audience members and offer constructive comments about the work.
- Ask: *How did the movement reflect what was happening in that scene? Did the movements flow together smoothly? What was most interesting about this performance?*

Lesson objectives
● To learn about the achievements of the earliest civilisations – a depth study of ancient Egypt.
● To regularly address and sometimes devise historically valid questions about change, cause, similarity and difference, and significance.
● To understand how our knowledge of the past is constructed from a range of sources.

Expected outcomes
● All children will know the Egyptians believed in life after death.
● Most children will give a basic description of the Egyptian belief about the afterlife.
● Some children will describe the ceremony of the weighing of the heart.

Resources
Photocopiable page 'The afterlife' from the CD-ROM; individual whiteboards or scrap paper

2: What did the Egyptians believe about the afterlife?

Introduction
● Draw a grid of four squares on the board and write a letter in each (P, A, S, T).
● Give children individual whiteboards or scrap paper and ask them to copy the grid.
● Challenge the children to fill each square with one or more words beginning with that letter and connected with ancient Egypt (for example: pharaoh, pyramid, Ptolemy; ankh, Amenhotep, amulet; scarab, Seth, sphinx; Tutankhamun, Thoth, treasure). Allow a minute for this.

Whole-class work
● Read and discuss photocopiable page 'The afterlife' from the CD-ROM, which summarises the weighing of the heart ceremony. Check that the children are clear as to which characters the arrows are pointing to. Explain that historians know about myths such as these from drawings, like the one on the photocopiable sheet.
● Draw two columns on the board. Write 'Light heart' in one and 'Heavy heart' in the other.
● As a class, talk about the kinds of deeds or characteristics that might make the heart lighter (such as kindness, sharing, showing respect, honesty, being trustworthy) and the kind of deeds that might make it heavier (such as lying, stealing, jealousy, being rude, hurting people).
● Talk about whether these things would be relevant in ancient Egypt or today or both.

Paired work or Independent work
● Ask the children to copy the columns into their books and write their own list in each.
● They can discuss ideas with a partner and think of things relevant to their own lives.

Differentiation
● Support: children might prefer to draw rather than write their ideas.
● Challenge: children could write more comprehensive lists, showing deeper reflection.

Review
● Ask some children to share their ideas; they should explain which are only relevant to themselves, or the present, and which were (also) relevant to the ancient Egyptians.
● Check the children's understanding of the Egyptians beliefs regarding the heart and the afterlife. Ask: *What did the Egyptians believe happened after death? Which god weighed the heart? Which god ruled the land of the dead? What happened if the heart was heavier than the feather?*

Week 3 lesson plans

This week, children explore the mummification process, reading about how embalmers prepared the body for the afterlife. Children write instructions for mummifying a body and then model their own canopic jars from clay.

Lesson objectives
- To learn about the achievements of the earliest civilisations – a depth study of ancient Egypt.
- To regularly address and sometimes devise historically valid questions about change, cause, similarity and difference, and significance.
- To understand how our knowledge of the past is constructed from a range of sources.

Expected outcomes
- All children will describe why Egyptians were mummified.
- Most children will describe the basic mummification process.
- Some children will describe the mummification process in detail.

Resources
Pictures of Egyptian mummies and sarcophaguses; photocopiable page 'Mummification'; photocopiable pages 'Mummification script' from the CD-ROM; internet access

1: How were people mummified?

Introduction
- Show the children some images of sarcophaguses (source online). Ask: *Do you know what this is? Does it look like anything that can be seen in churches or tombs today?* Explain that this is an Egyptian sarcophagus, which is a kind of coffin.
- Show a picture of an Egyptian mummy (source online). Ask: *Do you know what this is? What do you know about mummies?* The children may well talk about horror stories, and the idea of mummies coming to life.

Whole-class work
- Read and discuss photocopiable page 'Mummification' from the CD-ROM, which provides some general information about mummification.
- Ask the children to imagine that they are an experienced embalmer. They are about to retire and have been asked to write a set of instructions on how to mummify a body for their young apprentice.
- Talk about the features of an instructional text and create a list on the board for reference throughout the lesson: including an equipment list, clear steps, imperatives, words indicating order, adverbs, and so on.
- Refer to the section on the mummification process on the photocopiable sheet and model changing the first paragraph into a set of instructions.

Paired work or Independent work
- Ask the children to continue the task of turning the text into a set of instructions.
- As the children are writing, ask prompt questions if necessary, such as: *What equipment would the embalmer need to begin with? What would he do first? What would be the next step?*
- Alternatively, some children could rehearse the light-hearted script on photocopiable pages 'Mummification script' from the CD-ROM, which could be performed as part of an ancient Egypt assembly, or for the amusement of the class.

Differentiation
- Support: children could write very simple instructional texts or cut out the paragraphs from photocopiable pages 'Mummification' and glue them into their book in the correct order.
- Challenge: children should write a more advanced set of instructions.

Review
- Ask some children to share their instructions. The other children should listen and check to see if there is anything missing.
- Ask questions after the instructions have been read, such as: *Who would have carried out embalming?* (Priests) *Why did the Egyptians believe that bodies needed to be embalmed?* (To preserve them, so that the soul could recognise the body in the afterlife.)
- Explain that although Egyptians believed it was important to mummify bodies, only the rich would probably have been wealthy enough to do this.

2: What were canopic jars?

Lesson objectives
● To learn about the achievements of the earliest civilisations – a depth study of ancient Egypt.
● To regularly address and sometimes devise historically valid questions about change, cause, similarity and difference, and significance.
● To understand how our knowledge of the past is constructed from a range of sources.

Expected outcomes
● All children will create a canopic jar.
● Most children will create and describe a canopic jar.
● Some children will describe the four canopic jars and their uses.

Resources
Photocopiable page 'Canopic jars' from the CD-ROM; paper cups or small plastic containers/jars with lids; clay

Introduction
● Challenge pairs of children to come out to the front of the class to describe the steps involved in mummifying a body.
● As one child describes the process, the other could mime the actions.

Whole-class work
● Read the section about canopic jars on photocopiable page 'Canopic jars' from the CD-ROM. This explains: what the jars were used for; why they were used; how the lids were shaped as different animals; and that the jars represented the four sons of Horus, who were supposed to protect the organs in their journey to the afterlife.
● Ask the children to look at the pictures of the jars and consider the physical shape of the four heads and their key characteristics, in preparation for making their own jars. Draw the children's attention to some of the distinctive shapes, such as the jackal's ears, baboon's snout and falcon's beak.
● Demonstrate rolling a ball of clay, pressing it onto the lid to cover the outside of it, and then moulding it into the basic head shape.
● Talk about and model techniques that could be used to shape the clay – rolling, pulling, pressing and pinching. Demonstrate pinching some clay to make the jackal's ears.

Independent work
● Give each child a ball of clay and a cup or jar with lid.
● Ask them to choose their favourite canopic jar character and mould it with the clay to make the jar. If small jars are used, and there is enough clay, they could roll the clay flat to cover the jar as well.
● Optionally, children could also paint and glaze their jars.

Differentiation
● Support: children may need assistance with modelling the clay.
● Challenge: children should aim for greater detail in their models.

Review
● Look at some of the jars as a class.
● Ask: *Why did you choose to make this one? What animal is it? Which organ would it have contained?*

Week 4 lesson plans

This week, children explore Egyptian papyrus art, looking at examples and considering the colours, characters, scenes and poses used. They make paper in the papyrus style before creating their own Egyptian designs.

1: What was Egyptian art like? (1)

Lesson objectives
● To learn about the achievements of the earliest civilisations – a depth study of ancient Egypt.
● To regularly address and sometimes devise historically valid questions about change, cause, similarity and difference, and significance.
● To understand how our knowledge of the past is constructed from a range of sources.

Expected outcomes
● All children will create their own Egyptian-style art.
● Most children will describe at least one feature of Egyptian art.
● Some children will incorporate the features of Egyptian art in their work.

Resources
Media resource 'Egyptian art' on the CD-ROM; brown paper; glue; wax paper; pictures of Egyptian art (optional)

Introduction
● Show the media resource 'Egyptian art' on the CD-ROM and ask the children to comment on the artworks.
● Ask: *What colours have been used?* (Generally blue, orange, gold and green feature heavily in papyrus art.) *What are the pictures painted on?* (Papyrus paper, made from the pith of the papyrus plant, which grows on the Nile banks.) *What characters and scenes have been chosen? Which direction are the figures facing?* (Egyptian figures tend to have forward-facing torsos with head and limbs turned to the side.) *What poses are used? What evidence do the pictures give us about life in ancient Egypt?*

Whole-class work
● Go back to a few of the images. Invite groups of children to come out the front and adopt the poses in the pictures.
● Talk about the importance of papyrus (a Nile plant) to the Egyptians. Among other things, they used it to make baskets, paper and even small boats.
● Explain that, in this lesson, the children will make their own 'papyrus' paper and draft their Egyptian-style pictures. In the next lesson, they will draw their pictures onto their paper.
● Demonstrate creating the paper. You will need strips of brown paper, cut to around 25cm x 3cm; a mixture of one part glue and one part water; and a sheet of wax paper. Dip one strip of brown paper in the glue mixture and remove the excess liquid. Lay it vertically on the wax paper. Do the same with the next strip, so it slightly overlaps the first. Keep going until there are several in a row. Then repeat the process, laying the strips across the first layer, perpendicular to it. Smooth it down and leave it to dry. Explain that the paper strips represents strips of papyrus, which contains a natural glue-like substance.

Independent work
● Ask the children to create their paper and leave it to dry.
● They can then start on their draft designs, inspired by the ones they have seen on the CD-ROM. It may be helpful to have these on display throughout the lesson.

Differentiation
● Support: children are likely to need help with the paper making and, depending on time and ability, it may be appropriate to give them brown or yellow paper for their designs instead of asking them to make their own; children may need some help to create simple designs or they may wish to trace existing artworks.

Review
● Check the children's progress at the end of the lesson. Explain that next in the next lesson they will be copying their designs onto the paper they have made.
● Look at some of their designs so far. Ask other children to comment on how they are in the style of Egyptian pictures.

Lesson objectives
● To learn about the achievements of the earliest civilisations – a depth study of ancient Egypt.
● To regularly address and sometimes devise historically valid questions about change, cause, similarity and difference, and significance.
● To understand how our knowledge of the past is constructed from a range of sources.

Expected outcomes
● All children will create their own Egyptian-style art.
● Most children will describe at least one feature of Egyptian art.
● Some children will incorporate the features of Egyptian art in their work.

Resources
Paper made in the previous lesson; media resource 'Egyptian art' on the CD-ROM

2: What was Egyptian art like? (2)

Introduction
● Ask two or three children to show their draft designs and talk about how they have made them look like Egyptian art. This could be by their choice of characters, the clothing, the poses used, symbols or scenes depicted.

Independent work
● Children finish their draft designs and then recreate these on their papyrus paper. Ideally, they will draw the design lightly in pencil before going over it in felt-tipped pens.

Differentiation
● Support: ask the children additional prompt questions when talking about their designs to help them expand their answers to understand what particular features make it look like Egyptian art.

Review
● Look at some of the children's drawings as a class. Ask: *What design did you choose? How did you create your design? How did you make it look like Egyptian art? What was the most difficult thing about creating your artwork?*

Week 5 lesson plans

This week, children learn about why the Nile was so important to the ancient Egyptians and how its flooding helped the country to become wealthy and powerful. Children then begin their own end-of-year project, investigating a question of their choice and creating a poster with images and information.

Lesson objectives
● To learn about the achievements of the earliest civilisations – a depth study of ancient Egypt.
● To regularly address and sometimes devise historically valid questions about change, cause, similarity and difference, and significance.
● To construct informed responses that involve thoughtful selection and organisation of relevant historical information.
● To understand how our knowledge of the past is constructed from a range of sources.

Expected outcomes
● All children will describe one reason why the Nile was important to the Egyptians.
● Most children will describe several reasons why the Nile was important to the Egyptians.
● Some children will describe why the Nile helped Egypt become a wealthy civilisation.

Resources
Photocopiable page 114 'The Nile'; photocopiable page 115 'The Nile: question sheet'; internet access

1: Why was the Nile important to the ancient Egyptians?

Introduction
● Ask children the following riddle, giving extra clues until the children guess the correct answer, which is the River Nile: *I am called the backbone of Egypt. I give the people of Egypt many gifts. Farmers, travellers and traders love me. I am over 4000 miles long. I am the most important river in Egypt.*
● Tell the children to put up their hand when they think they know the answer, but don't ask for any answers to be suggested aloud until most children have their hand up.

Whole-class work
● Use satellite images online to view the Nile and its surrounding area from above. Invite children to comment on what they see. They should notice that there is a strip of green, fertile land along the river, which is surrounded by desert. Ask: *Why do you think the land is so green around the river?*
● Read and discuss the photocopiable page 114 'The Nile'. Children should now be able to answer the question as to why the satellite images show a green strip, more fully. Check their understanding of the sheet by asking different children to give one reason why the Nile was important to the ancient Egyptians.

Paired work or Independent work
● Ask the children to complete the comprehension questions on the photocopiable page 115 'The Nile: question sheet'.
● The activity challenge asks the children to imagine they are sailing down the Nile on a boat and to write about the things that they might see on the journey.

Differentiation
● Support: children should answer just the first six questions on the photocopiable sheet, which require straightforward answers; the final questions require deeper reflection.

Review
● Ask various children to provide answers to the questions on the photocopiable sheet. (Answers are: 1. around 4200 miles; 2. Akhet, Peret and Shemu; 3. grain, wheat, barley, vegetables and flax; 4. linen; 5. other work, such as building temples and pyramids; 6. a boat was needed to cross the Nile to get to the afterlife; 7. the Nile looks like a backbone running through the country, but it also acts as a support metaphorically, providing food and wealth; 8. the Nile enabled the ancient Egyptians to grow more food than they needed and the surplus could be used to trade.)
● Some children could share their descriptions of sailing down the Nile, with the rest of the class.

Lesson objectives

● To learn about the achievements of the earliest civilisations – a depth study of ancient Egypt.
● To regularly address and sometimes devise historically valid questions about change, cause, similarity and difference, and significance.
● To construct informed responses that involve thoughtful selection and organisation of relevant historical information.
● To understand how our knowledge of the past is constructed from a range of sources.

Expected outcomes

● All children will describe an aspect of life in ancient Egypt.
● Most children will create a poster dealing with an aspect of life in ancient Egypt.
● Some children will create a detailed poster or project dealing with an aspect of life in ancient Egypt.

Resources

Internet access or reference books about ancient Egypt

2: What was life like in ancient Egypt? (1)

Introduction

● Invite each child to say one thing about ancient Egypt that they didn't know before.
● Ask: *What have you enjoyed learning about most? Is there anything else you would like to find out?* Allow children one minute to discuss these questions with a talk partner before sharing their answers as a class.
● Note some key points on the board for reference throughout the lesson.

Whole-class work

● Creating a poster or project will allow children the opportunity to carry out some independent research into an area of their choice, answering their own historically valid question. It will be planned and put together over the next three lessons, although children could complete some of the work at home. Children can work on their posters individually or in pairs.
● List suggestions on the board for what the poster might cover, adding to the list already created on the board during the starter (for example, ancient Egyptian food, leisure activities, homes, temples, and so on). Children could choose a topic not yet covered or investigate a familiar area in more detail.
● Talk about how to turn children's areas of interest into historically valid questions that can be investigated, such as: What did the Egyptians do for fun? What did the Egyptians eat? What were Egyptian homes like?

Paired work or Independent work

● Children should start to plan their posters this lesson, thinking about where they will get information from and what text and images they will include. Provide reference books and internet access for the children to use for their research. Direct children to specific areas of websites, such as those of the BBC or British Museum.
● Children could create posters by hand or using computer software.

Differentiation
● Support: children could create simple posters containing bulleted facts and images.
● Challenge: children should be encouraged to choose a more complex topic and explore it in more detail in a poster or project.

Review

● Check the children's progress by asking them to tell you the historically valid questions they have chosen. Ensure that all children know which area they will be researching, and provide guidance if necessary.
● Check that the children have enough resources available to answer their questions. Assist them with finding additional websites online if necessary, or advise them to change their question if it is too narrow.

Week 6 lesson plans

This week, children continue work on their independent posters or projects, finding information to help answer their historically valid questions. Finally, they have the opportunity to share their work with the rest of the class.

1: What was life like in ancient Egypt? (2)

Introduction

- In pairs, invite children to talk about their poster or project work so far.
- Give children the opportunity to ask questions or request assistance if needed. Ask: *What are you finding enjoyable or difficult about independent work?*
- Is there anything the children have found out about at home, which they could share with the rest of the class?

Whole-class work

- Ask: *What makes a good poster?* Give the children two minutes to discuss this with a talk partner.
- Discuss their ideas and create a list on the board. This could include, eye-catching headings and images, clear and varied layout, bullet points, interesting facts, and so on.

Paired work or Independent work

- Give children time to work on their projects or presentations. Circulate around the class, helping where necessary.

> **Differentiation**
> - Support: children could create simple posters containing bulleted facts and images.
> - Challenge: children should be encouraged to choose a more complex topic and explore it in more detail in a poster or project.

Review

- Check the children's progress. Remind them that they will only have a short amount of time at the beginning of the next lesson before presenting their posters to the rest of the class.

Lesson objectives

- To learn about the achievements of the earliest civilisations – a depth study of ancient Egypt.
- To regularly address and sometimes devise historically valid questions about change, cause, similarity and difference, and significance.
- To construct informed responses that involve thoughtful selection and organisation of relevant historical information.
- To understand how our knowledge of the past is constructed from a range of sources.

Expected outcomes

- All children will describe an aspect of life in ancient Egypt.
- Most children will continue work on a poster dealing with an aspect of life in ancient Egypt.
- Some children will continue work on a detailed poster or project dealing with an aspect of life in ancient Egypt.

Resources

Internet access or reference books about ancient Egypt

Lesson objectives

● To learn about the achievements of the earliest civilisations – a depth study of ancient Egypt.
● To regularly address and sometimes devise historically valid questions about change, cause, similarity and difference, and significance.
● To construct informed responses that involve thoughtful selection and organisation of relevant historical information.
● To understand how our knowledge of the past is constructed from a range of sources.

Expected outcomes

● All children will describe an aspect of life in ancient Egypt.
● Most children will complete a poster dealing with an aspect of life in ancient Egypt.
● Some children will complete a detailed poster or project dealing with an aspect of life in ancient Egypt.

Resources

Internet access or reference books about ancient Egypt

2: What was life like in ancient Egypt? (3)

Introduction

● Remind the children of the kinds of criteria that make a good project or presentation, such as: eye-catching presentation and clear layout, including the use of subheadings and bullet points; images; interesting information or ideas).

Paired work or Independent work

● Give children time to put the finishing touches to their posters or projects; help where necessary.

Differentiation
● Support: children could create simple posters containing bulleted facts and images.
● Challenge: children should be encouraged to choose a more complex topic and explore it in more detail in a poster or project.

Review

● Give each child or pair the opportunity to show their poster or project to the class and talk through at least one thing they have learned.
● Invite children to offer constructive praise to their peers.

Lesson objectives
● To learn about the achievements of the earliest civilisations – a depth study of ancient Egypt.
● To develop a chronologically secure knowledge and understanding of British, local and world history, establishing clear narratives within and across the periods they study.

Resources
Interactive activity 'Y3 Summer 2 quiz' on the CD-ROM; sticky notes or card

Ancient Egypt quiz (1)

Revise
● Write the following words and phrases on the board and also on sticky notes or cards: mummy, Anubis, embalming, Osiris, River Nile, inundation, canopic jars, sarcophagus, Ammut, weighing of the heart, Thoth, Isis, natron salt, Horus.
● Play bingo using these terms in groups or as a whole class.
● Each player draws a three-by-three grid, writing a different term from the board in each cell.
● Choose children to select a card and provide a definition or description of the term (not the word or phrase itself). The other children must listen carefully and work out whether they have the related term.

Assess
● Ask the children to complete interactive activity 'Y3 Summer 2 quiz' on the CD-ROM, in which they answer multiple-choice questions covering the chapter content.
● Give children a set length of time (for example, 15 minutes) to answer the questions. This can be used as part of a formal assessment or as a fun challenge activity, giving children the opportunity to show what they have learned about the topic.
● Less confident readers may need adult support to read the questions aloud.

Further practice
● Ask children to create a glossary of terms relevant to ancient Egypt, which can be used for a class studying this period the following year.

Lesson objectives
● To learn about the achievements of the earliest civilisations – a depth study of ancient Egypt.
● To construct informed responses that involve thoughtful selection and organisation of relevant historical information.

Resources
Internet access or reference books about Ancient Egypt

Ancient Egypt mind maps

Revise
● Organise children into pairs and give them time to explore the information, images and activities on a specific web page, or page of a book (for example the British Museum's page on ancient Egypt).
● Talk about the way the information has been organised into categories.

Assess
● Ask children to create a mind map (model an example if necessary) containing as much information as they can remember about ancient Egypt (from this chapter and the previous one).
● Write the following words on the board as prompts: pyramids, hieroglyphics, King Tutankhamun, famous Egyptians, Great Sphinx, Rosetta Stone, Howard Carter, Seth and Osiris, mummification, weighing of the heart, Nile River.
● Less confident writers could share their ideas verbally with adult support. Some children may wish to draw labelled diagrams rather than write their answers.

Further practice
● Ask children to create an information booklet for a younger age group about ancient Egypt.

PHOTOCOPIABLE

The myth of Osiris and Seth

1. Long ago, Osiris was a great king. He ruled over Egypt with his beloved queen, Isis. Osiris was just and fair. He was loved and respected by his people.

2. Osiris had a brother named Seth. Seth was very jealous of Osiris and wanted to rule Egypt himself. One day, he could no longer bear his envy. He killed Osiris and cut his body into many pieces, scattering them across Egypt.

3. Isis was overwhelmed with grief. Her tears flowed into the Nile and the waters rose, flooding the land.

4. Isis went to her sister, Nephthys. The two women turned themselves into falcons, crying out their grief. They travelled across Egypt in search of the pieces of Osiris's body.

5. With Osiris and Isis gone, Seth became king. He was a cruel and strict ruler. The people feared him.

6. One by one, Isis and Nephthys collected the parts of Osiris's body. They brought the pieces to Thoth and Anubis, who carefully restored his body and embalmed him.

7. Osiris and Isis were together one last time and then he passed into the land of the dead. He became lord of the underworld. For all time he would sit in judgement of all the souls who entered.

8. Isis became pregnant and hid from Seth among the thick papyrus grasses on the banks of the Nile. There her son Horus was born. Horus was a weak child but his mother's love helped him to grow into a strong and brave man.

9. Horus decided to take revenge on Seth for murdering his father and challenge him to the throne. They battled for many days. Finally, Seth turned himself into a hippopotamus and attacked Horus. Horus grabbed his spear and stuck it deep into Seth's flesh. At last, Seth was defeated.

10. Horus became a fair and wise king, just like his father, Osiris. Once again, peace and order returned to Egypt.

The Nile

■ Read this text about the River Nile.

The Nile River is around 4200 miles long and is one of the longest rivers in the world. It is sometimes called the 'backbone of Egypt'. It is said to provide many 'gifts' to the people who live along its banks – fresh water, fish, papyrus plants, a place to wash, and much more.

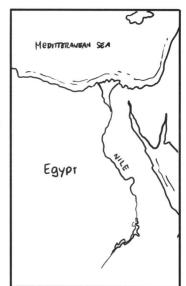

In ancient times, the Nile helped Egypt to become a rich and powerful civilisation. It flooded every year, watering the surrounding valley and keeping the land green and fertile. Because the farmers knew when the land would flood, they were able to time the planting of crops so that they always had a good harvest. This meant they had lots of food for themselves as well as extra that they could use to trade and make money. Farming was therefore very important to the Egyptians and pictures of farmers can often be found in Egyptian art.

The farming year was divided into three seasons:

■ **The flooding season (Akhet)** (June to September) – The Nile waters rose and flooded the surrounding plains. The flooding was called the 'inundation'. Farmers did other work during this time, including building temples and possibly even the pyramids.

■ **The growing season (Peret)** (October to February) – The Nile returned to normal. The plains were left with a layer of dark, fertile soil. Farmers ploughed the soil and planted crops. They grew grain, wheat, barley and vegetables, as well as plant called flax, which was used to make linen cloth.

■ **The harvest season (Shemu)** (March to May) – This was the time to harvest the crops. Wheat was used to make bread and barley was turned into beer. Farmers also raised animals like cattle and goats. They stored crops in preparation for the next flood.

As well as being important for food, water and farming, the Nile was also used for transport. The Egyptians travelled along the river in boats made from papyrus or wood. People could transport goods great distances to trade with other lands. Boats were also buried in tombs because the Egyptians believed that the dead person would have to cross the Nile to reach the afterlife.

PHOTOCOPIABLE

The Nile: question sheet

- Answer these questions and then complete the activity challenge.

1. How long is the River Nile?

_____

2. What were the Egyptian names for the three seasons?

_____

3. Which crops did farmers grow?

_____

4. What was flax used for?

_____

5. What did farmers do during the inundation?

_____

6. Why were boats buried in tombs?

_____

7. Why do you think the Nile was called the 'backbone of Egypt'?

_____

8. How did the Nile help Egypt become a rich country?

_____

- **Activity challenge:** imagine you are on a journey in a boat on the Nile. Write about the things that you see on the way

_____

_____

_____

_____

I can answer questions about the Nile.

How did you do?

Life in ancient Greece

The first half of Year 4 furthers children's understanding of the history of the wider world, as they are introduced to the topic of ancient Greece. This chapter focuses on ancient Greek life, including clothing, homes, warfare, architecture, the Acropolis, Sparta and the achievements of famous Greeks in such fields as literature, philosophy and science. Children also explore the interesting debate regarding the Elgin Marbles, which are sculptures controversially removed from the Parthenon and now housed in the British Museum. In the following chapters, children explore Greek religion, mythology and theatre, as well as the legacy of the Greeks throughout history to the present day.

Chapter at a glance

Curriculum objectives

• Ancient Greece – a study of Greek life and achievements and their influence on the western world.

Week	Lesson	Summary of activities	Expected outcomes
1	1	• Children examine a map of ancient Greece and place key events on a timeline.	• Can say when and where the civilisation of ancient Greece took place.
	2	• Children read about Greek clothing and then make their own garments for a Greek fashion parade.	• Can describe Greek clothing and hairstyles.
2	1	• Children read about Greek home life and compare it to the present day.	• Can compare Greek domestic life with that of today.
	2	• Children write names and messages using the Greek alphabet.	• Can compare the Greek alphabet to our own.
3	1	• Children use the internet and reference books to answer questions about the Athenian Acropolis.	• Can describe the Acropolis of Athens.
	2	• Children complete an interactive activity about the features of Greek temples before designing their own columns.	• Can design a Greek-style column.
4	1	• Children read about the Elgin Marbles and debate whether or not they should be returned to Greece.	• Can debate the pros and cons of the return of the Elgin Marbles to the Parthenon.
	2	• Children write about whether they would prefer to live in Sparta or Athens.	• Can compare the lives of people in Athens and Sparta.
5	1	• Children write a newspaper article about one of the battles of the Persian Wars.	• Can describe some main events of the Persian Wars.
	2	• Children perform a poem telling the story of the Trojan Horse.	• Can retell the story of the Trojan Horse.
6	1	• Children work in groups to create a campaign showing why their historical figure was 'The Greatest Greek'.	• Can describe the achievements of some famous Greeks.
	2	• Children work in groups to create a campaign showing why their historical figure was 'The Greatest Greek'.	• Can debate which Greek made the biggest impact.
Assess and review		• To review the half-term's work.	

Expected prior learning
● This chapter begins the fresh topic of ancient Greece. The topic is capable of standing alone and no prior learning is necessary, although a basic understanding of timelines would be useful.

Overview of progression
● Children will further develop their understanding of timelines, considering key events in ancient Greek history.
● They develop the skill of examining contrasting viewpoints and understanding why differing interpretations of the past occur, as they debate the return to Greece of the Elgin Marbles and consider whether the accepted account of the Persian wars, as recorded by Greek historian Herodotus, might be different if told from the Persian point of view.
● They also develop their understanding of the use of archaeological evidence as they explore the Acropolis and other Greek temples.
● They develop their understanding of the concept of 'significance', investigating the impact and legacy of a number of famous Greeks.

Creative context
● Cross-curricular opportunities include:
  ● debates and persuasive writing about the return of the Elgin Marbles to Greece; performance poetry on the theme of the Trojan Horse; writing a newspaper article about a battle of the Persian Wars; undertaking research;
  ● creating Greek garments; designing Greek columns or temples.

Background knowledge
● Wealthy Greeks lived in two-storey houses with separate areas for men and women. Household chores were carried out by slaves. Women weren't educated and enjoyed little freedom.
● The Acropolis in Athens is one of the most famous historical sites in the world. There are four main buildings – the Parthenon (the main temple, dedicated to Athena), the Propylaia (the gateway for entering the Acropolis), the Erechtheion (a temple dedicated to Athena and Poseidon) and the temple of Athena Nike.
● The Parthenon, built around 447–438BC, was once decorated with beautiful marble sculptures but these started to fall to ruin over the centuries. During a time of war, in 1687, it was used to store gunpowder. An explosion destroyed many of the remaining sculptures.
● In 1801, when Greece was under the rule of the Ottoman Empire, the British Ambassador, Lord Elgin, removed many of the sculptures from the Parthenon and took them to England. They were acquired by the British Museum and became known as the Elgin Marbles. In 1983, the Greek government began to demand that the sculptures be returned permanently to Athens. The British Museum refused and the prospect of returning the Marbles has sparked much debate.
● Much of the information we have about ancient Greek life comes from Athens, due to its written records and lasting architecture. Life in the city state of Sparta, however, was very different. Emphasis was on building the strength of the Spartan army. Sparta was ruled by two kings, as opposed to the democratic system of Athens.

Week 1 lesson plans

This week introduces children to the wider, world topic of ancient Greece. They use timelines and maps to determine when and where the ancient Greek civilisation took place. They then read about the type of clothing worn by the ancient Greeks and create their own Greek-style garments.

1: When and where did the civilisation of ancient Greece take place?

Lesson objectives
- To study ancient Greece – a study of Greek life and achievements and their influence on the western world.
- To develop a chronologically secure knowledge and understanding of British, local and world history, establishing clear narratives within and across the periods they study.
- To develop the appropriate use of historical terms.
- To regularly address and sometimes devise historically valid questions about change, cause, similarity and difference, and significance.

Expected outcomes
- All children will know some important ancient Greek events.
- Most children will place ancient Greek events on a timeline.
- Some children will discuss the relationship between different events on a timeline of ancient Greece.

Resources
Atlas, or map of Europe; photocopiable pages 131 and 132 'Ancient Greece map' and 'Ancient Greece timeline'; key events from photocopiable page 132 printed onto individual cards

Introduction
- Elicit what the children already know about ancient Greece. This could be done orally; alternatively, ask the children to create a spider diagram, or list of bullet points, in their books and refer back to this at the end of the topic to assess their progress.

Whole-class work
- Tell the children that they are going to find out where and when the ancient civilisation of Greece occurred.
- As a class, locate Greece on a map and its relationship to the UK.
- Give each child a copy of photocopiable page 131 'Ancient Greece map' to keep in their books. (The children will be learning about some of the areas on the map in the weeks to come.) Read through the names of the places on the map. Have the children heard of, or even been to, any of these places? Ask them to share anything they know already, or refer back to previous knowledge mentioned in the introductory activity.
- Read and discuss photocopiable page 132 'Ancient Greece timeline', which lists some key events in ancient Greek history, next to a timeline. Talk about the fact that some timelines run from left to right and others run vertically. This timeline is moving forward in time as it runs down the page. Remind children of the concepts of 'Before Christ' and 'Anno Domini'. These dates are BC, so the higher the number, the further back in time.

Paired work or Independent work
- Ask the children to complete the activity on the photocopiable sheet, which requires them to link the events to their correct position on the timeline.

> **Differentiation**
> - Support: children could work in a group with adult support to place a selection of the events on the photocopiable sheet in order.
> - Challenge: children can be expected to show more accuracy with the positioning of events along the timeline. As they progress through the topic, they may wish to add other important dates to the timeline.

Review
- Ask ten children to come to the front of the class and give each one a key event from the photocopiable sheet, printed onto card.
- Ask the rest of the class to put the children into the correct chronological order.

Lesson objectives

● To study ancient Greece – a study of Greek life and achievements and their influence on the western world.
● To develop a chronologically secure knowledge and understanding of British, local and world history, establishing clear narratives within and across the periods they study.
● To develop the appropriate use of historical terms.
● To regularly address and sometimes devise historically valid questions about change, cause, similarity and difference, and significance.

Expected outcomes

● All children will describe what ancient Greek clothing looked like.
● Most children will use the correct names for items of ancient Greek clothing.
● Some children will describe how ancient Greek clothing was affected by status.

Resources

Photocopiable page 'Ancient Greek clothing' from the CD-ROM; rectangular pieces of cloth of different sizes; safety pins; belts, rope or sashes

2: What did the ancient Greeks wear?

Introduction

● Ask: *What are you wearing today? Why are you wearing this?* (They will probably be wearing school uniform, because they have to.)
● Ask: *What will you wear after school today? What about at the weekend?* Talk about how they decide what clothes to wear and the factors that influence the decision: the weather, the occasion, their budget, fashion, and so on.

Whole-class work

● Ask: *What kind of clothes do you think they might have worn in ancient Greece? How do you think historians know what the clothes looked like?* Discuss the use of written texts and artworks (for example, pottery vases, and sculptures) in providing evidence about Greek clothing.
● Tell the children that they are going to be reading about Greek clothing and then having a go at making their own.
● Read about the different types of Greek clothing on photocopiable page 'Ancient Greek clothing' from the CD-ROM: the peplos and chiton (types of dress/tunic), himation and chlamys (types of cloak) and footwear and hairstyles.

Group work

● Ask the children to read the descriptions on the photocopiable sheet again, carefully, as well as the instructions on how to dress as an ancient Greek.
● Split the class into groups, distribute the dressing-up materials and challenge each group to dress one member of the group as an ancient Greek man or woman. (Alternatively, provide enough cloth, belts, and so on, for all the children to dress up.)

Differentiation
● Support: mixed-ability groups may be beneficial.
● Challenge: children could carry out wider research into the types of colours, styles and patterns worn by different occupations or members of society.

Review

● When the garments are ready, hold an ancient Greek fashion parade, asking the children to provide a commentary on what they, or their group members, are wearing.
● Ask: *What is it like wearing these garments? Why do you think the Greeks wore this type of clothing?* (The children might talk about comfort, suitability to the weather, status or aesthetic aspects of the clothing.)

Week 2 lesson plans

This week focuses on the skill of comparing aspects of ancient Greek life with modern life. Children explore ancient Greek homes and think about the ways in which they are similar to and different from today's home. They then learn about the Greek alphabet, comparing it with our alphabet and using it to write their names and messages.

1: How does ancient Greek domestic life compare with domestic life today?

Lesson objectives
● To study ancient Greece – a study of Greek life and achievements and their influence on the western world.
● To develop a chronologically secure knowledge and understanding of British, local and world history, establishing clear narratives within and across the periods they study.
● To regularly address and sometimes devise historically valid questions about change, cause, similarity and difference, and significance.

Expected outcomes
● All children will describe at least one feature of ancient Greek domestic life.
● Most children will describe several features of ancient Greek domestic life.
● Some children will compare ancient Greek domestic life with life today.

Resources
Photocopiable page 'Home life in ancient Greece' from the CD-ROM

Introduction
● Draw a grid of four squares on the board and ask children to suggest four rooms of a house (for example, kitchen, bedroom, bathroom and living room).
● Name a letter of the alphabet and give the children 30 seconds to try to write items beginning with that letter, which can be found in each room.

Whole-class work
● Read and discuss photocopiable page 'Home life in ancient Greece' from the CD-ROM, which shows an illustration of an ancient Greek home and describes who would have lived there.
● Ask: *What would it have been like to be a woman living in this house? What about a man/child/slave?*
● Select children to sit in the 'hot-seat' as these characters while other children interview them about their daily routine. Allow the children a few minutes to think of some questions to ask the different people. Encourage the children in the hot seat to give reasons for their answers.
● Talk about one or two things that are similar to or different from home life today. (For example, an ancient Greek home had a kitchen, bathroom and bedrooms like our homes today; but they also had separate rooms for men and women, and bedrooms for slaves.)

Group work or Paired work
● Split children into groups or pairs. Give each group a copy of the photocopiable sheet and a large sheet of sugar paper. Challenge them to write down ways in which ancient Greek home life was similar to and different from home life today.
● They should also consider the way the homes were used and organised (for example, the use of slaves; separate areas for men and women).
● If children are familiar with Venn diagrams, they could use one of these to show features of Ancient Greek homes and modern homes, as well as the features the two share.

Differentiation
● Support: mixed-ability groups may be beneficial.
● Challenge: children could conduct further research into domestic life in ancient Greece.

Review
● Ask some children or pairs to come to the front of the class to present and talk through their ideas. The other children should listen to see if there is anything they can add.
● Alternatively, create a class Venn diagram or table on the board, with different children contributing ideas.

Lesson objectives
• To study ancient Greece – a study of Greek life and achievements and their influence on the western world.
• To develop a chronologically secure knowledge and understanding of British, local and world history, establishing clear narratives within and across the periods they study.

Expected outcomes
• All children will know that the Greek alphabet is not the same as our own, Latin alphabet.
• Most children will write one or two words using the Greek alphabet.
• Some children will write a sentence using the Greek alphabet and will identify similarities and differences between the Greek alphabet and Latin alphabet.

Resources
Photocopiable page 133 'The Greek alphabet'

2: How does the Greek alphabet compare with ours?

Introduction
• Write the following list of school subjects on the board: science, reading and writing, history, PE, geography, PSHE, drama, maths, music.
• Ask: *Which do you think were the three main subjects taught to primary school aged children in ancient Athens?* (Answers are: reading and writing, PE, and music.)
• Ask: *How is this different from the subjects you are taught at school?* (Perhaps most notably, maths is missing from the Greek lessons, whereas children in Britain spend a lot of time developing numeracy skills, starting in Reception.)

Whole-class work
• Read and discuss photocopiable page 133 'The Greek alphabet', which gives some background information on how the Greek alphabet developed and also shows the Greek characters and letter names alongside our own alphabet.
• Ask the children:
  • *How many letters are there in the Greek alphabet?* (24)
  • *What similarities and differences are there between the Greek alphabet and ours?* (The Greek alphabet has fewer letters; the Greek letters have longer names; some of the Greek letters look the same as ours, but some are very different; a Greek upper-case letter can sometimes look very different from its lower-case version; they don't appear in the same order; Greek characters are sometimes made up of two of ours, for example 'ps'.)
  • *Which of our letters are missing?* (C, H, J, Q, V, W)

Independent work or Paired work
• Give each child a copy of the photocopiable sheet. Ask them to complete the activity, writing their name or a message using the Greek alphabet.
• Tell the children to swap work with a partner. They should then decipher each other's names or messages.

Differentiation
• Support: children could copy the Greek alphabet letters or use them to write their name.
• Challenge: children could use the Greek alphabet to write longer messages.

Review
• End the lesson by playing 'Hangman' using words written with the Greek letters.

Lesson objectives
● To study ancient Greece – a study of Greek life and achievements and their influence on the western world.
● To develop a chronologically secure knowledge and understanding of British, local and world history, establishing clear narratives within and across the periods they study.
● To understand how our knowledge of the past is constructed from a range of sources.

Expected outcomes
● All children will describe the main features of the Acropolis.
● Most children will research some information about the Acropolis.
● Some children will describe the strategic location of the Acropolis.

Resources
Pictures of the Parthenon (source online); photocopiable page 'The Athenian Acropolis' from the CD-ROM; internet access or references books about the Acropolis

Week 3 lesson plans

This week, children explore the Acropolis in Athens, using online resources to answer questions about the Parthenon and other Greek temples. They consider the features of Greek temples and the three main types of column – Doric, Ionic and Corinthian – before designing their own.

I: What was the Acropolis like?

Introduction
● Give the children one minute to write down as many famous buildings as they can (for example, the Empire State Building, Eiffel Tower, Sydney Opera House, St Paul's Cathedral).
● Select one or two examples and talk about why they are famous (for example, because they are tall, beautiful or historic).

Whole-class work
● Show children an image of the Parthenon in Athens. Ask: *Does anyone know what this building is? Where can it be found? How old is it? What material is it made from? What do you think it was used for?* At this stage don't give the correct answers, but listen to the children's ideas, and encourage them to give evidence to support their ideas.
● Tell the children that they are going to be carrying out their own research to find out more about the Parthenon and the Athenian Acropolis (the city on top of the hill in ancient Athens). Today, the remains of the Acropolis can be found in Athens. It is a popular tourist attraction and an important site of world heritage.
● Ask: *Why do you think the Acropolis was built on the hill like this?* Remind the children of any work they have done on Iron Age hill forts, and the fact that building on the top of a hill means that any enemies can be seen approaching from far away.

Group work or Paired work
● Split the class into small groups or pairs. Give each group or pair photocopiable page 'The Athenian Acropolis' from the CD-ROM. Explain that they need to carry out research in order to answer the questions on the sheet.
● Provide the children with reference books, or direct them to specific websites, such as the ancient Greece section of the British Museum's website www.ancientgreece.co.uk/acropolis.
● A virtual tour of the Acropolis is also available online at http://acropolis-virtualtour.gr.

Review
● Check that the children have answered the questions correctly. Ask various children to provide answers, and fill in any missing information as necessary.
● The children should mark their own sheets. Answers are:
  1. High city
  2. Pericles
  3. They had been left in ruins by the Persians
  4. Panathenaia
  5. Athena
  6. Seventeen
  7. Mnesikles
  8. Erectheion; columns in the shape of draped women
  9. Woollen or silk garments
  10. The Athenian victory over the Persians.

Lesson objectives
● To study ancient Greece – a study of Greek life and achievements and their influence on the western world.
● To develop a chronologically secure knowledge and understanding of British, local and world history, establishing clear narratives within and across the periods they study.

Expected outcomes
● All children will design a Greek column.
● Most children will identify the three main types of Greek column.
● Some children will describe the features of a Greek temple.

Resources
Interactive activity 'Greek temples' on the CD-ROM; an image of a Doric column, an Ionic column and a Corinthian column; pictures of Greek temples (source online); materials for model making (optional)

2: What are the features of Greek temples?

Introduction
● Give the children one minute to tell a partner as much as they can recall about the Acropolis.
● Discuss what they remember as a class.

Whole-class work
● Go through the first screen of the interactive activity 'Greek temples' on the CD-ROM, which requires the children to label the features of the temple.
● Display an image of Doric column, an Ionic column and a Corinthian column. Give the children clues to enable them to identify which column is which, such as: a Doric column is the most simple in design; an Ionic column looks like it has ram's horns at the top; a Corinthian column has elaborate decoration at the top.
● It may be useful for the class to come up with an arm gesture for each of the types of column, to aid children's memory (for example, arms raised at diagonals for Doric; arms curled underneath for Ionic; hands at the sides of face for Corinthian).
● Show some images of different Greek buildings (source online) such as: the Parthenon; Temple of Olympian Zeus; Temple of Athena Nike; Erechtheum; Temple of Hephaestus; Temple of Artemis. It may be useful to look at images of the temple ruins today as well as artists' depictions of the way the temples were. Ask: *Can you identify any of the features of these buildings? What are they made from? What geometric shapes can you see in these buildings? What type of columns do they have?*

Paired work or Independent work
● Tell the children to imagine that they are architects in ancient Athens. A new temple is to be built to honour the goddess Athena and they have been commissioned to create a design for it.
● Depending on time available and children's ability, they could design a new style of column, design the full temple or create a cardboard model of the temple. Specify that column designs need to be symmetrical, or leave them to children's imaginations.

Differentiation
● Challenge: children should be encouraged to think about the common features of Greek temples and incorporate these into their designs or models.

Review
● Create a class display of the designs and models, or ask some children to bring their work to the front of the class.
● Ask various children to identify the different features of ancient Greek temples in the work of their peers.

Week 4 lesson plans

This week provides opportunity for the children to develop their thinking and reflection skills. They learn about the history of the Elgin Marbles (sculptures from the Parthenon in the British Museum) and the two sides of the debate regarding whether or not they should be returned to Greece. Children then learn about the differences between the city states of Athens and Sparta, thinking carefully about which they would prefer to live in and why.

I: Why were the Elgin Marbles removed from the Parthenon?

Lesson objectives
● To study ancient Greece – a study of Greek life and achievements and their influence on the western world.
● To develop a chronologically secure knowledge and understanding of British, local and world history, establishing clear narratives within and across the periods they study.
● To note connections, contrasts and trends over time and develop the appropriate use of historical terms.
● To regularly address and sometimes devise historically valid questions about change, cause, similarity and difference, and significance.
● To construct informed responses that involve thoughtful selection and organisation of relevant historical information.
● To understand that different versions of past events may exist, giving some reasons for this.

Expected outcomes
● All children will know that some statues from the Parthenon were taken to Britain.
● Most children will describe why there is controversy regarding the Elgin Marbles' presence in Britain.
● Some children will analyse the two sides of the Elgin Marbles debate.

Resources
Pictures of the Elgin Marbles (source online); photocopiable page 'The Elgin Marbles' from the CD-ROM; internet access

Introduction
● Show some images of the Elgin Marbles, currently in the British Museum, and invite the children's comments. (Please be aware that the sculptures contain nudes.)
● Explain that they are referred to as 'marbles' because this is what they are made of.

Whole-class work
● Read and discuss the information on photocopiable page 'The Elgin Marbles' from the CD-ROM, which explains how the Elgin Marbles ended up in the British Museum, and gives reasons for and against returning them to Athens.
● This may be a good opportunity to talk about the difference between fact and opinion; identify facts and opinions in the presented arguments on the photocopiable sheet. (For example: it is a fact that Lord Elgin was given permission from the Ottoman Empire to take the Marbles; it's a matter of opinion as to whether he therefore had the right to take them.)
● Ask: *Do you think Lord Elgin was right or wrong to take the Marbles? Should the British Museum return them to Athens?* Talk about these issues as a class.

Independent work
● Ask the children to take a point of view and write a persuasive letter to the British Museum to urge them to either keep or return the Marbles.
● Talk about different persuasive devices that they might like to think about, such as biased wording (for example, 'Lord Elgin acquired the Marbles' as opposed to 'Lord Elgin stole the Marbles'), emotive language (for example, 'The loss of the sculptures would be a travesty for the millions of people who visit the British Museum every year.') and rhetorical questions (for example, 'Is it fair that the British Museum keeps hold of Greek property?').
● Alternatively, instead of writing a persuasive letter, four children could prepare speeches (two for and two against the return of the Marbles) for a class debate at the end of the lesson.

Differentiation
● Support: children could work in a group with adult support to discuss the debate.
● Challenge: children should be expected to show deeper reflection and analysis of both sides of the debate. They could read about the differing viewpoints at the websites of the British Museum and Acropolis Museum, or the British campaign site for the return of the sculptures (www.parthenonuk.com).

Review
● Ask some children to share their letters, or if four children have prepared a speech ask them to address the class.
● Allow other children to have their say and debate the issue as a class.
● Finally, hold a class vote.

Lesson objectives

- To study ancient Greece – a study of Greek life and achievements and their influence on the western world.
- To develop a chronologically secure knowledge and understanding of British, local and world history, establishing clear narratives within and across the periods they study.
- To note connections, contrasts and trends over time and develop the appropriate use of historical terms.
- To regularly address and sometimes devise historically valid questions about change, cause, similarity and difference, and significance.
- To understand that different versions of past events may exist, giving some reasons for this.

Expected outcomes

- All children will describe at least one difference between Athens and Sparta.
- Most children will be able to describe the main differences between Athens and Sparta.
- Some children will reflect on which city state they would prefer to live in.

Resources

Photocopiable page 'Athens versus Sparta' from the CD-ROM; photocopiable page 131 'Ancient Greece map'

2: How did life in Athens compare with life in Sparta?

Introduction

- Ask the children to look again at photocopiable page 131 'Ancient Greece map' and to locate the city states of Athens and Sparta. Explain that they are not just cities, but 'city states' – so the city rules over a wider area. (Note: the area covered by city states did change throughout the ancient Greek era – the photocopiable page should give a general idea.)
- Note that the two places are fairly close to each other; and that the city state of Athens is smaller and more spread out than that of Sparta.

Whole-class work

- Tell the children that much of the information we have about Greek life has come from Athens (they will consider why this is the case later).
- Explain that although the two city states weren't far apart, Spartan life was very different from Athenian life. They are going to find out about both and think about which city they would prefer to live in.
- Read and discuss photocopiable page 'Athens versus Sparta' from the CD-ROM, which shows some of the similarities and differences between the two places, in terms of leadership, homes, culture, education and the military.
- Ask: *Why do you think that so much of what we have learned about Greek life is based on Athenian life?* (Unlike Sparta, Athens valued culture and kept many written records from which we have learned about ancient Greek life. It also built grand buildings and artworks, which lasted through the centuries, providing archaeological evidence.)

Group work

- Split the class into discussion groups and ask the children to talk with their peers about which city state would be a better place to live. They should consider this from different perspectives: that of a man, woman and child.

Independent work

- Ask children to write a paragraph or more to explain which city state they would prefer to live in and why.

Differentiation

- Support: mixed-ability groups may be beneficial; children could discuss their ideas verbally rather than write them down.

Review

- Ask some children to read out the paragraphs they have written.
- Do the other children agree? Is there anything they can add to the debate?

Week 5 lesson plans

This week explores the Greeks at war. Children read about the three main battles between the Greeks and the Persians, creating a newspaper article about one of the battles. They then explore the legendary war against the city of Troy (in modern Turkey) with the story of the Trojan Horse. They read and perform a poem to tell this famous story.

Lesson objectives

● To study ancient Greece – a study of Greek life and achievements and their influence on the western world.
● To develop a chronologically secure knowledge and understanding of British, local and world history, establishing clear narratives within and across the periods they study.
● To understand how our knowledge of the past is constructed from a range of sources.

Expected outcomes

● All children will write some sentences about one of battles of the Persian wars.
● Most children will write a newspaper article about one of battles of the Persian wars.
● Some children will consider the events and outcomes of the Persian wars in more detail.

Resources

World map; photocopiable page 'The Persian wars' from the CD-ROM; newspapers; interactive activity 'Newspaper report template' on the CD-ROM

1: What happened during the Persian wars?

Introduction

● Write the word 'Marathon' on the board. Ask the children to share their ideas about its meaning (for example: long-distance run; Olympic event; held in London every year; 26 miles).
● Explain that the word comes from the name of a place, and battle, in ancient Greece. In this lesson they are going to find out about its origin.

Whole-class work

● Tell children that they are now going to learn more about the wars between the Greeks and the Persians (the Persian Empire covered modern-day Iran, Iraq, Turkey, Syria, Lebanon, Israel and parts of Egypt, Turkmenistan, Pakistan and Afghanistan). Locate the countries on a map to show how large the Persian Empire was compared with Greece.
● Read and discuss the events of the three main battles of the Persian wars on photocopiable page 'The Persian wars' from the CD-ROM.
● Tell the children that the main source of information about the wars comes from Herodotus, a Greek historian writing a few decades after the events. Introduce the idea of inaccuracy and bias towards the Greeks. Ask: *Do you think the account of what happened would be the same if it had been written by a Persian?*

Paired work or Independent work

● Give each child a copy of the photocopiable sheet. Tell the children that they are going to create a newspaper article about one of the Persian war battles. They can select which they would like to write about.
● Discuss the features of a newspaper article (show some examples) – headline, summary of key information, image and caption, columns, facts and opinions, quotes, past tense, paragraphs. Note these features on the board.
● Ask the children to come up with some possible headings for the battle of Thermopylae.
● Children can write their reports on paper or use the interactive activity 'Newspaper report template' on the CD-ROM.

Differentiation

● Support: children could write a few words or a sentence to answer the five key questions: What? Where? When? Who? Why?
● Challenge: children could think about bias and perspective in the writing, covering the event from both the Greek and Persian points of view.

Review

● Ask one or two children to show and read their reports. As a class, check the report against the list of newspaper features on the board.
● Ask: *Is this report biased in any way? Does it cover all the main points? Is there anything that could be added?*

Lesson objectives

● To study ancient Greece – a study of Greek life and achievements and their influence on the western world.
● To develop a chronologically secure knowledge and understanding of British, local and world history, establishing clear narratives within and across the periods they study.
● To understand how our knowledge of the past is constructed from a range of sources.

Expected outcomes

● All children will help to create a performance of a poem about the Trojan Horse.
● Most children will describe the basic story of the Trojan Horse.
● Some children will reflect upon the story of the Trojan Horse.

Resources

Internet access; photocopiable page 'The Trojan Horse' from the CD-ROM

2: What was the Trojan Horse?

Introduction

● Ask the children to locate Greece and the archaeological site of Troy (in Turkey) on a map. A description, map and photographs of the archaeological sites can be found on the UNESCO site.

Whole-class work

● Tell the children that there is a famous legend about a war between the Greeks and the Trojans. Explain that the war started because Paris of Troy took Helen from her husband Menelaus, King of Sparta.
● The war is said to have gone on for nearly a decade but the Greeks were not able to get through the high city walls of Troy to rescue Helen.
● Show children the picture of the Trojan Horse on photocopiable page 'The Trojan Horse'. Explain that this large wooden horse once helped the Greeks defeat their enemies, the Trojans. Can they think how?
● Read aloud the poem on the photocopiable sheet several times as a class.

Group work

● Split the class into groups. Depending on ability, you may wish the groups to perform the whole poem or one stanza each.

Differentiation

● Challenge: children could write their own stanzas or full poems on the same theme; or they could write poems about the battles of the Persian Wars as a comparison.

Review

● After a rehearsal period, bring the groups together to watch the performances. (Alternatively, develop this into a performance for assembly.)
● After the performances ask: *Do you think the Trojan Horse was a good plan? What might have gone wrong? How do you think the Trojans felt when they saw the horse?*

Week 6 lesson plans

This week, children explore the significance of some ancient Greek leaders, philosophers, writers and scientists who are still remembered today. They work in groups to explore their impact on the world. Children create a campaign for their Greek to be recognised as 'The Greatest Greek'.

Lesson objectives
● To study ancient Greece – a study of Greek life and achievements and their influence on the western world.
● To develop a chronologically secure knowledge and understanding of British, local and world history, establishing clear narratives within and across the periods they study.
● To regularly address and sometimes devise historically valid questions about change, cause, similarity and difference, and significance.
● To understand how our knowledge of the past is constructed from a range of sources.
● To understand that different versions of past events may exist, giving some reasons for this.

Expected outcomes
● All children will name some of the ancient Greeks who are remembered today.
● Most children will describe why some ancient Greeks are remembered today.
● Some children will describe the legacy of some famous ancient Greeks.

Resources
Photocopiable page 'Famous Greeks' from the CD-ROM; internet access and reference books

1: What are some of the achievements of individual Greeks?

Introduction
● Ask the children to name some modern-day celebrities and list them on the board.
● Ask: *Which of these famous people should be remembered in 2000 years' time? What is it about their achievements that makes them worthy of remembering?*

Whole-class work
● Tell the children that they are going to learn about some ancient Greeks that we still remember today.
● Read and discuss photocopiable page 'Famous Greeks' from the CD-ROM. Ask: *Why do we remember this person? What impact have they had on the world?* Note: some famous Greeks, such as Pythagoras, Socrates and Aesop, do not appear on the sheet as they are explored in greater depth in Spring 1 'Legacy of the Greeks'.

Group work
● Split the children into groups and allocate a famous Greek to each group. Alternatively, allow children to select which group they would like to join.
● Ask the children to imagine that one of these historical figures is to be chosen for a special hall of fame as 'The Greatest Greek'. Their job is to create a mini campaign and presentation to argue, before a panel of judges, that their Greek should be selected.
● Talk about the kinds of content that the children might include in their presentation (for example, achievements within the person's own lifetime, impact on others, legacy today).
● Give the children time to conduct further research into the achievements of their Greek. Provide reference books, or direct them to specific web pages, such as www.ancientgreece.com.
● Children could prepare an oral presentation, share their ideas on sugar paper or create a slideshow.
● They should be encouraged to be creative with their campaigns and may even wish to incorporate slogans or jingles to promote their Greek.

Differentiation
● Support: mixed-ability groupings may be beneficial. Although everyone should contribute, children's roles within the group can be organised according to their strengths (for example, researcher, presentation designer, speaker).

Review
● Check the children's progress at the end of the lesson. Remind them that they will only have a short time at the beginning of the following lesson to complete their presentations, before showing them to the rest of the class.

Lesson objectives

● To study ancient Greece – a study of Greek life and achievements and their influence on the western world.
● To develop a chronologically secure knowledge and understanding of British, local and world history, establishing clear narratives within and across the periods they study.
● To regularly address and sometimes devise historically valid questions about change, cause, similarity and difference, and significance.
● To understand how our knowledge of the past is constructed from a range of sources.
● To understand that different versions of past events may exist, giving some reasons for this.

Expected outcomes

● All children will name some of the ancient Greeks that are remembered today.
● Most children will describe why some ancient Greeks are remembered today.
● Some children will describe the legacy of some famous ancient Greeks.

Resources

Photocopiable page 'Famous Greeks' from the CD-ROM; internet access and reference books

2: Which Greek made the biggest impact?

Introduction
● Remind children of the kinds of criteria that make a good project or presentation (for example, it should be eye catching, clear, include subheadings and bullet points, images, interesting information or ideas; and it should be easy to see or hear).

Group work
● Give children time to work on their presentations; provide help where needed.

Differentiation
● Support: mixed-ability groups are suggested; children's roles within the group can be organised according to their strengths.
● Challenge: children could be encouraged to reflect on how we can measure the impact that the Greeks' achievements have had and their legacy today.

Review
● Allow groups to give their presentations one at a time.
● Invite children to offer constructive praise to their peers.
● Choose a 'winner', inviting other staff members or the rest of the class to act as judges, to vote (with a rule that they cannot vote for their own group).
● Discuss the fact that all of the Greeks have achieved great things in different but equally valuable fields and are worthy of being recognised.

Lesson objectives
● To study ancient Greece – a study of Greek life and achievements and their influence on the western world.
● To develop a chronologically secure knowledge and understanding of British, local and world history, establishing clear narratives within and across the periods they study.

Resources
Interactive activity 'Y4 Autumn I quiz' on the CD-ROM

Life in Ancient Greece

Revise

● Write the following words and phrases on the board: ancient Greek clothing, Persian Wars, Athens, Sparta, Acropolis, Elgin Marbles, ancient Greek homes, Trojan Horse, famous Greeks, Greek alphabet.
● Challenge children to talk for 30 seconds on one of the themes, without hesitation, repetition or deviation.

Assess

● Ask the children to complete interactive activity 'Y4 Autumn I quiz' on the CD-ROM, in which they answer multiple-choice questions covering the chapter content.
● Give children a set length of time (for example, 15 minutes) to answer the questions. This can be used as part of a formal assessment or as a fun challenge activity, giving children the opportunity to show what they have learned about the topic.
● Less confident readers may need adult support to read the questions aloud.

Further practice

● Ask children to discuss and answer the question: *Is Britain today more similar to Athens or Sparta? Why?*

Lesson objectives
● To study ancient Greece – a study of Greek life and achievements and their influence on the western world.
● To address and sometimes devise historically valid questions about change, cause, similarity and difference, and significance.

Resources
Photocopiable pages 'The Persian wars' and 'The Elgin Marbles' from the CD-ROM (optional)

Significant events in ancient Greece

Revise

● Write the following words, names and phrases on the board: chiton, Xerxes, Acropolis, Sparta, Trojan Horse, Lord Elgin, Alexander the Great.
● Tell the children that these are answers to questions. Challenge them to devise one or more questions for each answer.

Assess

● Ask children to answer (in writing or verbally) one of the following questions:
  ● How has the Athenian Acropolis changed over time? (Remind children that the original Acropolis was destroyed by Xerxes and the current one, including the Parthenon, was built under Pericles. It fell into disrepair, some of its artwork was removed by Lord Elgin and it is now a tourist attraction.)
  ● How do you think the Athenian people felt before, during and after the Persian invasion? (Remind children that Greece was still ruled by city states, but that some of these worked together to fight the Persians. The Greeks suffered a loss at Thermopylae but defeated the Persians during the Battle of Salamis.)

Further practice

● Ask children to use their knowledge of ancient Greece (from this and the previous chapter) to create a picture book for a younger age group.

Name: _____   Date: _____

Ancient Greece map

Ancient Greece timeline

■ Look at this timeline of ancient Greece.
For each event, draw an arrow to its correct place on the timeline.

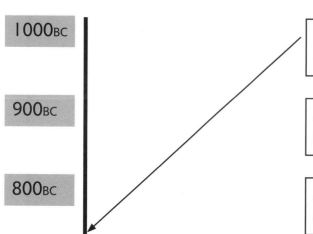

1000BC

900BC

800BC

700BC

600BC

500BC

400BC

300BC

200BC

100BC

776BC – The first Olympic Games is held in Olympia, Greece.

Around 750BC – The Greek alphabet is invented.

Around 750–700BC – Homer writes the epic poem 'The Odyssey'.

490BC – The Athenians beat the Persians at the Battle of Marathon.

480BC – The Persians defeat Spartans at the Battle of Thermopylae. Athenians beat the Persians at the Battle of Salamis at sea.

460BC – Pericles becomes leader of Athens and a 'Golden Age' begins.

447BC – Building commences on the Parthenon in Athens.

436BC – Alexander the Great becomes King of Macedonia.

287BC – The scientist Archimedes is born.

146BC – The Romans invade, conquer and rule Greece.

I can create a timeline of important events in ancient Greece.

How did you do?

The Greek alphabet

The Greek alphabet was first used around 750BC. It was adapted from the writings of another culture that the Greeks traded with: the Phoenicians. The Greeks used their alphabet to write down many things, such as plays, poems, stories, records of government meetings and business contracts. These documents have provided evidence for historians about life in ancient Greece.

The word 'alphabet' comes from the first two letters of the Greek alphabet – alpha and beta.

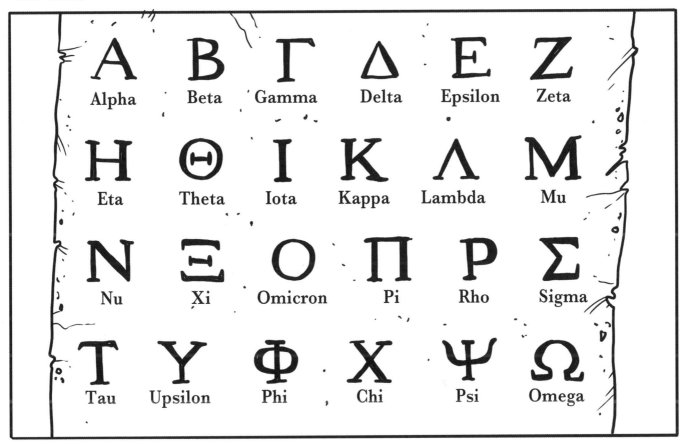

- Write your name or message here:

_____

_____

_____

_____

I can write some words using the Greek alphabet.

How did you do?

Ancient Greek culture

Having learned about everyday life for the Greeks in the previous chapter, children now focus on ancient Greek culture: beliefs, mythology, fables, art and theatre. Children explore these through a series of creative tasks, from dance, music and drama to arts and crafts. Children learn about the Greek gods and goddesses and about the heroes and creatures of mythology. They consider the legacy of Aesop's fables and why these are still popular today. They examine ancient Greek pottery art, using this as inspiration to create their own designs. Finally, they compare between ancient Greek theatre and present-day theatre.

Chapter at a glance

Curriculum objectives

• Ancient Greece – a study of Greek life and achievements and their influence on the western world.

Week	Lesson	Summary of activities	Expected outcomes
1	1	• Children complete an interactive activity in which they learn about the Greek gods and goddesses.	• Can describe some of the different gods and goddesses worshipped by the Greeks.
	2	• Children perform a playscript based on the characteristics of the Greek gods and goddesses.	• Can consider the characteristics of the Greek gods and goddesses.
2	1	• Children read the myth of Perseus and Medusa and write a blog entry from the viewpoint of Perseus on his journey.	• Can describe the myth of Perseus and Medusa.
	2	• Children work in groups to devise movement pieces based on the events of the myth of Perseus and Medusa.	• Can devise a performance using dance and movement to portray a Greek myth.
3	1	• Children hear the myth of Hades and Persephone and create musical compositions inspired by the changing seasons.	• Can describe the myth of Hades and Persephone.
	2	• Children read about Greek mythological creatures and use them as inspiration for a clay model.	• Can create a piece of art depicting a mythological creature.
4	1	• Children work in groups to develop a short play based on Aesop's fables.	• Can create a drama performance based on Aesop's fables.
	2	• Children perform short plays based on Aesop's fables and discuss their morals.	• Can discuss the moral of some of Aesop's fables.
5	1	• Children examine designs on Greek vases and pottery before designing their own.	• Can describe Greek pottery artefacts.
	2	• Children create their own Greek-style art on black card.	• Can create a piece of art in the style of ancient Greek pottery.
6	1	• Children look at images of ancient Greek theatre and theatre in the present day, comparing the two.	• Can describe what ancient Greek theatres were like.
	2	• Children create their own Greek theatrical masks and discuss how these would impact on the actors and audience.	• Can create Greek-style theatrical masks.
Assess and review		• To review the half-term's work.	

Expected prior learning

● This topic is capable of standing alone but it would be beneficial if children have completed the previous chapter and have an understanding of everyday life for the Greeks.

Overview of progression

● Through this topic, children will enrich their understanding of ancient Greek art and culture, considering how their legacy and influence are seen today, for example in theatre and in Aesop's fables. They analyse trends in the way artists through the ages have depicted Greek mythological creatures.

● They are given the opportunity to draw comparisons between ancient Greek theatre and present day theatre.

● They will also develop their understanding of the use of evidence from ancient artefacts to build a picture of the past, as they explore images on Greek pottery.

Creative context

● This is a highly creative chapter with strong links to the performing and visual arts, as well as literacy. Cross-curricular links include:

  ● drama activities to explore the characteristics of the Greek gods and the morals of Aesop's fables; using dance and movement to portray the myth of Perseus and Medusa; musical composition to portray the changing of the seasons;

  ● modelling mythological creatures out of clay; designing artwork inspired by Greek pottery; creating Greek theatrical masks;

  ● writing blogs and play scripts.

Background knowledge

● The ancient Greeks worshipped many gods and goddesses, each of whom had their own characteristics, symbolism and responsibilities for different aspects of life.

● Greek mythology featured Greek gods and goddesses, as well as heroes, and fantastical creatures such as centaurs, the Gorgons, Cyclops, the Minotaur and the Cerberus. Many such creatures can be found in modern literature, including the Narnia books and the Harry Potter series, and many films and books follow the structure of a myth, with a hero or heroine embarking on a quest. Throughout the centuries, mythology has also influenced many painters and sculptors, from Caravaggio to Salvador Dali.

● Little is known about the life of Aesop. He is believed to have been a Greek slave who became famous for his fables, which contain morals for good living. Some of the most famous include 'The Hare and the Tortoise', 'Belling the Cat' and 'The Town Mouse and the Country Mouse'.

● Theatre is one of the most powerful legacies of ancient Greece. Ancient Greek theatrical performances were held as part of festivals in honour of gods. Most plays were either tragedies or comedies. Sophocles, Euripides and Aeschylus were three of the most famous playwrights.

Week 1 lesson plans

This week introduces the creative unit on ancient Greek culture, with children learning about the gods and goddesses, their symbols, characteristics and responsibilities. Children engage in an interactive activity in which they match gods with their descriptions. In the second lesson, they read a light-hearted playscript involving some of the main gods, and create their own ending to the scene.

Lesson objectives
● To study ancient Greece – a study of Greek life and achievements and their influence on the western world.
● To regularly address and sometimes devise historically valid questions about change, cause, similarity and difference, and significance.

Expected outcomes
● All children will describe at least one Greek god or goddess.
● Most children will describe some Greek gods and goddesses, their symbols and responsibilities.
● Some children will describe how the Greek gods and goddesses were worshipped.

Resources
Image of the Parthenon (source online); interactive activity 'Greek gods and goddesses' on the CD-ROM; names of gods and goddesses from the interactive activity on scraps of paper in a 'hat'

1: What gods and goddesses did the Greeks worship?

Introduction
● Challenge a few children to talk about the topic of ancient Greece in front of the class for 30 seconds or one minute without hesitation, repetition or straying from the topic.

Whole-class work
● Show an image of the Parthenon. Ask: *Can you remember what this building is?* (Parthenon) *Where is it?* (Athens, part of the Acropolis) *Which god or goddess was it dedicated to?* (Athena)
● Tell the children that the Greeks worshipped many gods and goddesses. They built temples and held festivals in their honour. Each god or goddess was responsible for a different aspect of life and had certain characteristics and symbols. Athena, for example, was the goddess of war, wisdom, the arts, crafts and skills. Her special symbols were the olive tree and the owl. She was believed to have sprung from the forehead of the god Zeus, fully grown. She is normally portrayed wearing armour, carrying a shield and spear.

Group work or Paired work
● Ask children to work in groups or pairs to complete the interactive activity 'Greek gods and goddesses' on the CD-ROM, in which they must match names of some of the main gods with their descriptive profiles.

Differentiation
● Support: mixed-ability groups may be beneficial.
● Challenge: children could further research the ways that the gods and goddesses were worshipped.

Review
● Play a guessing game to check that the children are familiar with some of the gods and goddesses and their attributes: put all the names of the gods/goddesses in a hat or container. Invite one child to come to the front and pick a name out of the 'hat'; he or she describes the god or goddess, while the other children guess. Play in teams, and award each team a point for a correct guess.
● Alternatively, play 'Twenty questions' where the children still in their places ask yes/no questions of the child at the front, until one of them can guess the correct answer. For example: *Is the god/goddess male? Does he/she have a weapon for a symbol? Does he/she have a plant/fruit as a symbol?*

Lesson objectives
- To study ancient Greece – a study of Greek life and achievements and their influence on the western world.
- To regularly address and sometimes devise historically valid questions about change, cause, similarity and difference, and significance.

Expected outcomes
- All children will describe at least one Greek god or goddess.
- Most children will describe some Greek gods and goddesses.
- Some children will consider the personalities of the Greek gods and goddesses.

Resources
Interactive activity 'Greek gods and goddesses' on the CD-ROM; photocopiable pages 'Greek gods playscript' from the CD-ROM

2: What were the Greek gods and goddesses like?

Introduction
- As a class, go through the interactive activity 'Greek gods and goddesses' on the CD-ROM to see how quickly the children can match the gods with their descriptions.
- Alternatively, write/draw some of the symbols on the board and ask children to identify which god is associated with it (for example: an owl for Athena; a trident for Poseidon; a lyre for Apollo; a thunderbolt for Zeus; winged sandals for Hermes).

Whole-class work
- Read through photocopiable pages 'Greek gods playscript' from the CD-ROM, selecting children to play the roles. The script depicts a dating programme scenario, in which Athena has to choose between Apollo, Pan and Poseidon.
- The script is light-hearted but suggests the personalities of some of the gods, as well as mentioning some of the myths associated with them.

Group work or Paired work
- Depending on the ability of the class, children could engage in one or more of the following activities:
  - rehearse and perform the play script in groups;
  - write or improvise their own ending to the scene (the script provided only goes up to the point at which Athena has to make her decision, and leaves it there, as a cliff-hanger);
  - write a dating profile for one of the other gods or goddesses in which they give reasons why they would be a good date;
  - write their own play script based on the Greek gods and goddesses.

Differentiation
- Support: mixed-ability groups may be beneficial; children could engage in the simpler task of rehearsing the existing playscript, while more able children could create their own.

Review
- Watch the scenes rehearsed by the children. At the end of the performances ask: *Which god do you think Athena should choose? Why?*
- Ask any children who have written their own endings to read or perform these now. Ask: *Why did you choose to end the script like this?*
- Ask any children who have written dating profiles for other gods to read these now. Ask: *Do you think Athena would be more suited to one of these gods instead?* Hold a class vote.
- Consider the gods that the children don't think are a good match for Athena. Ask: *Which goddess might you match with each of these gods?*

Week 2 lesson plans

This week, the children explore the Greek myth of Perseus and Medusa. They read the myth and create a blog entry from the point of view of Perseus, describing his quest. In the second lesson, children work in an open space to create a dance and movement piece to depict different scenes from the myth.

1: What was the myth of Perseus and Medusa? (1)

Lesson objectives
● To study ancient Greece – a study of Greek life and achievements and their influence on the western world.
● To regularly address and sometimes devise historically valid questions about change, cause, similarity and difference, and significance.
● To understand how our knowledge of the past is constructed from a range of sources.

Expected outcomes
● All children will describe at least one part of the myth of Perseus.
● Most children will write a blog entry from the viewpoint of Perseus.
● Some children will consider how Perseus might have felt during his quest.

Resources
Photocopiable pages 149 and 150 'Perseus and Medusa (1) and (2)'

Introduction
● Tell the children that a myth is a traditional story, a bit like a fairy tale.
● Ask them if they are already familiar with any Greek myths, or characters from Greek mythology (for example, King Midas, Theseus and the Minotaur, Icarus, or Pandora).

Whole-class work
● Read photocopiable pages 149 and 150 'Perseus and Medusa (1) and (2)', which tells the story of Perseus and Medusa, and also Andromeda.
● Talk about how Perseus might have felt at the different stages of his quest, for example, when he: is instructed to kill Medusa; is helped by Athena; finds the Graeae; finds the Hesperides; slays Medusa; rescues Andromeda; returns home and shows Medusa's head to King Polydectes.

Paired work or Independent work
● In pairs, or individually, ask the children to write a blog entry from the point of view of Perseus on his quest.
● If the children are unfamiliar with blogs, explain that they are online diaries. Talk through their main features and show some examples (many charity and school websites include one). Discuss the differences and similarities between a blog and a traditional diary. Note that blogs often contain photographs, or even video clips, and invite the reader to comment on what they've read; the blogger can then reply to the reader's comment, making a blog much more interactive than a printed diary.
● There are numerous free blogging sites designed for school children, where children can publish their blogs online. Examples include kidsblog.org and edublogs.org.
● Depending on the children's ability, they could write a single blog entry with a few sentences about one of the events of Perseus' journey, or a series of blog entries covering the different events of the quest (for example, stealing the eye from the Graeae, seeking out the Hesperides, slaying Medusa, rescuing Andromeda).

Differentiation
● Support: children could write simple sentences about one of the events in the myth.
● Challenge: children should consider the character and personality of Perseus in their writing, indicating his feelings during the different stages of his journey.

Review
● Invite some children to share all or part of their blog with the rest of the class. Then ask other children to write a comment in response to what they've just heard, as if commenting on a blog.

2: What was the myth of Perseus and Medusa? (2)

Introduction
● In a large, open space, ask the children to warm up their bodies by travelling around the space as different characters, for example: Perseus (the hero) striding bravely; one of the Graeae hobbling around; Medusa stealthily creeping up on Perseus; Pegasus flying through the air; the sea monster slithering towards Andromeda.
● Use a cardboard cut-out of Medusa's head: the children must turn to stone (freeze) whenever it is held up.

Whole-class work
● Tell the children that they are going to be portraying some of the scenes from the myth of Perseus and Medusa through movement and dance.
● Ask different children to recap the key events of the story (Perseus is instructed to kill Medusa when he fails to bring a gift to the king's party; he is helped by Athena, who tells him how to find the Graeae; they tell him how to find the Hesperides, who give Perseus gifts from the gods to help him in his quest; Perseus slays Medusa; on the way home he rescues Andromeda; finally, he returns home and shows Medusa's head to King Polydectes, who dies when he looks upon it.)
● If necessary, read the myth to the children again.

Group work
● Split children into groups.
● Give each group a copy of photocopiable pages 149 and 150 'Perseus and Medusa (1) and (2)' to remind them of the myth, and challenge them to create a dance or movement piece to represent three parts of the story: the Graeae searching for their eye; Perseus slaying Medusa (with her writhing snakes for hair); Pegasus springing from Medusa's blood.
● Ask the children to combine their three movements, linking them with a smooth transition to create a fluent piece.

Differentiation
● Support: mixed-ability groups may be beneficial.
● Challenge: children should encourage the other children in their group to try to incorporate different levels in the piece to make it more visually interesting.

Review
● One at a time, ask the groups to perform their piece to the rest of the class.
● Invite constructive praise/criticism from the 'audience'.

Week 3 lesson plans

This week, children further explore Greek mythology, listening to the myth of Persephone and creating musical compositions to depict the changing of the seasons as Persephone journeys to and from the Underworld. They then investigate some of the fantastical creatures found in Greek mythology and consider how these have been depicted in art through the ages. They create their own versions using clay modelling.

Lesson objectives
● To study ancient Greece – a study of Greek life and achievements and their influence on the western world.
● To regularly address and sometimes devise historically valid questions about change, cause, similarity and difference, and significance.
● To understand how our knowledge of the past is constructed from a range of sources.

Expected outcomes
● All children will describe at least one part of the myth of Hades and Persephone.
● Most children will help to create a musical composition, inspired by the myth of Hades and Persephone.
● Some children will create contrasting musical compositions, inspired by the myth of Hades and Persephone.

Resources
Media resource 'The myth of Persephone' on the CD-ROM; various tuned and untuned musical instruments

1: What is the myth of Hades and Persephone?

Introduction
● Show the children the musical instruments. Check that they know what each one is, and how to play it.
● Tell the children to pass the instruments around and give them a few minutes to play them and become familiar with the different sounds.

Whole-class work
● Tell the children that they are going to be hearing another well-known Greek myth – the story of Hades and Persephone, which describes how the seasons came to change throughout the year. (Persephone was the daughter of Demeter, goddess of the harvest. Other important characters in the story include Hermes, the gods' messenger, and Hades, god of the Underworld.)
● Read the story of Hades and Persephone using media resource 'The myth of Persephone' on the CD-ROM. Note that this is just one version of the story: the number of pomegranate seeds Persephone eats, and the amount of time she spends on the earth each year varies between different versions of the story.
● Ask: *How would you describe the personalities of Hades and Persephone? How might Demeter feel when Persephone must travel to the Underworld? How might she feel when her daughter returns?*

Group work
● Tell the children that they are going to work in groups to use musical instruments to represent the journey of Persephone into the Underworld and back to the world above – the passage of autumn and winter into spring and summer.
● Talk about the kinds of sound that might represent the seasons (for example, icy wind blowing in the wintertime; birds chirping at the beginning of spring). Ask: *How could these be portrayed using instruments?*
● Give children time to work on their pieces, which could use different instruments, pitches, tempos, timbres, dynamics and so on to show the contrast between Demeter's sorrow and joy.

Differentiation
● Support: children could try to identify 'happy' and 'sad' sounds in different instruments.
● Challenge: children could portray different moods through tuned instruments (for example, minor key to provoke a sadder or more anxious mood).

Review
● Ask each group to perform their musical interpretation of the story at the end of the lesson; other groups should comment on what they have heard. Ask: *Was there a clear contrast between the different times of the year? How was this contrast shown?*

Lesson objectives

● To study ancient Greece – a study of Greek life and achievements and their influence on the western world.
● To develop a chronologically secure knowledge and understanding of British, local and world history, establishing clear narratives within and across the periods they study.
● To regularly address and sometimes devise historically valid questions about change, cause, similarity and difference, and significance.
● To understand how our knowledge of the past is constructed from a range of sources.

Expected outcomes

● All children will model a creature from Greek mythology.
● Most children will model and describe a creature from Greek mythology.
● Some children will create a model of their own mythological creature.

Resources

Photocopiable page 151 'Mythological creatures'; pictures of Medusa (source online); modelling clay

2: What creatures existed in Greek myths?

Introduction

● Draw Medusa's head on the board with ten wavy lines as snakes coming out of it.
● Ask the children to come up with an adjective describing her for each of the snakes. Suggestions might include: gruesome, hideous, repugnant, repulsive, ghastly, odious, and so on.

Whole-class work

● Tell the children that one feature common to most myths is that they contain fantastical beasts and creatures. For example, the myth of Perseus involves the Gorgons, Pegasus and the sea monster.
● Read and discuss photocopiable page 151 'Mythological creatures', which describes some of the key creatures that appear in Greek myths: centaurs, griffins, nymphs, satyrs, the Minotaur, Cerberus, and so on.
● Tell the children that mythological creatures have been depicted in art throughout the ages. Show some examples, such as the portraits and sculptures of Medusa by the artists Bernini, Cellini, Dali, Canova, Caravaggio, Rubens and Böcklin. Ask the children to comment on the way each artist has portrayed the creature. Do they all show it to be terrifying? Are some more sympathetic than others?

Independent work

● Give some clay to each child and ask them to sculpt a mythological creature. They can either portray an existing creature (for example, Medusa, Hydra, Cyclops) or create their own.
● Talk through modelling techniques, such as creating texture by poking the clay with objects, or rolling out the clay to make snakes for Medusa's head.

Differentiation
● Support: children can create a more simple design, such as a ball of clay with 'snakes' attached to create Medusa's head.
● Challenge: children could invent their own creature and describe its characteristics; if creating a creature from Greek mythology, they could consider how to present it (for example, emphasising its 'monstrousness' or showing it in a more sympathetic light).

Review

● Create a class display of the different models and invite children to come and look at them.
● Ask questions such as: *Can you identify the creatures from Greek mythology? How can you tell this is the Minotaur/Medusa/Hydra? What techniques have been used to create it?*

Week 4 lesson plans

This week focuses on Aesop's fables. Children work in groups to create a performance based on one of the fables (over two lessons) and perform it for the rest of the class. The children then discuss the morals of the fables and consider why Aesop's tales are still popular today.

1: Why is Aesop remembered today? (1)

Introduction
● Ask children to discuss with a talk partner their experience of stories. Ask: *What are your favourite stories? What do you like about them? Where and when do you read them? Does someone read stories to you?*

Whole-class work
● Tell the children that storytelling was very important to the ancient Greeks. Stories were told aloud and passed down through the generations. One of the most famous storytellers was Aesop. He told a special type of story called a fable, which had a moral – a message suggesting how to live a good life.
● Read or tell the children the fable of 'The Hare and the Tortoise' (one of the most famous) and discuss the meaning of the moral: slow and steady wins the race. Ask: *Why might this be good advice?*

Group work
● Split children into groups and allocate each a fable. Aesop's work can be found on various websites, including: www.aesopfables.com and www.taleswithmorals.com. Suggested fables are: 'The Lion and the Mouse'; 'The Ant and the Grasshopper'; 'Belling the Cat'; 'The Lion and the Shepherd'; 'The Town Mouse and the Country Mouse'; 'The Four Oxen and the Lion'.
● Tell the children that they are going to work with their group to create a short drama performance to tell the story of their fable. Their performance should help their audience to guess what the moral or message might be.
● Alternatively, allow the children to incorporate props or costumes and challenge them to find imaginative ways to get the fables across (for example, puppetry, mime, film).
● Give children time to prepare their performance, which they will present during the next lesson.

> **Differentiation**
> ● Support: mixed-ability groups may be beneficial.

Review
● Check the children's progress at the end of the lesson; ensure that each group has chosen which one of Aesop's fables they are going to perform and that they have allocated roles and have a good idea as to how they are going to relate the tale.
● Remind the children that they will only have a short time at the beginning of the next lesson to practise their performance.

Lesson objectives
● To study ancient Greece – a study of Greek life and achievements and their influence on the western world.
● To develop a chronologically secure knowledge and understanding of British, local and world history, establishing clear narratives within and across the periods they study.
● To regularly address and sometimes devise historically valid questions about change, cause, similarity and difference, and significance.
● To understand how our knowledge of the past is constructed from a range of sources.

Expected outcomes
● All children will describe one of Aesop's fables.
● Most children will help to create a drama performance based on one of Aesop's fables.
● Some children will discuss the morals of some of Aesop's fables.

Resources
Aesop's fables (available online); costumes and props (optional)

Lesson objectives
● To study ancient Greece – a study of Greek life and achievements and their influence on the western world.
● To develop a chronologically secure knowledge and understanding of British, local and world history, establishing clear narratives within and across the periods they study.
● To regularly address and sometimes devise historically valid questions about change, cause, similarity and difference, and significance.
● To understand how our knowledge of the past is constructed from a range of sources.

Expected outcomes
● All children will describe one of Aesop's fables.
● Most children will help to create a drama performance based on one of Aesop's fables.
● Some children will discuss the morals of some of Aesop's fables.

Resources
Internet access or print outs of Aesop's fables; (optional) costumes and props

2: Why is Aesop remembered today? (2)

Introduction
● Again discuss the fable and moral of 'The Hare and the Tortoise'. Discuss any other interpretations of the moral, other than 'slow and steady wins the race' (for example: don't judge a book by its cover; don't give up even if the odds are stacked against you; being arrogant and egotistical can lead to failure).
● Ask: *How could we adjust or adapt the story to bring it up to date?* Give the children time to discuss this with a talk partner.
● Discuss some of their ideas (for example, a pupil boasting about their ability in maths and not studying for a test, only to be beaten by a humble pupil who studied hard and worked slowly and diligently.).

Whole-class work
● Have the moral for each of the fables written on the board. Make sure that the children are clear on what the morals mean: write them in more child-friendly language as appropriate, for example:
  ● 'The Lion and the Mouse': even the smallest friend can be a big help.
  ● 'The Ant and the Grasshopper': always be prepared.
  ● 'Belling the Cat': it is easy to suggest an impossible solution.
  ● 'The Lion and the Shepherd': be kind to everyone, as one day you might need kindness from someone else.
  ● 'The Town Mouse and the Country Mouse': it is better to live a simple life in safety, than a rich life in fear.
  ● 'The Four Oxen and the Lion': we are stronger if we work together.
● Tell the children that when they are preparing their retelling of their fable they need to make sure that the moral is clearly presented to the audience through their performance.
● Ask the children to discuss which morals they think go with which stories. Ask: *Do you think these morals are good messages for life? Why?*
● It time allows, ask the children to choose one moral and write a modern-day example to demonstrate it.

Group work
● Give the groups time to practise and polish their performances (started in the previous lesson).

Differentiation
● Support: mixed-ability groups may be beneficial.

Review
● Ask each group to perform its fable, while the rest of the class acts as audience.
● After each performance, ask the children in the audience to offer positive criticism on what they have seen. Ask: *Was the moral of this fable made clear? What did you like about this performance? What would you have done differently?*
● When all the groups have finished, ask: *Why do you think that these fables are still popular today? Do the morals still apply? Can any of the stories be interpreted differently – with a moral other than that stated at the end of the tale?*

Week 5 lesson plans

This week explores ancient Greek pottery art. Children examine examples of pots and vases, considering the colours, patterns, characters and scenes used to decorate them. They then create their own designs over two lessons.

1: What was Greek pottery art like? (1)

Introduction

● Select an image of a piece of pottery art, for example a red-figure bell krater (source online). These vessels would have been used for mixing wine, and typically were illustrated with gods and goddesses, scenes from Greek mythology, or people drinking/socialising. Note: the style of red-figure pottery continued from around 520–320BC.
● Ask three children to come to the front of the class and give different descriptions of what is happening in the picture, in the style of 'Call My Bluff'. If available, share the actual information about what the image portrays.

Whole-class work

● Show the children some examples of Greek pottery art, both red- and black-figure pottery (source online, for example at www.ancientgreece.co.uk or www.metmuseum.org). Ask: *What are these made from?* (Clay.) *Which colours have been used?* (Black and shades of brown, yellow and orange.) *What patterns are there? What is being shown in the pictures?* (Vases and pots often showed scenes from mythology or daily life, including agriculture, death and burial, education, slavery and music and entertainment.)
● Tell the children that they are going to create their own designs in a similar style. They should think about the scene they wish to depict – it could be an aspect of Greek life or a scene or character from Greek mythology. They should also consider the colours they will use to replicate the pottery.

Independent work

● Give children a piece of A4 paper to create a draft design. Keep some images of Greek pottery on display for them to use as a starting point.
● They should begin by folding their paper in half vertically (from portrait layout). They can then draw and cut out half a vase shape on one side so that it will create a symmetrical vase when opened out.
● They should then draw their draft designs in the vase shape. They could also include Greek-style patterns.
● In the next lesson, they will re-create their designs on black card.

> **Differentiation**
> ● Support: children can create simpler designs and may need help in drawing and cutting the vase shape.
> ● Challenge: children should aim to replicate the style of the original designs as much as possible in the subject matter chosen, layout and colours.

Review

● Check the children's progress at the end of the lesson.
● Ask some children to show their rough designs to the rest of the class. Ask other children to say how the design imitates ancient Greek pottery art.
● Remind the children that in next lesson they will be re-creating their designs on black card.

Lesson objectives
● To study ancient Greece – a study of Greek life and achievements and their influence on the western world.
● To develop a chronologically secure knowledge and understanding of British, local and world history, establishing clear narratives within and across the periods they study.
● To regularly address and sometimes devise historically valid questions about change, cause, similarity and difference, and significance.
● To understand how our knowledge of the past is constructed from a range of sources.

Expected outcomes
● All children will describe at least one feature of Greek pottery art.
● Most children will create their own artwork, inspired by Greek pottery.
● Some children will closely replicate the style of Greek pottery in their artwork.

Resources
Images of Greek pottery art (source online); A4 paper or thin card

Lesson objectives

● To study ancient Greece – a study of Greek life and achievements and their influence on the western world.
● To develop a chronologically secure knowledge and understanding of British, local and world history, establishing clear narratives within and across the periods they study.
● To regularly address and sometimes devise historically valid questions about change, cause, similarity and difference, and significance.
● To understand how our knowledge of the past is constructed from a range of sources.

Expected outcomes

● All children will describe at least one feature of Greek pottery art.
● Most children will create their own artwork, inspired by Greek pottery.
● Some children will closely replicate the style of Greek pottery in their artwork.

Resources

Black A4 card; chalk pastels (particularly browns, oranges and yellows)

2: What was Greek pottery art like? (2)

Introduction

● Choose a character from a myth or fable (for example Andromeda, Hermes, the Tortoise) and see if the children can guess who or what it is in fewer than 20 questions. They may only ask questions with 'yes' or 'no' answers.

Whole-class work

● Ask one or two children to show their draft vase designs and talk through what they have chosen to depict. Have any children chosen to illustrate scenes or characters from Greek myths or fables?

Independent work

● Give each child a piece of black A4 card (have some spares handy in case some of the designs go wrong).
● Children should place their cut-out vase shapes on the A4 black card and trace around them, and then cut their vases out of the black card.
● Children can use a pencil to draw in their designs lightly. They can then go over these with chalk pastels. They can either keep the black background, and draw their designs using yellow, orange or brown chalk pastels, or they can shade around the background with the pastels and leave the black card as the images in the foreground.

Differentiation
● Support: children can create more simple designs.
● Challenge: children should aim to replicate the style of the original designs as much as possible in the subject matter chosen, layout and colours.

Review

● Create a class display of the finished designs.
● Look at the display in small groups, or as a class. Ask: *What different scenes can you see? Do the designs imitate the style of ancient Greek pottery? Which design do you think is closest to the Greek style? Why?*

Week 6 lesson plans

This week, children explore ancient Greek theatre, considering how it was different from and similar to theatre in the present day. They look at images of ancient and modern theatres, comparing the two. Children then examine Greek-style theatrical masks and think about the benefits and disadvantages for actors and audience. Finally, they create their own masks to depict a character or emotion.

1: What was it like to go to the theatre in ancient Greece?

Lesson objectives
● To study ancient Greece – a study of Greek life and achievements and their influence on the western world.
● To develop a chronologically secure knowledge and understanding of British, local and world history, establishing clear narratives within and across the periods they study.
● To regularly address and sometimes devise historically valid questions about change, cause, similarity and difference, and significance.
● To understand how our knowledge of the past is constructed from a range of sources.

Expected outcomes
● All children will describe at least one fact about ancient Greek theatre.
● Most children will draw basic comparisons between ancient Greek and modern theatre.
● Some children will draw more complex comparisons between ancient Greek and modern theatre.

Resources
Photocopiable page 'Ancient Greek theatre' from the CD-ROM

Introduction
● Ask if any of the children have been to the theatre. Ask them to describe what they went to see and what the experience was like.
● Write some of their observations on the board for the benefit of any who have not been to the theatre.

Whole-class work
● Tell the children that the ancient Greeks loved going to the theatre. Explain that theatres at the time shared some similarities and some differences with present day theatre; they are going to find out what it was like to go to the theatre in ancient Greece and compare it with the modern day.
● If feasible, this lesson would be ideal after a class trip to a local theatre.

Group work
● Split the children into small groups and ask them to look at and discuss photocopiable page 'Ancient Greek theatre' from the CD-ROM. As they read through the sheet they should consider the differences between the description of ancient Greek theatres, and the observations of modern-day theatre noted on the board from the beginning of the lesson.
● The groups should write down their observations about the similarities and differences between ancient Greek theatre and present-day theatre (for example, the use of up to three actors in ancient Greece versus modern plays involving many actors; outdoors versus indoors; the use of props, costumes, scenery, curtains, and so on).

Differentiation
● Support: mixed-ability groups may be beneficial.
● Challenge: children should show deeper reflection about the experience of the actors and audience.

Review
● Ask one group to come to the front of the class to present their lists of similarities and differences.
● At the end of the presentation, ask the rest of the class to check their own lists to see if there's anything the group at the front has missed.
● Ask the following additional questions: *Would it be better to be an actor in ancient Greece or now? How does the experience of the audience compare? How have the actors' costumes changed?*

Lesson objectives

- To study ancient Greece – a study of Greek life and achievements and their influence on the western world.
- To develop a chronologically secure knowledge and understanding of British, local and world history, establishing clear narratives within and across the periods they study.
- To regularly address and sometimes devise historically valid questions about change, cause, similarity and difference, and significance.
- To understand how our knowledge of the past is constructed from a range of sources.

Expected outcomes

- All children will know that masks were worn by actors in ancient Greece.
- Most children will create their own Greek-style theatrical masks.
- Some children will describe how masks were used by actors in ancient Greek theatre.

Resources

Images of ancient Greek theatrical masks (source online); materials for mask making

2: What were Greek theatrical masks like?

Introduction

- Write the following words on the board and ask the children to identify the odd one out: actors, stage, audience, curtains, masks. (The answer is curtains: there were no curtains in ancient Greek theatre.)

Whole-class work

- Show some images of ancient Greek theatrical masks (source online). Ask: *What do you think they were made from? What types of character might these masks represent? Thinking about the layout of Greek theatres, what would be the benefit of wearing the masks? Would there be any disadvantages for the actors?* (Masks were made from lightweight materials such as linen, cork, leather or wood. Since the masks were made from organic materials, no physical evidence of them remains; what we know about them has been deduced from vase paintings. As there were only three actors in a Greek play, masks enabled one actor to take on several roles without being recognised; they also enabled changes to a character's appearance to be made apparent – such as the blinding of Oedipus; and the exaggerated emotions of the masks would have made the mood of the play very clear – especially as the members of the chorus would all have worn the same mask; the mouth shape of the mask was also designed to amplify the sound of the actor's voice. However, the masks wouldn't have allowed the subtle changes of mood or emotion which are common in present-day theatre.)

Independent work

- Ask children to design and create their own Greek-style theatrical masks. These could represent a specific character from a myth or be more generic, portraying an emotion. Remind children of the characters from Greek myths, and Greek gods and goddesses that they have studied in previous lessons (for example, Perseus, Medusa, Hades, Persephone, Athena, Pan and Dionysus).
- Encourage the children to consider what the character they have chosen might look like. Model an example using a mythical character such as Hades. Ask: *What sort of character is Hades? How could you show this in a mask? What kind of eyes/hair/mouth/nose/eyebrows might he have? What sort of expression might he usually have on his face?*
- Basic masks can be made out of cardboard; more advanced masks could be made out of clay or papier mâché.
- Children could also improvise short scenes around their characters.

Differentiation

- Children's masks can be as simple or complicated as they wish.
- Challenge: children could portray an emotion in their mask; they could also research how these masks were used.

Review

- Any children who have prepared short scenes could perform these at the end of the lesson.
- Show some of the completed masks to the class and ask: *Which character might this be used for? How do you know? What is the emotion of this mask?*

Lesson objectives
● To study ancient Greece – a study of Greek life and achievements and their influence on the western world.
● To develop a chronologically secure knowledge and understanding of British, local and world history, establishing clear narratives within and across the periods they study.

Resources
Sticky notes; interactive activity 'Y4 Autumn 2 quiz' on the CD-ROM

Ancient Greece quiz

Revise

● Write the following names on sticky notes: Zeus, Aphrodite, Poseidon, Hades, Medusa, Perseus, Persephone, Minotaur, Cerberus, Athena.
● Ask children to come to the front of the class and place a sticky note on their forehead. They must guess who they are and can ask the rest of the class up to 20 questions (requiring a 'yes' or 'no' answer) in order to find out.

Assess

● Ask the children to complete the interactive activity 'Y4 Autumn 2 quiz' on the CD-ROM, in which they answer multiple-choice questions covering the chapter content.
● Give children a set length of time (for example, 15 minutes) to answer the questions. This can be used as part of a formal assessment or as a fun challenge activity, giving children the opportunity to show what they have learned about the topic.
● Less confident readers may need adult support to read the questions aloud.

Further practice

● Ask the children to create their own ancient Greek quiz to test their friends.

Lesson objectives
● To study ancient Greece – a study of Greek life and achievements and their influence on the western world.
● To construct informed responses that involve thoughtful selection and organisation of relevant historical information.

Resources
Video cameras (optional)

Ancient Greece mind maps

Revise

● Organise the class into two quiz teams and select several children's self-devised quizzes from the previous assessment task with which to test the teams (with the children who wrote them sitting out while their quiz is used, or reading the questions aloud).

Assess

● Ask children to create a mind map (model an example, if necessary) containing as much information as they can remember about ancient Greece, including information on the three chapters covering this period.
● If children are struggling, write the following words on the board as prompts: ancient Greek clothing, Persian Wars, Athens, Sparta, Acropolis, Elgin Marbles, homes, Trojan horse, famous Greeks, theatre, philosophy, alphabet, gods and goddesses, mythology, Aesop's fables, Olympic Games.
● Less confident writers could share their ideas verbally with adult support. Some children may wish to draw labelled diagrams rather than write their answers.

Further practice

● Ask children to incorporate what they have learned about ancient Greece into a short video presentation, which could be uploaded to the school learning platform. Children could work in groups, each selecting a different aspect of ancient Greek life on which to focus.

Perseus and Medusa (1)

Perseus was the son of Zeus and a beautiful mortal woman named Danae. Polydectes, king of the island of Seriphos, fell in love with Danae and tried to force her to marry him, but Perseus protected her.

The king hatched a wicked plan to get rid of Perseus. He held a feast and insisted that all who attended bring a gift. When Perseus arrived empty handed, because he was too poor to bring anything, Polydectes pretended to be furious.

"Name any gift you wish," cried Perseus, "and I will bring it for you." Polydectes asked Perseus to bring him the head of Medusa, one of the Gorgons. The Gorgons were three sisters, vile creatures with writhing snakes for hair. Anyone who looked upon them was immediately turned into stone. Perseus began his quest but it seemed hopeless.
He didn't even know where to find Medusa.

The goddess Athena took pity on Perseus and decided to help him. She told him to seek out the Graeae, who could tell him how to find the nymphs known as the Hesperides. These nymphs had the weapons needed to defeat Medusa and knew where she dwelt.

The Graeae were three hideous old women who had only one eye and one tooth between them. Perseus approached and asked the wretched hags for their help.

"Help? Ha! Why should we help you?" cackled one, peering at Perseus through the one eye. She threw the eye to her sister. Perseus dashed forward and grabbed it, threatening to keep the eye unless they told him where to find the Hesperides. The Graeae begrudgingly cooperated. Perseus returned the eye and continued on his journey.

Perseus reached the beautiful garden of the Hesperides. The nymphs welcomed him and gave him gifts from the gods and goddesses of Olympus. These included a special sword, which was stronger than diamond; the helm of Hades, which had the power to turn the wearer invisible; the winged sandals of Hermes; Athena's polished shield; and a magic sack to contain Medusa's head.

Perseus and Medusa (2)

Following the nymphs' directions, Perseus arrived at the Gorgons' lair. The entrance was strewn with statues, their faces contorted in terror. Perseus realised that these were men who had been turned to stone by the Gorgons. Looking only in the reflection of the polished shield, Perseus entered the cave and found the Gorgons asleep. Taking the sword, he slashed off the head of Medusa. As he collected the head and shoved it into the magic sack, the winged horse Pegasus was born, springing from Medusa's bleeding neck. Medusa's sisters awakened and pursued Perseus in a violent rage but he used the winged sandals to escape.

On his way home, Perseus noticed a beautiful maiden tied to a rock on the ocean shore. He flew down to her. She told him that her name was Andromeda and that she was being sacrificed to a sea monster, to stop it from attacking her father's kingdom. Perseus slew the creature and rescued Andromeda, taking her with him to Seriphos.

When Perseus at last arrived home, he found that King Polydectes had pestered his mother so much that she had gone into hiding.

Thinking Perseus dead, the king was shocked to see him striding into his court. Perseus reached into the magic sack and lifted out Medusa's head. Before he realised what was happening, the evil king caught sight of the gruesome head and was turned immediately into stone.

Perseus rescued his mother, telling her that she could now live in peace. Perseus and Andromeda were married and lived a long and happy life. When they eventually died, they joined the stars that we still see in the night sky.

PHOTOCOPIABLE

Mythological creatures

Centaurs – a race of creatures that were human down to the waist with the body and legs of a horse.

Cerberus – a three-headed dog, which guarded the entrance to the Underworld and was used by Hades to stop the souls of the dead from escaping.

Chimera – a fire-breathing beast that was part lion and part goat, with a snake for a tail.

Cyclops – a race of giants with one eye in the middle of the forehead.

Griffin – a creature with the body and back legs of a lion and head, claws and wings of an eagle.

Hydra – a poisonous beast with a dragon's or snake's body, and many heads. When one head was cut off, two grew back in its place. It was eventually killed by Hercules, who burned the flesh when he cut off each head, in order to stop new ones growing back.

Minotaur – a creature with the body of a man and the head of a bull. It guarded the great maze of King Minos, known as the Labyrinth, but was slain by Theseus.

Nymphs – nature spirits with the appearance of beautiful young women. There were many different types, including water nymphs, called 'Nereids' and tree nymphs, called 'Dryads'.

Satyrs – creatures with the head and torso of a man and the legs and horns of a goat

Scylla and Charybdis – two sea monsters that lived on either side of the narrow body of water, the Strait of Messina. Ships would sail to one side of the Strait to avoid one monster but would then be attacked by the other.

Legacy of the ancient Greeks

In this final topic, covering the civilisation of ancient Greece, children learn about the legacy of the Greeks, which can still be felt in many aspects of present day life. Through a wide range of cross-curricular activities, children explore ancient Greek influence on science and mathematics, through the work of Archimedes and Pythagoras. They discuss the wisdom of the ideas of well-known Greek philosophers and the Greek system of democracy. Children explore the structure of Greek myths, which can be found in countless book and film narratives, and investigate the way our language has been influenced by ancient Greek. Finally, they draw comparisons between the ancient and modern Olympic Games.

Chapter at a glance

Curriculum objectives

• Ancient Greece – a study of Greek life and achievements and their influence on the western world.
• A study of an aspect or theme in British history that extends pupil's chronological knowledge beyond 1066: the legacy of Greek culture on later periods in British history, including the present-day.

Week	Lesson	Summary of activities	Expected outcomes
1	1	• Children read an excerpt of *The Persians* by Aeschylus, practising reciting text in the style of a Greek chorus.	• Can read an excerpt of an ancient Greek play.
	2	• Children carry out an experiment based on Archimedes' principle.	• Can describe some Greek contributions to science.
2	1	• Children review the features of a Greek temple and consider how these have been incorporated into buildings around the world.	• Can identify examples of Greek architecture in modern buildings.
	2	• Children experience three systems of decision making in order to understand the democratic systems of ancient Greece and Britain today.	• Can describe what democracy is and how it began, in ancient Athens.
3	1	• Children carry out an investigation based on Pythagoras' theorem.	• Can investigate Pythagoras' theorem.
	2	• Children discuss in groups and share their ideas about a series of quotations from famous Greek philosophers.	• Can discuss some of the ideas of ancient Greek philosophers.
4	1	• Children discuss how Greek myth structure and mythological creatures can be found in many stories and films, before planning their own myths.	• Can discuss how Greek myths have influenced modern stories and films.
	2	• Children write their own myths, using the Greek myth structure.	• Can use Greek myths as inspiration for their own writing.
5	1	• Children examine Greek prefixes and suffixes that have been used to form English words.	• Can name English words that are derived from ancient Greek.
	2	• Children use online research to find out about the ancient Greek Olympic Games.	• Can describe the Olympic games in ancient Greece.
6	1	• Children research the modern Olympics and compare them to the ancient Greek Olympic Games.	• Can compare the ancient Greek Olympics with those in the present day.
	2	• Children participate in their own Greek-style Olympic Games.	• Can participate in a Greek-style Olympic Games.
Assess and review		• To review the half-term's work.	

Expected prior learning
● The topic is capable of standing alone but it would be beneficial if children have completed the previous Year 4 chapters about ancient Greece.

Overview of progression
● Children will gain a deeper understanding of the abstract concept of 'legacy', considering the many ways that the culture and knowledge of the ancient Greeks has impacted on modern Britain. This skill helps to prepare children for later consideration of the legacy of the Romans in Britain.
● This chapter focuses on the key skills of drawing comparisons and analysing trends over time, for example identifying the influence of ancient Greek architecture in modern buildings.

Creative context
● Cross-curricular opportunities include:
  ● performing a Greek playscript; debating different systems of government (also linking to citizenship); writing new myths; consolidating knowledge of prefixes and suffixes by considering English words derived from ancient Greek;
  ● a science investigation based on Archimedes' principle; a mathematics investigation based on Pythagoras' theorem;
  ● discussing the meaning of the words of famous ancient Greek philosophers, and their relevance to our lives today;
  ● staging a Greek-style Olympic Games.

Background knowledge
● Greek plays are still performed around the world, including the works of the great tragedians, Euripides, Sophocles and Aeschylus, and the eleven surviving comedies of Aristophanes. Modern plays, musicals and operas sometimes incorporate a Greek-style chorus of actors.
● Archimedes famously discovered the relationship between buoyancy and water displacement while having a bath. Archimedes' principle has influenced the engineering of sea craft for over 2000 years. The principle states that an object will sink if it weighs more than the weight of the water it displaces. Ships hulls are shaped to displace the maximum amount of water, so they can float.
● Democracy (translated as 'people power') in ancient Athens involved a Council of 500 decision makers, who were drawn by lot from Athens' free, adult male citizens. They decided upon policies to do with the day-to-day running of Athens and decided which issues would be raised at the weekly Ecclesia, an assembly of all free, adult male Athenians that met on the Pnyx hill to debate proposed laws.
● Pythagoras was an ancient Greek mathematician. His famous geometrical theorem states that the square of the hypotenuse of a right-angled triangle is equal to the squares of the other two sides.
● The ancient Greek Olympic Games were first held at Olympia in 776BC, and ran until around AD393. The event was linked to religious festivals in honour of the god Zeus. During the Games, a truce was drawn between the city states, which were usually at war, and so the event encouraged good relations between them. The modern Olympics began in 1896, founded on the principle of fostering peaceful relations between the countries of the world.

Week 1 lesson plans

This week, children focus on the legacy of the ancient Greeks, which can still be felt in Britain and around the world today. The first lesson extends children's learning about Greek theatre from the previous topic, as children practise reading an excerpt from a Greek play script. In the second lesson they focus on Greek science, carrying out an investigation to test Archimedes' principle.

1: What were Greek plays like?

Lesson objectives
● To study ancient Greece – a study of Greek life and achievements and their influence on the western world; the legacy of Greek culture on later periods in British history, including the present day.
● To develop a chronologically secure knowledge and understanding of British, local and world history, establishing clear narratives within and across the periods they study.
● To note connections, contrasts and trends over time.
● To understand how our knowledge of the past is constructed from a range of sources.

Expected outcomes
● All children will describe an excerpt from a Greek play.
● Most children will help to perform an excerpt from a Greek play.
● Some children will reflect on the style and meaning of an excerpt from a Greek play.

Resources
Image of an amphitheatre (source online); photocopiable page 168 'A Greek play'; media resource 'The Persians audio' on the CD-ROM; Greek theatre masks (optional)

Introduction
● Show an image of an ancient Greek amphitheatre (source online).
● Give the children two minutes to share with a talk partner everything they can remember (from the previous topic) about theatre in ancient Greece.
● Children might remember the different parts of the theatre (the skene, where the actors can change clothes; the seats for the audience; the orchestra, where the action takes place), the different kinds of play that would have been performed (mostly comedies and tragedies), the masks, and so on.

Whole-class work
● Ask the children to imagine that they are actors in ancient Greece. Talk about what it would be like to perform in an amphitheatre. Ask: *How would you use your voice? How would you use gesture?*
● Tell children that the plays of some famous playwrights in ancient Greece are still performed today. Discuss the concept of 'legacy' as an idea handed down through the ages.
● Explain to the children that they are going to be acting out an excerpt from an ancient Greek play – *The Persians* by Aeschylus, which tells the plight of the Persian people after Xerxes' defeat by the Greek navy at the Battle of Salamis. It was first performed in 472BC. In the excerpt on photocopiable page 168 'A Greek play', a messenger arrives in Susa, one of the capitals of the Persian Empire, to tell the chorus of old men gathered there that the Greeks have defeated the Persians in bloody battle. The Persians lament their losses.
● The media resource 'The Perisians audio' on the CD-ROM includes an audio recording of the script, which could be used as a starting point.
● Read through the playscript as a class, selecting one child to play the messenger and the rest to act as members of the chorus. Make sure the children understand what they are reading, clarifying any words they are not familiar with. If necessary allow them time to work in pairs to write a summary of each section in modern English, and then go through this as a class.
● Go through the scene several times, practising speaking together in unison.
● It might be beneficial to practise in an open space. Movement could also be added to the piece, with the chorus travelling and gesturing as one, and even wearing Greek-style masks, if available.

Differentiation
● All children should participate; however some may prefer to act as audience members, giving feedback to the performers.

Review
● At the end of the lesson, gather all the children together and ask: *What did we do well and what could have been improved? How did we imitate the style and features of an ancient Greek performance?*

Lesson objectives

● To study ancient Greece – a study of Greek life and achievements and their influence on the western world; the legacy of Greek culture on later periods in British history, including the present day.
● To develop a chronologically secure knowledge and understanding of British, local and world history, establishing clear narratives within and across the periods they study.
● To note connections, contrasts and trends over time.
● To regularly address and sometimes devise historically valid questions about change, cause, similarity and difference, and significance.
● To understand how our knowledge of the past is constructed from a range of sources.

Expected outcomes

● All children will know that Archimedes' principle has influenced ship building.
● Most children will carry out an experiment based on Archimedes' principle.
● Some children will understand how Archimedes' principle is used in ship building.

Resources

Image of a ship (source online); photocopiable page 167 'Archimedes principle'; water; scales; containers; trays; jugs; wooden blocks; objects that float or sink; modelling clay

2: How did the Greeks contribute to scientific knowledge?

Introduction

● Have a number of objects made from different materials at the front of the class (for example a pencil, coin, rubber, apple), as well as a clear tank or jug of water.
● Hold up each object in turn and ask the children whether they think it will float or sink. Ask them to explain why they think this.

Whole-class work

● Ask for children's ideas around whether or not metal objects can float and why they think this. (Children are likely to say that metal cannot float because it is too heavy.)
● Show children an image of an iron or steel ship, such as an aircraft carrier. Tell them what it is made from and ask why it might be able to float. Tell them that it floats because of a scientific principle that was discovered by an ancient Greek scientist called Archimedes (children may remember him from the lesson on famous Greeks).
● Read and discuss photocopiable page 167 'Archimedes' principle', which explains the principle.

Group work

● Organise children into small groups. Give each group a copy of the photocopiable sheet and the materials needed for the investigation (a tray, wooden block, scales, container for water, jug, modelling clay, objects that float or sink).
● Depending on the children's ability, children could complete all of the activities, or just one.

Differentiation

● Support: mixed-ability groups may be beneficial; children should complete only the third activity on the photocopiable sheet (or first and third).
● Challenge: children should complete all three activities on the photocopiable sheet. They should show deeper reflection about the way the shape of an object affects the water it displaces and how this has informed ship building.

Review

● Ask different children to share their findings. They should have noticed that the wooden block weighed the same as the water that it displaced. Objects that weighed the same as the water they displaced floated. Objects heavier than the displaced water sank. The modelling clay's shape could be altered to enable it to displace more water and eventually float (by flattening it into a wide bowl shape, like the hull of a boat).
● Ask: *How do you think Archimedes' principle has influenced ship building?* (A ship's hull is shaped in such a way that as the ship sinks into the water it displaces more and more liquid until a balance is reached between the mass of water displaced and the mass of the ship. This allows a ship to be built of strong metals, such as iron and steel, and carry a lot of passengers or cargo.)

Week 2 lesson plans

This week, the children look at the way Greek architecture has influenced buildings all over the world, from the British Museum to the Capitol Building in Washington DC. They review the features of an ancient Greek temple and then create a slideshow of modern examples. Children then gain practical experience of three systems of decision-making in order to understand the democratic process of ancient Greece and in Britain today.

Lesson objectives
● To study ancient Greece – a study of Greek life and achievements and their influence on the western world; the legacy of Greek culture on later periods in British history, including the present day.
● To develop a chronologically secure knowledge and understanding of British, local and world history, establishing clear narratives within and across the periods they study.
● To note connections, contrasts and trends over time.
● To regularly address and sometimes devise historically valid questions about change, cause, similarity and difference, and significance.
● To construct informed responses that involve thoughtful selection and organisation of relevant historical information.
● To understand how our knowledge of the past is constructed from a range of sources.

Expected outcomes
● All children will describe at least one feature of ancient Greek architecture.
● Most children will identify features of ancient Greek architecture in modern architecture.
● Some children will describe how modern architecture had been inspired by ancient Greece.

Resources
Interactive activities 'Greek temples' and 'Greek architecture today' on the CD-ROM; photographs of buildings showing features of ancient Greek architecture (optional)

I: How has Greek architecture influenced today's buildings?

Introduction
● As a class, revisit interactive activity 'Greek temples' on the CD-ROM, in which children label architectural features on an ancient Greek temple.

Whole-class work
● Look at one of the photographs from the interactive activity 'Greek architecture today' on the CD-ROM. The slideshow includes photographs of famous buildings around the world that have been built in the ancient Greek style: the British Museum; Oslo Trading Building in Norway; Trevi Fountain in Rome; Capitol Building and the Supreme Court in Washington DC; Glyptothek in Munich.
● Ask: *What features of ancient Greek architecture can you see on this building?* Discuss the features (different types of column, statues, friezes, pediments, tiled roofs, and so on).
● Tell the children the name of the building, and explain that it was built much later than the ancient Greek era, but was influenced by ancient Greek architecture. Remind the children of the term 'legacy' introduced in the previous week's lessons.

Group work
● Organise children into groups and ask them to look at the rest of the images.
● Tell the children that they should be prepared to talk about the photographs, pointing out the Greek features of the different buildings.

> **Differentiation**
> ● Support: mixed-ability groups may be beneficial.
> ● Challenge: children should be able to search for their own examples of modern architecture containing Greek features.

Review
● Ask one or two groups to share their slideshows with a class, discussing the Greek features they identified. Children who are listening should be prepared to make comments, or note any additional Greek features at the end of the presentation.
● Ask: *Why do you think the Greek style is so popular?*

Lesson objectives

● To study ancient Greece – a study of Greek life and achievements and their influence on the western world; the legacy of Greek culture on later periods in British history, including the present day.
● To develop a chronologically secure knowledge and understanding of British, local and world history, establishing clear narratives within and across the periods they study.
● To note connections, contrasts and trends over time.
● To regularly address and sometimes devise historically valid questions about change, cause, similarity and difference, and significance.

Expected outcomes

● All children will comment on the fairness of different systems of decision making.
● Most children will describe and compare different systems of decision-making.
● Some children will compare the systems of government in ancient Greece with the UK's democratic system.

Resources

Image of the Pnyx (source online)

2: How has the Greek system of democracy influenced modern government?

Introduction

● Show the children a picture of the Pnyx. Ask: *Where do you think this is? What do you think might have happened here?*
● Explain that this is the Pnyx, a hill opposite the Acropolis in Athens on which the male citizens met to vote on important issues. It is said to be the birthplace of democracy, which is the system of government in the UK and many other countries today. Explain that 'democracy' can be translated as 'rule by the people'.

Whole-class work

● Explain to the class that they are going to test out three systems of governance.
● Note: this lesson could tie in with a voting opportunity within the school, such as school council, house captains or class president.
● Over the course of a day (or three days if preferred) use the following systems of decision-making within the class (such as deciding which subject the class does next or choosing a game for the class to play):
    ● Choose one child to be sole ruler and make all the decisions (akin to a monarchy or dictatorship).
    ● Select five class members at random to act as decision-makers, though any member of the class can make a suggestion, which the decision makers can choose to put to class vote (reminiscent of the democratic system of ancient Greece in which a Council of 500 were chosen at random from the adult, free male population and decided which issues would be put to vote at weekly assemblies of citizens).
    ● Have the class vote for five representative decision-makers, who in turn vote on a leader. Each class member has one vote each and the five with the most votes form the 'parliament' (akin to Britain's democratic system).

Group work

● Organise the children into discussion groups to reflect on the three systems of decision-making they've experienced. Ask them to consider the benefits and disadvantages of each system, and which they found the fairest.

> ### Differentiation
> ● Challenge: children could further research the democratic process in ancient Greece and Britain today.

Review

● Ask different groups to share their thoughts on the different systems; hold a class vote on which is the best system.
● Share how the three systems relate to historic and present-day systems of government, as described above.
● Refer to the results of the class vote on different systems of governance and ask: *Is the Greek legacy of democracy a good or a bad thing?*

Week 3 lesson plans

This week, children explore some of ancient Greece's greatest thinkers. Firstly, they investigate Pythagoras' theorem, which states that the square of the hypotenuse of a right-angled triangle is equal to the sum of the squares of the other two sides. Children then read and discuss some famous quotes from ancient Greek philosophers: Socrates, Plato, Aristotle, Epicurus and Democritus.

1: How did the Greeks contribute to mathematics?

Lesson objectives
● To study ancient Greece – a study of Greek life and achievements and their influence on the western world; the legacy of Greek culture on later periods in British history, including the present day.
● To develop a chronologically secure knowledge and understanding of British, local and world history, establishing clear narratives within and across the periods they study.
● To note connections, contrasts and trends over time.
● To regularly address and sometimes devise historically valid questions about change, cause, similarity and difference, and significance.

Expected outcomes
● All children will know that Pythagoras was a famous Greek mathematician.
● Most children will test Pythagoras' theorem.
● Some children will demonstrate a solid understanding of Pythagoras' theorem.

Resources
Map of Greece; 1cm grid paper; calculators

Introduction
● Tell the children that they are going to be learning about one of the famous discoveries of the ancient Greek mathematician, Pythagoras.
● Locate the island of Samos, where Pythagoras was born on a map.

Paired work
● Ask the children to draw a right-angled triangle on 1cm grid paper, with sides 3cm and 4cm and a 5cm hypotenuse (be aware the children will not yet have learned this term). Tell them to multiply each side by itself ($3 \times 3 = 9$, $4 \times 4 = 16$, $5 \times 5 = 25$).
● Ask: *What do you notice about the totals?* Help children to see the relationship between the hypotenuse squared and the sum of the squares of the other sides ($9 + 16 = 25$).
● Ask the children to repeat this to see if it works for other right-angled triangles: 5cm, 12cm and 13cm; 8cm, 15cm and 17cm.
● Tell the children that this was a discovery made by Pythagoras over 2000 years ago. He found that in a right-angled triangle, the hypotenuse multiplied by itself (squared) was always equal to the squares of the other two sides added together. This is normally written as:

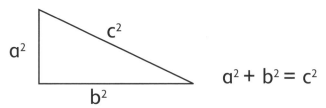

$$a^2 + b^2 = c^2$$

● To help prove the rule, ask children to draw three squares on the grid paper: 3×3cm, 4×4cm and 5×5cm. They should colour the smaller ones in different colours. Children should then cut the smaller squares into 1cm squares and arrange them on the larger square to check that the area is the same.

> ### Differentiation
> ● Support: mixed-ability pairings may be beneficial; this is a challenging lesson mathematically and may not be appropriate for all children; the final activity involving cutting out the squares could be omitted.
> ● Challenge: children can experiment with more advanced calculations.

Review
● Ask: *Why was Pythagoras' discovery significant? What sort of tasks might be easier if you know about Pythagoras' theorem?*
● Allow the children one minute to discuss these questions with a talk partner, before discussing as a class. (Perhaps the most obvious use of Pythagoras' theorem is in building work, as builders use this knowledge to keep right angles in floors and windows, calculate the dimensions of roofs, and so on. Many artists use knowledge of Pythagoras's theorem when they use triangles as a drawing tool – triangles are often used to map 3D environments in computer games.)

Lesson objectives

● To study ancient Greece – a study of Greek life and achievements and their influence on the western world; the legacy of Greek culture on later periods in British history, including the present day.
● To develop a chronologically secure knowledge and understanding of British, local and world history, establishing clear narratives within and across the periods they study.
● To note connections, contrasts and trends over time.
● To regularly address and sometimes devise historically valid questions about change, cause, similarity and difference, and significance.
● To understand how our knowledge of the past is constructed from a range of sources.

Expected outcomes

● All children will read quotations of ancient Greek philosophers.
● Most children will discuss quotations of ancient Greek philosophers.
● Some children will reflect more deeply on quotations of ancient Greek philosophers.

Resources

Photocopiable page 'Greek philosophy' from the CD-ROM; quotations from the photocopiable page printed onto card (optional)

2: What were some of the ancient Greeks' philosophical ideas?

Introduction

● Have one or two 'big questions' written on the board, such as: *What is the meaning of life? How do we achieve happiness?* Ask the children to discuss the answers with a talk partner.
● Discuss as a class.

Whole-class work

● Tell the children that one of the legacies of ancient Greece is the ideas of its philosophers, who thought deeply about big questions like the meaning of human existence. Today, many people read their work and are inspired by the wisdom of their ideas.
● Tell the children that they are going to be reading and discussing some of the ideas of some famous Greek philosophers, such as Plato, Aristotle and Socrates.

Group work

● Organise children into small groups and give each of them philosophical quotation from photocopiable page 'Greek philosophy' from the CD-ROM. The sheet includes five quotations for discussion; one each from Plato, Epicurus, Aristotle, Socrates and Democritus. It is helpful if these can be supplied on cards.
● Allow five minutes for the children to read and discuss the meaning of the quotation and their ideas around it.
● After five minutes, ring a bell and ask the groups to pass their cards to the next group.
● Keep going so that the cards rotate around the room and each group is able to discuss each quotation.

Differentiation
● Support: mixed-ability groups may be beneficial; alternatively, group less confident children together so that the conversation can be facilitated by an adult.

Review

● As a class, discuss each of the quotations. Ask: *What do you think the quotation means? How might it be said today? Do you agree? Is it still relevant to life today? In what sort of situation might it apply?*
● Can the children think of anything they have experienced that exemplifies any of the quotations? Ask: *Have you ever had to try really hard to achieve something? How did you feel when you finally achieved it?* (See the Epicurus quotation.) Ask: *Have you ever had to work with someone you don't normally get on with (mentioning no names...) in order to solve a problem, or overcome a danger?* (For example, when towns have flooded in Britain in recent years, communities have pulled together; see the Aristotle quotation.) Ask: *Have you ever done something wrong and then felt really terrible afterwards – perhaps worse than the person affected by the wrong thing you did?* (See the Democritus quotation.)

Week 4 lesson plans

This week focuses on the way that Greek mythology has influenced many of the books and films with which children will be familiar. Children discuss the structure of a myth and identify examples of its use elsewhere before planning and writing their own myths. They also consider the appearance of mythological creatures in books and films.

Lesson objectives
● To study ancient Greece – a study of Greek life and achievements and their influence on the western world; the legacy of Greek culture on later periods in British history, including the present day.
● To develop a chronologically secure knowledge and understanding of British, local and world history, establishing clear narratives within and across the periods they study.
● To note connections, contrasts and trends over time.
● To regularly address and sometimes devise historically valid questions about change, cause, similarity and difference, and significance.
● To understand how our knowledge of the past is constructed from a range of sources.

Expected outcomes
● All children will describe the basic structure of Greek myths.
● Most children will plan simple stories following the Greek myth structure.
● Some children will plan more complex stories following the Greek myth structure.

Resources
Photocopiable page 151 'Mythological creatures'

I: How has Greek mythology influenced modern culture? (I)

Introduction
● Challenge a few children to come to the front of the class to see if they can summarise the myth of Perseus and Medusa in less than 30 seconds. (Key points are: Perseus didn't take a gift to the king's party, so was sent on a mission to bring back Medusa's head; Athena helped him by telling him where to find the Graeae; the Graeae told him where to find the Hesperides; they gave him some gifts from the gods, helping him to find and slay Medusa; on the way home he rescued Andromeda; when he returned, the king looked upon Medusa's head and was turned to stone.)

Whole-class work
● Talk about the key structure found in many myths: a hero or heroine embarks on a quest or adventure. There are challenges but then the goal is achieved (for example, beast defeated or treasure found) and the hero returns home victorious.
● Discuss some of the stories or films with which children are familiar that follow a similar structure (for example, the Percy Jackson series, *The Lion King*, *The Hobbit*, *Star Wars*, *Labyrinth*, *The Hunger Games*).
● Tell children that they are going to be using this structure to create their own myths. In this lesson they will plan their stories, which will be written in the next lesson.

Independent work
● Ask children to use the following guidance and questions to plan their myths:
1. Describe your hero or heroine.
2. What will they have to do for their quest?
3. Where will they travel?
4. Who will go with them?
5. Describe the creature they will meet.
6. What will happen?
● They could also refer to photocopiable page 151 'Mythological creatures' for inspiration.
● When they have planned their myths, children can begin writing them.

Differentiation
● Support: children could glue or draw a picture of a mythological creature into their books and write sentences to describe it, or create a storyboard with pictures and simple sentences showing the basic myth structure.
● Challenge: children should follow the myth structure, ensuring their climax builds the reader's excitement. They may wish to describe their own mythological creatures or include a twist in the story.

Review
● Check the children's progress. Ask some children to share their ideas with the rest of the class. Ask other children to say how the plan imitates the style of a Greek myth.

Lesson objectives

● To study ancient Greece – a study of Greek life and achievements and their influence on the western world; the legacy of Greek culture on later periods in British history, including the present day.
● To develop a chronologically secure knowledge and understanding of British, local and world history, establishing clear narratives within and across the periods they study.
● To note connections, contrasts and trends over time.
● To regularly address and sometimes devise historically valid questions about change, cause, similarity and difference, and significance.
● To understand how our knowledge of the past is constructed from a range of sources.

Expected outcomes

● All children will describe the basic structure of Greek myths.
● Most children will plan simple stories following the Greek myth structure.
● Some children will plan more complex stories following the Greek myth structure.

Resources

Photocopiable page 151 'Mythological creatures'

2: How has Greek mythology influenced modern culture? (2)

Introduction

● Write a list of Greek mythological creatures on the board or revisit photocopiable page 151 'Mythological creatures'.
● Ask the children to identify other books or films in which some of these appear (for example: centaurs, Cerberus and chimera in the Harry Potter series; centaurs, satyrs and the Minotaur in the Narnia series; satyrs and Cyclops in the Percy Jackson series).

Whole-class work

● Select two contrasting mythological creatures and work with the class to write detailed descriptions of them to help paint a picture in the readers' imagination, including devices such as powerful adjectives, alliteration, simile and metaphor.
● Provide sample sentences for children to improve. For example: The Minotaur had sharp horns and smelly breath. ➜ The piercing horns of the Minotaur jutted forwards like daggers and the stench of his breath fouled the air like the rotting corpses of those who had tried to defeat him.
● Encourage children to use this level of description when writing their stories.

Independent work

● Children begin or continue writing their own myths.
● Circulate the class, providing help where necessary.
● Periodically ask one or two children to share some of what they have written, to inspire children who might be struggling, and to allow all children to have a break from writing.
● If children finish early, they may choose to illustrate their myths.

Differentiation
● Support: children could glue or draw a picture of a mythological creature into their books and write sentences to describe it, or create a storyboard with pictures and simple sentences showing the basic myth structure.
● Challenge: children should follow the myth structure, ensuring their climax builds the reader's excitement. They may wish to describe their own mythological creatures or include a twist in the story.

Review

● When the children have finished, ask one or two of them to share their work with the class, while the rest of the children consider how their work has been influenced by Greek myths.
● Collect all the myths and create a special class *Book of Myths*, which everyone can read.

Week 5 lesson plans

This week explores the way the English language has been influenced by prefixes and suffixes based on ancient Greek, as children explore the Greek words and their meanings. Children then begin a depth study of the Olympic Games, learning about what it was like to attend the Games in ancient Greece.

1: How has ancient Greek influenced the English language?

Introduction
● Write the following words and countries on the board and ask children to match the word to the country of origin: shampoo (India), hamburger (Germany), courgette (France), circus (Italy – Romans), photography (Greece). This task introduces children to the idea of foreign words that have become part of the English language, leading to the consideration of words of Greek influence.
● Allow children time to discuss their ideas with a talk partner before matching the pairs as a class.

Paired work or Independent work
● Tell the children that the Greek language has influenced many modern English words.
● Give each child copy of photocopiable page 169 'Greek language'. Ask them to work individually, or in pairs. They need to match ancient Greek prefixes and suffixes to create familiar English words, and then use a dictionary to find the meaning of each word.

Whole-class work
● Talk through children's answers on the photocopiable sheet. Write the children's words on the board. Have any words been missed? (Answers include: biology, biography, biosphere, photometer, photography, geography, geology, geosphere, telephone, telescope, microscope, microsphere, microphone, thermometer, hemisphere, tricycle.)
● Write some of the following additional Greek words on the board and ask the children to identify words that contain them and then guess at their meanings: 'auto-' (self – automatic, automobile, autobiography); 'anti-' (opposite of – antiseptic, antisocial); 'archa'- (ancient – archaeology); 'chrono'- (time – chronological); 'demo-' (people – democracy); 'dyna-' (energy – dynamite); 'extra-' (beyond – extraordinary, extra-terrestrial), 'giga-' (a billion – gigabyte).

> **Differentiation**
> ● Support: children could work in a group with adult support; prefixes and suffixes could be printed on card to be joined together and the word meanings discussed.
> ● Challenge: children could research additional words derived from ancient Greek and discuss how the Greek meanings apply to the related English words.

Review
● Play a game of 'Splat': write a mixture of prefixes and suffixes on the board. Invite two children to come to the front, and give them the meaning of one of the prefixes or suffixes (for example, small). The child who touches – splats – the correct word (micro) on the board first, wins that round. The winner stays at the front; invite another child to come to the front and try to beat them.
● Repeat the activity until all the prefixes and suffixes have been used at least once.

Lesson objectives

● To study ancient Greece – a study of Greek life and achievements and their influence on the western world; the legacy of Greek culture on later periods in British history, including the present day.
● To develop a chronologically secure knowledge and understanding of British, local and world history, establishing clear narratives within and across the periods they study.
● To note connections, contrasts and trends over time.
● To regularly address and sometimes devise historically valid questions about change, cause, similarity and difference, and significance.
● To understand how our knowledge of the past is constructed from a range of sources.

Expected outcomes

● All children will describe at least one feature of the ancient Greek Olympic Games.
● Most children will describe what happened at the ancient Greek Olympic Games.
● Some children will consider what it was like to attend the ancient Greek Olympic Games.

Resources

Map of Greece; photographs of the ruins at Olympia (source online); sugar paper and marker pens (optional); internet access

2: How did the Olympic Games begin?

Introduction

● Locate Olympia on a map of Greece and look at some photographs showing the ruins there.

Whole-class work

● Tell children that, over the next three lessons, they are going to be finding out about the ancient Greek Olympic Games and how these compare to the modern Olympics, such as the Games in London 2012. In the last lesson, they will participate in their own version of the Olympic Games.
● This lesson they will consider and make notes about what it was like to attend the ancient Olympic Games.
● Ask children to come up with questions that could be researched about the ancient Games, such as: When were the Games first held? Who participated in the Games? Which events were held? What did athletes wear? What prizes did the winners receive? Were there ceremonies for winners? Were the Olympics the only Games in Greece?
● Write their questions on a sheet of sugar paper or on the whiteboard (to be kept for next lesson).

Group work

● Children should use the internet to explore the ancient Greek Olympic Games and make notes about them. Encourage them to make bullet points about anything that interests them, or that they didn't know before, rather than copying out paragraphs of text.
● Direct the children to websites, such as:
    ● www.bbc.co.uk
    ● www.olympic.org
    ● www.ancientolympicgames.org
    ● www.ancientgreece.co.uk

Review

● Ask some children to share some of the information they have discovered about the Games. Can any of the questions on the board be answered?
● Discuss features of the ancient Olympics, such as: the statue of Zeus; the truce between the city states; events such as sprinting, javelin, discus, chariot racing and the race for hoplites (men wearing armour); prizes of wreaths; the squalid conditions; and the fact that married women weren't allowed to spectate.
● Tell the children to keep their notes safe, as they will need them for the following lesson in which they will compare the ancient and modern Olympics.

Week 6 lesson plans

This week, the children further explore the ancient Greek Olympic Games, comparing them to the modern Olympics of London 2012 to see what has changed and what has remained similar. Children then prepare for and participate in their own Greek-style Olympic Games.

Lesson objectives

● To study ancient Greece – a study of Greek life and achievements and their influence on the western world; the legacy of Greek culture on later periods in British history, including the present day.
● To develop a chronologically secure knowledge and understanding of British, local and world history, establishing clear narratives within and across the periods they study.
● To note connections, contrasts and trends over time.
● To regularly address and sometimes devise historically valid questions about change, cause, similarity and difference, and significance.

Expected outcomes

● All children will describe at least one difference between the ancient Greek and modern Olympic Games.
● Most children will draw basic comparisons between the ancient Greek and modern Olympic Games.
● Some children will draw more complex comparisons between the ancient Greek and modern Olympic Games.

Resources

Notes from the previous lesson (on sugar paper, or saved onto the whiteboard); sugar paper and marker pens; internet access

1: How did the ancient Olympic Games compare with those in London 2012?

Introduction

● Ask: *If you could go to the Olympic Games in ancient Greece, which event would you most like to see and why?*
● Remind the children of some of the events, if necessary: sprinting, javelin, discus, chariot racing, the race for hoplites (men wearing armour), wrestling, boxing, long jump and pentathlon.

Whole-class work

● Look at questions from the previous lesson. Ask: *How many of these questions could be used to investigate the modern Olympics? Are there any questions we should add?*
● Show the children photos or video footage of past Olympic Games (optional), for example at: www.olympic.org.

Group work

● In their groups (switch groups around if desired), ask children to research the modern Olympic Games and to use the information to draw comparisons with the ancient Olympics, making notes to share with the class at the end of the lesson. They could create a table of differences and similarities on large sheets of sugar paper.
● The official Olympic website contains images of the modern Games, and information about sports, athletes and participating countries.
● Part of this lesson could also be used to have children prepare materials for their own Greek-style Olympic Games in the following lesson (for example, wreaths for event winners).

Differentiation
● Support: mixed-ability groups may be beneficial.

Review

● Discuss the children's findings. Similarities between the ancient and modern Olympics might include: some of the events are the same (running, discus, long jump, boxing, and so on); people travel from far and wide to watch; both have prizes; there is a common spirit of uniting different places. Differences might include: there are more events now and the Games go on for longer; competitors and spectators come from around the world, not just Greece; women can participate and spectate; events are more regulated (no biting in the wrestling!); events such as chariot racing and racing in armour are no longer included.
● Ask prompt questions, if necessary, such as: *Would it be better to be an athlete in ancient Greece or now? In what way do the modern Olympic Games share the principles of the ancient Greek Olympics? How has the role of women changed? Which Olympics would you prefer to attend? Why?*

Lesson objectives

● To study ancient Greece – a study of Greek life and achievements and their influence on the western world; the legacy of Greek culture on later periods in British history, including the present day.
● To develop a chronologically secure knowledge and understanding of British, local and world history, establishing clear narratives within and across the periods they study.
● To note connections, contrasts and trends over time.
● To regularly address and sometimes devise historically valid questions about change, cause, similarity and difference, and significance.

Expected outcomes

● All children will watch a mini Olympic Games.
● Most children will participate in a mini Olympic Games.
● Some children will describe ways in which their mini Olympics reflects the ancient Greek Olympic Games.

Resources

Equipment for a mini Olympic Games; open space (for example, playground, hall)

2: What might it be like to be an Olympic athlete?

Introduction

● In an open space (for example, the playground, or hall), organise children into their city state groups (see below); allow children time to dress as Olympians (optional); ensure that all the necessary preparations have been made in terms of marking out a race track, preparing prizes, gathering equipment such as foam javelins, and so on.

Whole-class work

● The idea is to stage a mini Olympic Games within the school to take place over a whole or half day. It can be organised by teachers, or a group of confident children could be selected to act as an 'Olympic Committee' to make the preparations, based on their research into the ancient Greek Olympic Games. The day should incorporate historical elements, such as a dedication to Zeus, presentation of wreaths to the winners, or perhaps a feast to end proceedings. Greek costume could be worn.
● The event works well with children or classes organised into three city states, for example Athenians, Spartans and Corinthians.
● A number of events should be organised in which the athletes will participate. These could be fun sports, such as an egg-and-spoon race, obstacle course, foam javelin or paper plate discus, but could incorporate other subjects, such as a spelling or times-table event.
● Each child should participate in one event only (with two or three representatives from each city state per event). The children will cheer on their city state for all other events.
● Children could be allocated to appropriate events, based on their strengths, or they could pick their event out of a hat. They should not be forced to participate in an event if they don't wish to.

> ### Differentiation
> ● Children can be allocated to the different events according to their own strengths.

Review

● At the end of the event, ask the children to evaluate it. Ask: *Did you enjoy being an Olympian? How do you think your experience was like that of an ancient Greek, or modern, Olympian? How was it different?*

Lesson objectives
● To study ancient Greece – a study of Greek life and achievements and their influence on the western world; the legacy of Greek culture on later periods in British history, including the present day.
● To develop a chronologically secure knowledge and understanding of British, local and world history, establishing clear narratives within and across the periods they study.

Resources
Interactive activity 'Y4 Spring 1 quiz' on the CD-ROM

Ancient Greek legacy (1)

Revise

● Write the following words on the board: theatre, government, language, science, mathematics, architecture, philosophy, mythology, sport.
● Challenge children to come to the front of the class and talk for 30 seconds about how the ancient Greek idea influenced the world today, without hesitation, repetition or deviation.

Assess

● Ask the children to complete interactive activity 'Y4 Spring 1 quiz' on the CD-ROM, in which they answer multiple-choice questions covering the chapter content.
● Give children a set length of time (such as 15 minutes) to answer the questions. This can be used as part of a formal assessment or as a fun challenge activity, giving children the opportunity to show what they have learned about the topic.
● Less confident readers may need adult support to read the questions aloud.

Further practice

● Ask the children to put together a list of recommended focus questions for subsequent classes studying the ancient Greeks.

Lesson objectives
● To study ancient Greece – a study of Greek life and achievements and their influence on the western world; the legacy of Greek culture on later periods in British history, including the present day.
● To note connections, contrasts and trends over time.

Resources
Cameras (optional)

Ancient Greek legacy (2)

Revise

● Write the following words on the board: theatre, government, language, science, mathematics, architecture, philosophy, mythology, sport.
● Hold a class debate around the question: Which of these ancient Greek ideas has had the biggest influence on modern Britain?

Assess

● Ask children to select one topic they have learned about, concerning the legacy of the ancient Greeks in Britain and the world today (for example, theatre, democracy). They should write a paragraph about how it has influenced modern life and compare and contrast the modern and ancient versions.

Further practice

● Ask the children to look around the local area for things that are in some way influenced by ancient Greek life or culture (for example: objects featuring Greek words such as a microscope or photograph; buildings; theatre; election materials). They could take photographs and create a class album featuring these.

Name: _____   Date: _____

Archimedes' principle

The story of Archimedes' discovery

Have you ever noticed that when you get into the bath, the water level rises? The ancient Greek scientist Archimedes noticed this when he was using the public baths one day. This led him to the discovery of what is known today as Archimedes' principle. According to legend, he was so excited by his discovery that he jumped out of the bath and ran naked through the streets shouting, "Eureka!" – which means "I have found it!".

Archimedes' principle helps us to explain why some objects float and some objects sink. When an object is submerged or floats in water, it pushes some of that water aside. This is called displacement. If the object weighs the same as the water it displaces, it will float. If the object is heavier than the water it displaces, it will sink.

Challenge 1: carry out the following investigation, based on Archimedes' principle.

You will need:
■ wooden block
■ scales for weighing
■ container for water (big enough for the block of wood)
■ tray
■ jug for pouring

Instructions:
1. Weigh the wooden block and the tray separately and note down their weight.
2. Place the container in the tray. Use the jug to fill the container to the brim with water.
3. Float the wooden block carefully on the water. It will displace some of the water, which will spill into the tray.
4. Remove the container and weigh the tray containing the displaced water. Subtract the weight of the tray. This should give you the weight of the displaced water.
5. Compare the weight of the displaced water with the weight of the wooden block. What do you notice?

Challenge 2: repeat the above investigation with other objects that float or sink. What do you notice?
How does an object's shape affect the amount of water it displaces?

Challenge 3: take a ball of modelling clay and place it in a container of water. Does it float or sink?
Can you change its shape in a way to make it float on the surface of the water?

A Greek play

This is an excerpt from an ancient Greek play – *The Persians* by Aeschylus.
It tells the story of the Persian people after their defeat by the Greek navy at the
Battle of Salamis.

Excerpt from *The Persians* by Aeschylus

A messenger enters.

MESSENGER

Wo to the towns through Asia's peopled
realms! Wo to the land of Persia, once
the port. Of boundless wealth, how is
thy glorious state. Vanish'd at once, and
all thy spreading honours. Fall'n, lost!
Ah me! unhappy is his task. That bears
unhappy tidings: but constraint
Compels me to relate this tale of wo.
Persians, the whole barbaric host is fall'n.

CHORUS *(chanting)*

O horror, horror! What a baleful train.
Of recent ills! Ah, Persians, as he speaks.
Of ruin, let your tears stream to the earth.

MESSENGER

It is ev'n so, all ruin; and myself,
Beyond all hope returning, view this light.

CHORUS *(chanting)*

How tedious and oppressive is the weight.
Of age, reserved to hear these hopeless
ills!

MESSENGER

I speak not from report; but these mine
eyes. Beheld the ruin which my tongue
would utter.

CHORUS *(chanting)*

Wo, wo is me! Then has the iron storm,
That darken'd from the realms of Asia,
pour'd. In vain its arrowy shower on
sacred Greece.

MESSENGER

In heaps the unhappy dead lie on
the strand. Of Salamis, and all the
neighbouring shores.

CHORUS *(chanting)*

Unhappy friends, sunk, perish'd in the sea;
Their bodies, mid the wreck of shatter'd
ships, mangled, and rolling on the
encumber'd waves!

MESSENGER

Naught did their bows avail, but all the
troops. In the first conflict of the ships
were lost.

CHORUS *(chanting)*

Raise the funereal cry, with dismal notes
Wailing the wretched Persians. Oh, how ill
They plann'd their measures, all their
army perish'd!

Name: _____ Date: _____

Greek language

■ Match the prefixes (starts of words) on the left with suffixes (ends of words) on the right to make some English words. Note: some prefixes might go with more than one suffix.

■ Use a dictionary to write the meaning of each word in the table.

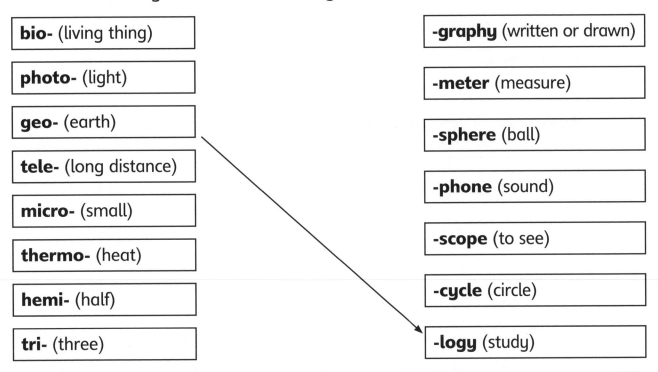

| **bio-** (living thing) | | **-graphy** (written or drawn) |

| **photo-** (light) | | **-meter** (measure) |

| **geo-** (earth) | | **-sphere** (ball) |

| **tele-** (long distance) | | **-phone** (sound) |

| **micro-** (small) | | **-scope** (to see) |

| **thermo-** (heat) | | **-cycle** (circle) |

| **hemi-** (half) | | **-logy** (study) |

| **tri-** (three) | | |

English word	**Meaning**
geology	the scientific study of the Earth

I can create some English words using Greek prefixes and suffixes.

How did you do?

Rome and its empire

This chapter introduces the children to international history and furthers their understanding of timelines and the way that historical knowledge is constructed from evidence. Children explore the Roman Empire at its height, including social, military and cultural aspects of life in ancient Rome in order to gain a grounded understanding of who the Romans were and how they lived. This chapter prepares children for the continuation of the chronological narrative of British history with the Roman invasion of Britain in the next chapter.

Chapter at a glance

Curriculum objectives

• The Roman Empire and its impact on Britain: the Roman Empire by AD42 and the power of its army.

Week	Lesson	Summary of activities	Expected outcomes
1	1	• Children compare maps of the Roman Empire with modern maps and place the Roman Empire on a timeline.	• Can say when and where the Roman Empire took place.
	2	• Children use past and present images to discuss famous Roman buildings, including the Colosseum, Forum and Pantheon.	• Can describe some famous buildings in ancient Rome and consider their purpose.
2	1	• Children investigate the features of a Roman villa, incorporating these features into a design for a modern home.	• Can identify and describe the main features of a Roman villa.
	2	• Children research domestic life in an ancient Roman villa and write a schedule for a Roman's day.	• Can describe the domestic life of the different Roman social classes.
3	1	• Children read about gladiators and chariot races and create a poster advertising an event.	• Can demonstrate understanding of a Roman leisure activity.
	2	• Children learn and perform a rap about Roman gods and goddesses.	• Can describe some of the different gods and goddesses worshipped by the Romans.
4	1	• Children enact Roman battle strategies (for example, testudo) before writing a description of how a testudo is formed.	• Can describe what life was like for a Roman soldier, describing some of the army tactics used.
	2	• Children construct their own Roman onager.	• Can describe some of the weapons used by the Roman army.
5	1	• Children compare Roman and modern British coins before designing their own.	• Can identify similarities and differences between Roman and modern coins.
	2	• Children examine examples of Roman mosaics before creating their own.	• Can create Roman-style artwork.
6	1	• Children locate Pompeii on a map and read excerpts from Pliny the Younger's account of the eruption of Vesuvius.	• Can describe what happened to Pompeii in AD79.
	2	• Children learn about the way that the preservation of Pompeii has been used to piece together information about Roman life.	• Can describe how knowledge of Roman life has been constructed from Pompeii's archaeological site.
Assess and review		• To review the half-term's work.	

■ SCHOLASTIC
www.scholastic.co.uk

Expected prior learning

● This chapter can be taught without prior knowledge of the Romans.
● To continue the chronological learning of history, it would be useful if the children have some knowledge of British pre-history from the Stone Age through to the Iron Age Celts.

Overview of progression

● Children will build on their enquiry skills, using a variety of different methods to research what life was like for the ancient Romans.
● They will respond to written and pictorial accounts of Roman life and learn about the way archaeological evidence from Rome and Pompeii has contributed to our historical knowledge.
● They will also develop their ability to draw comparisons, as they consider similarities and differences between Roman times and the modern day.

Creative context

● Cross-curricular opportunities include:
  ● speech and drama activities; reading information texts; persuasive writing; diary writing;
  ● exploring maps and diagrams showing the extent of the Roman Empire; locating cities (Rome and Pompeii);
  ● designing Roman-style coins; constructing an onager; creating mosaics.

Background knowledge

● The city of Rome was founded in 753BC. It became a republic in 509BC and the Roman Empire was established from 27BC (with the first emperor, Augustus) until its decline and fall, which most historians set as AD476 for the western Roman Empire and 1453 for the eastern (Byzantine) Empire, with the fall of Constantinople to the Ottoman Turks. Roman wealth, power and military strength saw its empire expand to control just over a fifth of the world's population.
● Roman social classes were split into three main levels. Patricians were the wealthy, upper-class citizens, who wielded most of the power. The richest and most powerful patricians formed the Senate. There was also a sub-class, the equestrians, who performed important public jobs like bankers and tax collectors. The plebeians were the lower classes of free men, such as craftsmen. There were also slaves, who had no rights at all but could sometimes earn their way to freedom if they worked hard and pleased their masters.
● The Romans worshipped many different gods and goddesses, each responsible for a different aspect of the world. Many of these, and the myths surrounding them, were adapted from the deities of ancient Greece. For example, the king of the gods, Zeus, was renamed Jupiter by the Romans.
● The Roman army was made up of two types of soldier. Male Roman citizens aged over 20 could become legionaries; they received good wages and a pension. Auxiliary soldiers were not Roman citizens and were paid less than legionaries; they were recruited from conquered countries and could be rewarded with Roman citizenship after serving in the army. Soldiers remained in the army for 25 years. They were highly skilled and trained to march over 30 miles a day, carrying heavy equipment.
● Pompeii was a busy Roman city with a population of around 2000. In AD79, a nearby volcano, Mount Vesuvius, erupted and buried the whole city in volcanic ash. The city was rediscovered in 1748; it was well preserved and the findings have taught historians a lot about ancient Roman life.

Week 1 lesson plans

This week introduces the children to the history of the wider world as they develop understanding of the term 'empire'. They discuss how and why empires rise and explore when the Roman Empire took place and the area of the world that it covered. Children then explore the city of Rome through its famous buildings.

1: When and where did the Roman Empire take place?

Introduction

- Ask the children to locate Italy and Rome on a map of the world. Have any of the children been there for a holiday? Show some images of modern day Rome blending new and ancient buildings, inviting comment. Ask: *What can you tell me about Rome from looking at these images?*
- Show a picture of the Colosseum. *Ask: What do you notice about this building? How old do you think it is? What do you think it was used for?*

Whole-class work

- Write the word 'Empire' on the board and ensure children understand its meaning (a group of countries or peoples ruled by one emperor or sovereign).
- Tell the children that the Roman Empire took place from around 27BC (with the first emperor, Augustus) to AD476, when the western part of the Empire fell, though the city of Rome had already existed for around 700 years. If appropriate, draw this period on a timeline in relation to the periods that have already been studied by the children.
- Explain that this topic will focus on the period around AD42, when the Roman Empire was very powerful.

Group work

- Discuss the reasons for the rise of empires. Give children a focus question, such as: *What makes an empire successful, and able to expand?* Collect one or two examples as a class before allowing the children time for groups to come up with their own ideas. (These might include: the accumulation of wealth, land, resources and slaves; military power; strong leadership).
- Ask groups to share their ideas and add these to the list already started as a class.

> **Differentiation**
> - Support: children may need support with map work and could be paired with a more confident child.
> - Challenge: children could create their own maps of the Roman Empire or look at the expansion of the Empire over a period of time.

Review

- Ask the children to write down the most interesting thing they have learned this lesson. Ask some children to share what they've written with the rest of the class.

Lesson objectives

- To understand the Roman Empire and its impact on Britain, including the Roman Empire by AD42 and the power of its army.
- To develop a chronologically secure knowledge and understanding of British, local and world history, establishing clear narratives within and across the periods they study.
- To develop the appropriate use of historical terms.
- To regularly address and sometimes devise historically valid questions about change, cause, similarity and difference, and significance.
- To understand how our knowledge of the past is constructed from a range of sources.

Expected outcomes

- All children know what an 'empire' is.
- Most children can describe where and when the Roman Empire occurred.
- Some children can provide reasons as to how and why the Roman Empire rose.

Resources

Maps of the world; images of modern-day Rome and the Colosseum (source online); map of the Roman Empire; map of modern Europe, North Africa and the Middle East; internet access

2: The ancient city of Rome

Lesson objectives
● To understand the Roman Empire and its impact on Britain, including the Roman Empire by AD42 and the power of its army.
● To develop a chronologically secure knowledge and understanding of British, local and world history, establishing clear narratives within and across the periods they study.
● To develop the appropriate use of historical terms.
● To regularly address and sometimes devise historically valid questions about change, cause, similarity and difference, and significance.
● To understand how our knowledge of the past is constructed from a range of sources.

Expected outcomes
● All children will be able to name some famous Roman buildings.
● Most children will describe some of the features of Roman architecture.
● Some children will be able to describe how Roman buildings tell us about life in ancient Rome.

Resources
Information on famous buildings from ancient Rome (books or websites); internet access

Introduction
● Tell the children that the centre of the Roman Empire was the city of Rome. It was said that all roads led to Rome.
● Explain that one of the reasons we know so much about the Romans is because they built grand buildings that have lasted over the centuries.

Whole-class work
● Show the children images of a range of Roman buildings as they are now, for example: the Colosseum, Pantheon, Curia Julia, Arch of Septimus Severus, Temple of Vesta and Temple of Saturn. Explain that these are the ruins of ancient Roman buildings, all to be found in Rome itself.
● Ask: *What materials are used in these buildings?* (stone) *What design features do you notice?* (columns, pediments, archways, ornate carvings, domes – all on a grand scale) Some children may notice similarities between Roman and Greek architecture, if ancient Greece has been studied previously.

Group work
● Split the class into groups and give each one a different Roman building to research. Each group should write facts about their building.
● Provide a selection of age-appropriate reference books, or access to the internet. (This would tie in with work on researching using the internet: how to skim and scan material; how to choose the most useful keywords when searching; how to recognise a respected or reputable source, and so on.)
● Provide guidance questions, such as: *When was your building built? What was its purpose? Who used it?*

Differentiation
● Support: mixed-ability groups may be beneficial.

Review
● Towards the end of the lesson, groups should present their information to the rest of the class. After all the presentations have been delivered, ask: *What are some of the main features of Roman buildings? What do they tell us about ancient Rome?*
● Show the children some illustrations of ancient Rome as it was (optional).
● Ask them to look for examples of Roman-style architecture (such as arches and columns) when they are out and about. They could take photographs to show the class.

Week 2 lesson plans

This week focuses on Roman domestic life. Children investigate the layout and features of a Roman villa, considering which features can still be found in modern buildings. They then explore what domestic life was like in ancient Rome, considering the daily activities in which villa owners and their servants might engage.

1: What was it like to live in a Roman villa?

Introduction
- Ask the children to describe the kind of house they would like to live in if they had lots of money.
- Tell them that some wealthy Romans lived in luxurious country houses called villas. Ask: *What features do you think villas might have?*

Whole-class work
- Tell the children that floor plans are used to show the layout of a house. Historians have been able to draw up floor plans of ancient Roman villas through investigating archaeological ruins of Roman buildings. Show images of Cerro da Vila in Portugal as an example (source online).
- Read and discuss photocopiable page 185 'Roman villa floor plan'. Ask: *How is this villa similar to houses of today? What features can be found in your home? Who might live here? What would it have been like to live here?*
- Show the children an artist's impression of a completed villa, or a photograph of a reconstructed villa, such as Villa Borg in Germany (source online), so that the children can put the floor plan into context.

Independent work or Paired work
- Tell the children that they are going to be architects for the day. They need to imagine that their client is a history buff who has asked them to design a modern home including one or more of the features from a Roman villa.
- Depending on ability, children could either create a floor plan of their house or draw a specific room (for example, bedroom or bathroom). They should include at least one feature from a Roman villa, such as mosaic tiles, columns or arches.
- Tell the children to write a sentence describing how they have included the feature in their design.

Differentiation
- Support: children may need help with their designs and could work with adult support.
- Challenge: children may wish to create a model of a Roman villa or a section of the building, using the floor plan as a guide.

Review
- Ask some children to present their designs to the rest of the class. Ask other children: *What features of a Roman villa does this design include? Would you like to live in a house like this?*
- Ask further questions about Roman villas in general, such as: *Which features were designed to make the villa more attractive? Which served a practical purpose? Which Roman features can we find in modern buildings?*

Lesson objectives
- To understand the Roman Empire and its impact on Britain, including the Roman Empire by AD42 and the power of its army.
- To develop a chronologically secure knowledge and understanding of British, local and world history, establishing clear narratives within and across the periods they study.
- To note connections, contrasts and trends over time.
- To regularly address and sometimes devise historically valid questions about change, cause, similarity and difference, and significance.

Expected outcomes
- All children will know that wealthy Romans lived in villas.
- Most children will describe the main features of a Roman villa.
- Some children will be able to compare Roman villa features with those of modern houses.

Resources
Images of Cerro da Vila in Portugal and Villa Borg in Germany (source online); photocopiable page 185 'Roman villa floor plan'

Lesson objectives
● To understand the Roman Empire and its impact on Britain, including the Roman Empire by AD42 and the power of its army.
● To develop a chronologically secure knowledge and understanding of British, local and world history, establishing clear narratives within and across the periods they study.
● To note connections, contrasts and trends over time.
● To regularly address and sometimes devise historically valid questions about change, cause, similarity and difference, and significance.

Expected outcomes
● All children will describe one or more aspects of Roman domestic life.
● Most children will create a more detailed description of daily domestic life in ancient Rome.
● Some children will compare the domestic life of Romans of different social classes.

Resources
Photocopiable page 186 'Roman social classes'; information on domestic life in ancient Rome (books or websites)

2: What was domestic life like for the Romans?

Introduction
● Tell children that they are going to explore day-to-day life in a Roman villa. Ask: *Who might live there? What types of activities might the people do throughout the day?*

Whole-class work
● Read and discuss photocopiable page 186 'Roman social classes'. Ask: *Was Roman society fair? How is our society similar, or different? Would you rather be a plebeian or a patrician?*
● Ask children to think about the types of activity that people of the different classes might engage in during their daily lives. Allow one or two minutes for the children to discuss this with a talk partner, before sharing their ideas as a class.

Independent work or Paired work
● Ask the children to select one of the people who would have lived in a Roman villa (for example, the owner of the villa, his wife, or a slave). Tell them that they are going to put together a schedule for this person showing his or her daily activities (for example, a slave rising early to light the fires, then scrub the mosaic floor, then help the villa owner to dress, then walk the children to school, then prepare a bath). They could use the photocopiable sheet, books, or the internet to research the kinds of activity that might have taken place.
● Discuss how to set out a schedule, perhaps using the class timetable for the day.
● Try to ensure that a range of characters is being considered by the class as a whole.

> **Differentiation**
> ● Support: children could work in a group with adult support to think about suitable activities and create a simple schedule.
> ● Challenge: children could write a day's diary rather than a schedule, including the character's thoughts and feelings about his or her life. They could draw comparisons between Romans of different social classes.

Review
● Invite children who have written about different types of Roman to share their schedules or diaries.
● Ask: *How does the daily life of the villa owner differ from that of his wife? How does a servant's or slave's day differ from that of a tradesman? How was domestic life in ancient Rome similar to and different from today?*

Lesson objectives
● To understand the Roman Empire and its impact on Britain, including the Roman Empire by AD42 and the power of its army.
● To develop a chronologically secure knowledge and understanding of British, local and world history, establishing clear narratives within and across the periods they study.
● To note connections, contrasts and trends over time
● To regularly address and sometimes devise historically valid questions about change, cause, similarity and difference, and significance.
● To construct informed responses that involve thoughtful selection and organisation of relevant historical information.

Expected outcomes
● All children will be able to name two Roman leisure activities.
● Most children will describe what these activities were like.
● Some children will demonstrate detailed understanding of why Romans enjoyed these activities, making comparisons with modern society.

Resources
Photocopiable pages 'Chariot races and gladiators' from the CD-ROM; A3 paper; posters of local or sporting events (optional); reference books about gladiators, or internet access (optional)

Week 3 lesson plans

This week focuses on aspects of Roman culture and religion. Children explore two popular Roman leisure activities – chariot racing and gladiator fights – comparing them to modern day sporting events and designing a poster to advertise a fictitious up-and-coming event. Children then use speech and drama to learn about Roman mythology and the characteristics of different gods and goddesses worshipped by the Romans.

1: How did the Romans spend their leisure time?

Introduction
● Ask the children to describe their favourite leisure activities – the things they do for fun in their spare time. Ask: *What kinds of leisure and entertainment events are popular in the UK?*
● Tell the children that the ancient Romans also enjoyed leisure activities and that two of the most popular were watching chariot races and gladiator fights. (Note: Romans also played board games, went hunting for fun, visited the theatre and spent time in baths.)

Whole-class work
● Read through photocopiable page 'Chariot races and gladiators' from the CD-ROM, as a class. Ask: *What do you think of this description of chariot racing – would you like to watch something like this for fun? Is it like any sporting event today?*
● Read the section of the sheet about gladiators. Ask: *What do you think of these event? Would you like to watch something like this? Are they similar to any modern sporting events?*

Group work
● Ask the children to consider how chariot racing, in terms of popularity, is similar to football today.
● In groups, children should discuss the following question: *What are the similarities and differences between a Roman chariot race and a modern day football match?*
● They should record a list of similarities and differences.

Paired work or Independent work
● Tell the children that they should select one of the Roman leisure activities and create a poster to advertise an up-and-coming event. Ask: *What kinds of information would be needed by someone who wished to attend? How could you make the poster eye-catching?*
● If available, analyse some posters for existing events in the local community and discuss what makes them appealing and how they could be improved.

Differentiation
● Support: children may need support with writing phrases for the poster and could be paired with more confident children.
● Challenge: children could create a brochure with a more detailed description of what will take place at their event.

Review
● Show some of the children's posters to the rest of the class, inviting positive criticism. Ask: *Who might the poster be aimed at? How does the poster attract attention? How has the author made the event sound appealing?*

■SCHOLASTIC
www.scholastic.co.uk

Lesson objectives
● To understand the Roman Empire and its impact on Britain, including the Roman Empire by AD42 and the power of its army.
● To develop a chronologically secure knowledge and understanding of British, local and world history, establishing clear narratives within and across the periods they study.
● To note connections, contrasts and trends over time.

Expected outcomes
● All children will be able to name some Roman gods/goddesses.
● Most children will describe a number of gods/goddesses and their responsibilities.
● Some children will be able to describe the role that religion played in Roman life.

Resources
Photocopiable page 187 'Roman gods rap'; reference books about Roman gods, or internet access; costumes and props for the different gods/goddesses (optional), video or sound recorders (optional)

2: Roman gods and goddesses

Introduction
● Ask: *Can you name the planets in our solar system?* Write them on the board: Mercury, Venus, Earth, Mars, Jupiter, Saturn, Uranus, Neptune, and dwarf planet Pluto.
● Explain that all the planets (except Earth) were named after Roman gods and goddesses – the Romans named the five planets visible to them with the naked eye (Mercury, Venus, Mars, Jupiter and Saturn). When the other planets were discovered, the tradition continued.

Whole-class work
● Tell children that the Romans worshipped many different gods and goddesses. Each had a different responsibility (similar to the gods of ancient Greece): for example, Apollo was god of the sun; Poseidon was god of the sea.
● Read the rap aloud several times as a class (using photocopiable page 187 'Roman gods rap').

Group work
● Ask the children to rehearse the rap in groups. They could include specific actions, musical theme tunes or sound effects for each god or goddess. They could use costumes and props and they could record their performance using a video camera or sound recorder.
● Children should write a final verse to the rap; they will need reference books to find out about another god or goddess, or access to the internet.
● They could also conduct further research into Roman religious practices and mythology. They could research questions such as: *What role did the gods and goddesses play in Roman life? Where and how did worship take place?*

Differentiation
● Support: mixed-ability groups may be beneficial; those who are less confident with performance may wish to direct, film or add sound effects.

Review
● Invite each group to perform the rap to the rest of the class.
● If any children have carried out further research into Roman gods and goddesses, ask them to report on their findings.
● Ask questions such as: *What did the Romans believe? Why were the gods and goddesses important to Romans? Can you describe some of the gods or goddesses and what they were responsible for?*
● If the children have studied the ancient Greeks, they could consider how Roman gods are similar to Greek gods.

Lesson objectives
• To understand the Roman Empire and its impact on Britain, including the Roman Empire by AD42 and the power of its army.
• To develop the appropriate use of historical terms.

Expected outcomes
• All children will describe a Roman soldier.
• Most children will describe some of the weapons and tactics of the Roman army.
• Some children will describe advantages and disadvantages of Roman testudo formation.

Resources
Photocopiable page 'Roman army' from the CD-ROM; objects weighing 2.5kg and 10kg (optional); materials to act as Roman shields (such as sugar paper); beanbags or tennis balls

Week 4 lesson plans

This week involves practical activities focusing on the Roman army, its battle strategies and weaponry. Children consider ways in which the army's effectiveness helped the Romans to conquer enemies and expand their empire. They practise forming a testudo and build their own onager (catapult).

1: What was it like to be a soldier in the Roman army?

Introduction

• Tell the children that they are going to be recruited to the Roman army for the day.
• Role play a Roman soldier and have the class interview you about your life and battle experience (see information on the photocopiable sheet, or in the background information at the beginning of this chapter for information about the Roman army.)
• Read through and discuss photocopiable 'Roman army' from the CD-ROM. Talk about what life might have been like for the soldiers and the advantages and disadvantages of the weapons they carried.
• Note: optional additional activities could include making and painting Roman shields, using cardboard, before the lesson begins; demonstrating the weight of the pilum (javelin) and scutum (shield) using objects weighing 2.5kg and 10kg.

Whole-class work

• Split the class into two groups of even numbers and give each child a shield, or sheet of sugar paper to act as a shield.
• In an open space (hall or playground), have the groups practise marching and, on the blow of a whistle, forming a testudo (close together, with shields over their heads and around the sides – see photocopiable sheet) and marching forward. After some practice time, ask the first group to form their testudo while the other group stands to the front or sides and tries to 'attack' the Roman soldiers with beanbags or tennis balls to see how impenetrable the formation is.
• Swap to allow the other group a chance to be the Roman soldiers.

Paired work or Independent work

• Ask the children to write a description of the testudo and how it helped the Roman army (optional).

Differentiation
• Support: children could engage in group discussion with adult support.
• Challenge: children could further research and evaluate other Roman weapons and battle strategies.

Review

• If the children have written about the testudo, some could share their work with the rest of the class.
• Allow the children a few minutes to discuss reasons why the testudo was a useful battle strategy, with a talk partner. Ask: *How did tactics like this help the Romans to conquer their enemies?* (Clever battle strategies and well-trained, disciplined soldiers made the Roman army very effective against enemy forces that were often disorganised.) *What would be the advantages and disadvantages of the testudo formation?* (The testudo protected Roman soldiers from enemy arrows and other missiles. They could move forward in this formation, but progress was slow and the formation was not very suited to hand-to-hand fighting.)

Lesson objectives
● To understand the Roman Empire and its impact on Britain, including the Roman Empire by AD42 and the power of its army.
● To develop the appropriate use of historical terms.

Expected outcomes
● All children will participate in making an onager.
● Most children will describe how the onager works.
● Some children will investigate ways to make the onager more effective.

Resources
Photocopiable page 'How to build an onager' from the CD-ROM; materials for model making (such as rubber bands, lolly sticks, bottle cap or plastic spoon, modelling clay)

2: What weapons did Roman soldiers use?

Introduction
● Give the children a quick quiz to recap facts about the Roman army, its strategies and weapons. Ask: *What does the word 'testudo' mean?* (tortoise) *Name two weapons that each soldier carried.* (javelin and dagger) *What did soldiers wear on their feet?* (sandals)

Whole-class work
● Tell children that they are going to work in groups or pairs to build their own catapult (called an 'onager').
● Read through the first paragraph of photocopiable page 'How to build an onager' from the CD-ROM, which explains what an onegar is.
● Tell the children to imagine that the Roman army wishes to purchase a new catapult that will hurl large stones a great distance. The groups/pairs will be in competition with each other to build the onager that can fling a ball of modelling clay the farthest.
● Read through the rest of the photocopiable sheet. This might be a good opportunity to link in with literacy work, discussing the photocopiable sheet in terms of the features of an instructional text (for example, steps, imperatives, diagrams).

Group work or Paired work
● Give each group or pair of children a copy of the photocopiable sheet and the materials needed to build the catapult.
● Model the different steps, if necessary, before setting the children to work.
● If time allows, children could investigate changing the design in different ways to make the onager more effective.

Differentiation
● Support: mixed-ability groups may be beneficial; children could work in a group with adult support.
● Challenge: children could experiment by adjusting the catapult to see if it can be made more effective (for example, by using a longer spoon).

Review
● Gather the children together to test each catapult to see which can fling the modelling clay the farthest. This might be a good opportunity to bring in aspects of fair testing (for example: using the same size, weight and shape of modelling clay; using the same starting point; measuring in the same way).
● Ask the children:
  ● *How do you think the Romans might have used this weapon?* (Onagers were mainly used as siege weapons to attack settlements and forts. Heavy stones were sometimes doused in flammable materials so that they could set enemy buildings alight.)
  ● *What advantages and disadvantages might it have?* (Onagers enabled soldiers to break through or damage the enemy's settlements. However, they would be heavy and awkward to transport over great distances and would require the use of heavy stones, which would need to be found locally or transported.)

Week 5 lesson plans

This is a creative week with children investigating Roman coins before designing their own. They then explore examples of mosaic art and create their own picture in a similar style.

1: How similar were Roman coins to modern coins?

Introduction
● Ask the children to suggest how we use money (coins and notes) in daily life.
● Ask: *What are the coins that make up British currency? Can anyone remember what can be found on those coins?*

Whole-class work
● Show the children some examples of modern coins (these could be British or foreign currency). Ask them to describe the coins. Ask: *Whose head is found on these coins? What is on the other side? Why have these designs been chosen? Is there any writing on the coins? What shape are they? What are they made of?*

Group work
● Ask the children to research (using books or the internet) different examples of Roman coins and comment on their designs. (Some libraries or local historical societies have examples that they are willing to lend to schools. Alternatively, a large database of Roman coin images can be found at http://finds.org.uk/romancoins and www.romancoins.info.)
● Provide some focus questions, such as: *What is on each coin? What is it made of? What shape is it?*
● Discuss the similarities and differences between Roman coins and modern coins. (For example: Roman coins are also mostly round, made of metal, and have the date and a profile of the emperor on one side along with his name – in the same way that British coins include a profile of the queen. However, the reverse side of British coins generally shows the royal shield or arms, (or segments of these) or symbols of the different countries of the UK, whereas Roman coins often show images of gods and goddesses, or symbolic images of victory in battle. Roman coins were made from bronze, silver and gold, whereas modern British coins are made from alloys of copper, zinc and nickel.)

Paired work or Independent work
● Tell the children to imagine that they are the new emperor or empress of Rome. They are going to design a coin featuring their profile and some writing of their choice. They should also think about an appropriate design for the back of the coin. Before creating their designs, the children should consider the message that they want their coin design to give to the citizens of Rome.

> **Differentiation**
> ● Support: children could have a large pre-cut coin for their design and could glue on images from magazines instead of drawing their own pictures.
> ● Challenge: children could research and discuss some of the common themes found on Roman coins (animals, gods and goddesses, buildings, and so on).

Review
● Create a class display of the coin designs. Ask: *How are these coins similar to the coins of ancient Rome? What would they have been made of? How are they similar to the coins we use today?*
● Look at specific examples and ask: *What message does this coin send to the citizens of Rome and its empire?*

Lesson objectives
● To understand the Roman Empire and its impact on Britain, including the Roman Empire by AD42 and the power of its army.
● To develop a chronologically secure knowledge and understanding of British, local and world history, establishing clear narratives within and across the periods they study.
● To note connections, contrasts and trends over time and develop the appropriate use of historical terms.
● To regularly address and sometimes devise historically valid questions about change, cause, similarity and difference, and significance.
● To understand how our knowledge of the past is constructed from a range of sources.

Expected outcomes
● All children will comment on examples of Roman mosaic art.
● Most children will create a mosaic based on Roman mythology.
● Some children will describe how they created their artwork and what it depicts.

Resources
Images of Roman mosaic art; information on Roman mythology (books or websites); photocopiable page 151 'Mythological creatures' (optional); A3 paper; magazines or coloured paper

2: What art did the Romans create?

Introduction
● Write the word 'mosaic' on the board and ask the children if they know its meaning.
● Explain that skilled Roman craftsmen created pictures out of small stones or tiles, called 'mosaics'.

Whole-class work
● Look at some examples of Roman mosaic art (source online; for example, the BBC's history site has a gallery of Roman mosaics linked to their ancient history page on Roman Britain). Ask: *How have the pictures been formed? What do they show?* (The mosaics often depicted scenes from Roman mythology, gods, or gladiators.) *What materials have been used? What colours have been used? What do you like or dislike about this form of art?*
● Tell the children that they are going to produce their own mosaics, based on Roman myths and legends.

Group work or Paired work
● This outcome of this activity might work better if carried out over two or more lessons.
● Ask the children to research some of the creatures from Roman mythology (such as Medusa, Cerberus, Cyclops, the Minotaur, Pegasus), using reference books or the internet. They may be familiar with some of these creatures already, if they have completed work on ancient Greece (see photocopiable page 151 'Mythological creatures').
● They should select a creature (or invent their own) and draw a basic design on an A3 sheet of paper, also thinking about which colours will be needed.
● Provide the children with magazines or coloured paper to cut into little squares of around 1–2cm (provide pre-cut squares if appropriate).
● Carefully, using glue, the children should stick their squares over their design to create their mosaic.

Differentiation
● Support: children with poor fine motor skills may need assistance cutting and gluing their squares; children could use a computer package to create their mosaics; some photo-editing software enables a mosaic effect to be added to any image.

Review
● Create a class display of the mosaics, or show some examples at the front of the class. Ask: *How is this like a Roman mosaic? What mythological creature does this mosaic show? What have historians learned about the Romans from mosaics?*

Week 6 lesson plans

This week focuses on the story of Pompeii and how it has been used by historians to build up a picture of life in Roman times. The children investigate both written evidence about what happened and archaeological findings.

Lesson objectives
● To understand the Roman Empire and its impact on Britain, including the Roman Empire by AD42 and the power of its army.
● To regularly address and sometimes devise historically valid questions about change, cause, similarity and difference, and significance.
● To understand how our knowledge of the past is constructed from a range of sources.

Expected outcomes
● All children will explore written evidence of what happened to Pompeii.
● Most children will discuss what the letters of Pliny the Younger tell us about Roman life.
● Some children will consider the advantages and disadvantages of eyewitness accounts.

Resources
Maps of Italy; photocopiable page 'Pompeii' from the CD-ROM; media resource 'Letters from Pliny the Younger'

1: What can written evidence tell us about Pompeii?

Introduction

● Show the children a map of Italy (or view the satellite images online) and ask them to find the city of Pompeii (just south of Naples).
● Explain that the city was destroyed in AD79. Ask them to look closely at the map and guess how it might have been destroyed. (Note: some children may already know the story of Pompeii, as it features in an episode of *Dr Who*.)
● Point out Mount Vesuvius to the north-west of the city and explain that the volcano's eruption buried the city in volcanic ash. This preserved it and excavations of the site have given us a good picture of Roman life.

Whole-class work

● Tell the children that one way historians investigate the past is through written documents. Listen to media resource 'Letters from Pliny the Younger' on the CD-ROM, or read the letters on photocopiable page 'Pompeii' from the CD-ROM, which give an account of his uncle's death during the eruption of Vesuvius in AD79. The full letters can be found online if you search for 'Letters from the Pliny Younger'.
● Discuss the advantages and disadvantages of eyewitness accounts, in terms of reliability.

Paired work or Independent work

● Ask the children to read again the letters of Pliny the Younger on the photocopiable sheet and to answer the following questions: *What do the letters tell us about what happened to Pompeii?* (They describe the volcano, the ash, swaying buildings, and so on – but not from inside Pompeii itself.) *What do they tell us about Pliny the Elder?* (He seems to have been well educated, wealthy; he was a naval commander; he could write.) *What do they tell us about Roman life?* (The Romans believed in gods; the houses were made of, or contained, pumice stone; they used pillows; they didn't have as much knowledge of volcanoes and when they might erupt, as we have today, and so on.)
● Write the questions on the board. The children should divide their page into three and go through the letters, writing bullets points to answer each question using quotations from the text.

Differentiation
● Support: children could go through the letter as a group with adult support, highlighting relevant words or phrases to answer each question.
● Challenge: children should provide more in-depth analysis of the text, using quotations and inference.

Review

● Ask different children to answer the questions on the board, completing the three columns as a class.

Lesson objectives
● To understand the Roman Empire and its impact on Britain, including the Roman Empire by AD42 and the power of its army.
● To regularly address and sometimes devise historically valid questions about change, cause, similarity and difference, and significance.
● To understand how our knowledge of the past is constructed from a range of sources.

Expected outcomes
● All children will describe why the archaeological site at Pompeii is important to historians.
● Most children will write a letter showing why preserving Pompeii is important.
● Some children will provide a detailed analysis of the problems faced by archaeological sites and the reasons they should be preserved.

Resources
Media resource 'Pompeii' on the CD-ROM; report about Pompeii (source online) (optional)

2: What can archaeological evidence tell us about Pompeii?

Introduction
● Look at the images of Pompeii provided on media resource 'Pompeii' on the CD-ROM; the images are of the present day ruins of Pompeii.
● Ask: *What might this building have been used for? What might have happened here? Who might have lived here?*

Whole-class work
● Ask: *Why do you think Pompeii is an important place for historians?* (Talk about the fact that Pompeii was preserved largely intact, due to being covered very quickly with volcanic ash. This meant that it avoided changing under subsequent generations and became like a time capsule, providing valuable information about daily life during that period and how Roman cities were built. Many artefacts – everyday items as well as valuable artworks and possessions – were found on the site.)
● Explain that the ruins of Pompeii have been neglected over the years, falling into a poor state of repair, and that the Italian government has now appointed a special commissioner to preserve them. Read a report in the national media, if desired.
● Hold a class discussion around the kinds of issues faced by archaeological sites (such as weathering, erosion and damage caused by visitors, looting, the cost of upkeep, and so on) and why it is important to raise funds to protect them. (The children should consider what we have learned about Roman life from Pompeii, and why they think it is important to find out about, and connect with, the past.)
● List some of their ideas on the board.

Group work or Paired work
● The children should write a persuasive letter requesting funds to preserve Pompeii's archaeological site. They should think carefully about how to structure their argument and present their case.
● Create a class list of the features of persuasive writing, if necessary.

Differentiation
● Support: children could work with a letter-writing template or discuss their ideas verbally.
● Challenge: children may wish to put together a presentation or campaign for funds.

Review
● Tell the children to swap their work with a partner. Ask: *Would the letter persuade you to donate some money – does it convince you that it's a good cause? What reasons have been presented in the letter for preserving the site? Have any reasons been presented that you hadn't thought of?*
● Ask some children to read good examples of each other's work.

Lesson objectives
• To understand the Roman Empire and its impact on Britain, including the Roman Empire by AD42 and the power of its army.
• To develop a chronologically secure knowledge and understanding of British, local and world history, establishing clear narratives within and across the periods they study.

Resources
Interactive activity 'Y4 Spring 2 quiz' on the CD-ROM

Roman Empire quiz

Revise

• Organise the children into groups and ask them to make a list of questions about the Roman Empire that they have investigated during the chapter – these can show an overview (for example: What were Roman homes like? What gods did the Romans worship? What did the Romans do for fun? What was life like for a soldier in the Roman army?) or depth study (for example: How did an onager work? What was the god Neptune responsible for? How many people could the Colosseum hold?)

• Discuss ideas together as a class and write some of these on the board.

Assess

• Ask the children to complete interactive activity 'Y4 Spring 2 quiz' on the CD-ROM, in which they answer multiple-choice questions covering the chapter content.

• Give children a set length of time (for example, 15 minutes) to answer the questions. This can be used as part of a formal assessment or as a fun challenge activity, giving children the opportunity to show what they have learned about the topic.

• Less confident readers may need adult support to read the questions aloud.

Further practice

• Ask the children to write a poem or story covering an aspect of ancient Rome.

Lesson objectives
• To understand the Roman Empire and its impact on Britain, including the Roman Empire by AD42 and the power of its army.
• To develop the appropriate use of historical terms.

Resources
Sets of cards featuring the following historical terms from the ancient Romans: charioteer, gladiator, Colosseum, pilum, testudo, onager, hypocaust, frigidarium, mosaic, patrician, plebeian, slave, Jupiter, Neptune, Juno

Roman Empire historical terms

Revise

• Organise the class into groups and give each group a set of cards of the historical terms.

• Ask children to work together collaboratively to sort the cards into groups. Provide categories, or let the children could devise their own categories (such as: Roman leisure, the Roman army, features of a villa, social classes, gods and goddesses).

• Discuss how the children have grouped their cards.

Assess

• Choose one of the words from the cards and model writing a glossary definition of the word and a sentence to show it in context.

• Ask the children, working independently, to select five words from the cards. Each word must belong to a different group from the sorting activity. For each word they should write a definition and then use the word in context.

• Less confident writers could share their ideas verbally with adult support.

Further practice

• Ask children to create a glossary of terms relevant to the ancient Romans, which can be used for a class studying this period the following year.

Roman villa floor plan

Wealthy Romans often lived in villas made from timber and stone. Villas were used to show how rich the owner was – the wealthier the owner, the larger and more luxurious the villa. Rooms were usually arranged in rows around a central courtyard. Every villa was different. Some contained a single building, while others had several buildings and included accommodation for slaves and a barn for animals.

Columns and arches: provided support as well as making the villa look grand.

Bathhouse: most villas had either a bathing room or a special bathhouse, which might contain a hot bath (caldarium) and cold bath (frigidarium).

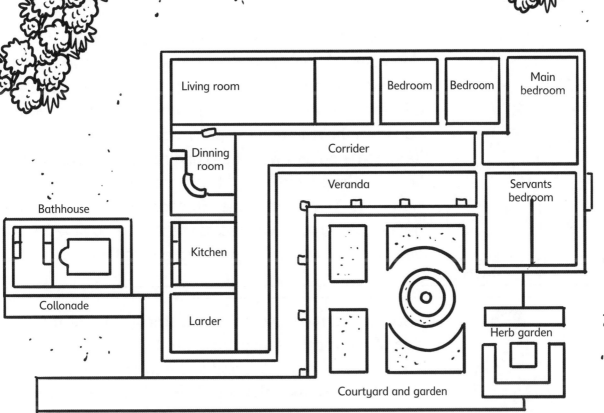

Living room

Bedroom   Bedroom   Main bedroom

Corrider

Dinning room

Veranda

Servants bedroom

Bathhouse

Kitchen

Collonade

Larder

Herb garden

Courtyard and garden

Mosaic floors: important rooms in Roman villas were decorated with mosaic artworks.

Central heating (hypocaust system): certain rooms in the house had under-floor heating. Floors were built on top of brick columns. A fire was lit beneath the floor so that the air heated up and kept the room warm.

Roman social classes

Patricians – I am a patrician, one of the wealthy, upper-class citizens of Rome. We have more power and advantages than the other classes. I own a large villa surrounded by vineyards just outside of Rome and have bought many slaves to help my family. I received a good education and can afford to buy beautiful clothing. I spend most days bathing, feasting and resting. The richest and most powerful members of my class are the senators. There are also equestrians, who perform important public jobs such as bankers and tax collectors.

Plebeians – I am a plebeian, one of the lower-class citizens of Rome. I make a living making and selling clay vases in my shop in Rome. I live in a flat above the shop with my father, my wife and children. Our home is comfortable but small. We have to fetch our water each day from the river and use public toilets and baths. I'm lucky to be able to work hard and make a decent living. Some of the people in my class are extremely poor – slaves who have earned their freedom. We plebs have our own special groups; we discuss the laws set by the Senate and protest if we don't agree with one of the laws.

Slaves – I am a slave. I live in a small room at the side of my master's villa. I used to be a plebeian but I couldn't pay my debts and so I had to become a slave. Some of the other slaves in the villa come from lands that Rome has conquered. We farm my master's land, prepare and serve his family's meals, assist him dressing after his bath, clean the villa and go to the market to buy the things he wants. I work really hard from early morning until late evening. If my master isn't happy with my work, he might sell me to another master at a slave market. If I please him, he might eventually grant me my freedom.

Roman gods rap

- Read the rap about Roman gods and goddesses.
- Write your own verse about another Roman god or goddess (for example, Diana, Minerva, Apollo or Mercury).

Jupiter

King of the gods and lord of the sky
I'm Jupiter and I'm the top guy
I'm renowned as a bit of a ladies' man
I hurl lightning bolts... because I can!

Juno

Queen goddess is my claim to fame
Protector of women, Juno's my name
I can get jealous, you bet your life
It isn't easy being Jupiter's wife

Neptune

I'm Neptune, the mighty god of the sea
Sometimes my mood's as calm as can be
But if I'm angry, hope you're feeling brave
My trusty trident can sure make waves

Pluto

I'm Jupiter's brother, Pluto's my name
The underworld is my domain
Dead souls cross the River Styx to my home
But soon they're reborn again in Rome

Venus

I'm Venus, the goddess of love and beauty
Bet you've never seen a woman as lovely as me
Some call me haughty, some call me vain
But if you looked like me, you'd feel the same

Mars

I'm Mars and I'm the god of war
I'm a really big fan of blood and gore
I'm Jupiter's son, I love causing strife
No one likes me much but... hey, that's life.

I can perform a rap about Roman gods and goddesses.

How did you do?

Roman Britain (1)

This chapter picks up the chronological narrative of Britain's history with the Roman invasion. Having explored Rome and its way of life in the previous chapter, children learn about the main events of the three Roman invasions of Britain. They compare Celtic and Roman life and consider the impact that the invading Romans had on the British population. Children also learn about the resistance from Caratacus and Boudica. In the next chapter they consider the on-going impact of Roman rule in Britain, and its legacy.

Chapter at a glance

Curriculum objectives

• The Roman Empire and its impact on Britain: Julius Caesar's attempted invasion in 55–54BC; the Roman Empire by AD42 and the power of its army; successful invasion by Claudius and conquest, including Hadrian's Wall; British resistance; 'Romanisation' of Britain and the impact of technology, culture and beliefs.

Week	Lesson	Summary of activities	Expected outcomes
1	1	• Children discuss and write down similarities and differences between numerous aspects of Celtic and Roman ways of life.	• Can draw comparisons between Celtic and Roman ways of life.
	2	• Children use physical theatre to represent the differences between the Celtic warriors and the Roman army.	• Can compare and contrast the Celtic warriors with the Roman army.
2	1	• Children consolidate their understanding of BC/AD and create a timeline of important events in Roman Britain's history.	• Can create a timeline showing important events in Roman Britain.
	2	• Children write a persuasive letter to the Roman leaders showing reasons for invading Britain.	• Can identify reasons why the Romans invaded Britain.
3	1	• Children learn about the life of Julius Caesar and debate his merits and faults.	• Can discuss the merits and faults of Julius Caesar.
	2	• Children role play Celtic tribe members reacting to a potential Roman invasion, before reading about what happened.	• Can describe what happened during Julius Caesar's invasions of Britain in 55BC and 54BC.
4	1	• Children read about the invasion by Claudius and answer comprehension questions.	• Can describe the main events of the Roman invasion of AD43.
	2	• Children perform a poem about the deeds of Caratacus.	• Can describe how Caratacus resisted the Roman invaders.
5	1	• Children label a map of Roman Britain with Roman towns and cities.	• Can describe where the Romans settled in Britain.
	2	• Children use a written description of Boudica to draw a portrait of her.	• Can describe how written evidence has helped us to understand what Queen Boudica was like.
6	1	• Children create a storyboard showing the events of Boudica's rebellion.	• Can describe the main events of Boudica's rebellion.
	2	• Children write about Boudica from the point of view of a Celt and a Roman.	• Can identify why Celts and Romans may have differed in their opinions of Boudica.
Assess and review		• To review the half-term's work.	

Expected prior learning

● In order to continue the chronological narrative of British history, it would be useful if the children have learned about the Stone Age through to the Iron Age Celts before looking at this period.

● Children should also have covered the previous chapter on Rome and its Empire, and therefore be familiar with Roman domestic life, customs, religion, military strength and so on.

Overview of progression

● Children develop their understanding that different views exist about historical people and events, and that historical records can be biased.

● They debate the merits and faults of significant historical figures such as Julius Caesar and Boudica.

● They speculate about the Roman reasons for invading Britain and the feelings of the Celts about the Roman invaders, taking different characters' points of view.

● They also build on their understanding of the use of written evidence to piece history together.

Creative context

● Cross-curricular links include:
  ● engaging in a number of debate and role-play activities; developing skills in reading comprehension and persuasive writing; performance poetry;
  ● exploring maps and diagrams showing the location of important Roman towns in Britain;
  ● using their bodies, in PE and dance, to portray the different battle styles of the Celts and Romans;
  ● creating portraits of Boudica; storyboarding events of her rebellion.

Background knowledge

● Britain was under Roman rule from AD43 until AD410, although it was invaded twice prior to that by Julius Caesar, in 55BC and 54BC.

● Motivated by Britain's natural resources (grain, tin and lead), Emperor Claudius led a successful invasion in AD43. Many Celtic tribes surrendered to the Romans, while others chose to fight. The Celts were ultimately defeated by the highly skilled Roman army with their superior weapons and training.

● British resistance was led by Caratacus, leader of the Catuvellauni tribe. He fought for many years but was eventually pushed back into the Welsh mountains. He then fled to the Brigantes tribe in Northern England and was handed over to the Romans by its leader, Queen Cartimandua. He was taken to Rome, where his boldness impressed the emperor, and he was allowed to live there for the rest of his life. He famously remarked, 'And can you, then, who have got such possessions, and so many of them, covet our poor tents?'

● Boudica, Queen of the Iceni tribe, led a major revolt against the Romans in AD61. Boudica's warriors ruthlessly attacked the Roman cities of Camulodunum (Colchester), Londinium (London) and Verulamium (St Albans), killing both Romans and Britons.

● A troop of 10,000 well-trained Roman soldiers went to battle against around 100,000 of Boudica's warriors. The Britons were defeated. Boudica poisoned herself in order to avoid becoming the Romans' prisoner.

● The Romans eventually conquered much of Britain (though struggled with Scotland). The British population learned to live under Roman rule and actually benefited from the technology and wealth the Romans brought with them.

Week 1 lesson plans

This week brings the historical focus back to the chronological narrative of Britain. Children recall what they have previously learned about the Iron Age Celts and draw comparisons between Celtic and Roman life. They use physical theatre and movement to portray Celtic warriors and Roman soldiers and consider the advantages and disadvantages of each side. These activities prepare them for the following lessons covering the Roman invasion of Britain.

1: How did Celtic life compare with Roman life?

Introduction

- Elicit what the children remember from their topic on the Iron Age Celts.
- Allow them one or two minutes to discuss what they remember with a talk partner, before asking them to share their ideas with the rest of the class.

Whole-class work

- Divide the board in two and ask the children to share their ideas about how the Celts and Romans differed.
- For a more challenging activity, use a Venn diagram and ask the children to suggest items for Celts, Romans or both (for example: the Celts had basic dwellings, lived in tribes and were ruled by kings and queens; the Romans had luxurious villas for the rich, were united under the Roman Empire and were ruled by the emperor; both loved jewellery, used coins and enjoyed feasting).
- Read through photocopiable page 203 'Celts and Romans' as a class, which contains a table for the children to complete with information about the Celtic and Roman ways of life.

Group work or Paired work

- Divide children into groups or pairs and give each a copy of the photocopiable sheet. Ask them to complete the table, either by using their existing knowledge or by using books or the internet to research information. Children could select one or two categories to write about, or challenge them to cover them all.

Differentiation

- Support: children could work in a small group with adult support.
- Challenge: children should analyse the similarities between Celts and Romans as well as the differences.

Review

- Tell each group to swap their work with a different group; they should add any points they missed to their own table. Repeat this activity one or more times, until each group has roughly the same information.
- In class discussion, check that they have covered all the key points. Ask questions such as: *What was the same/different about Roman and Celtic homes/clothes/leisure activities?* (The Celts lived in roundhouses, which were very simple compared with the Roman villas; the Romans wore togas and tunics, while the Celts wore brightly coloured, often checked trousers, skirts or dresses; both enjoyed board games, hunting and feasting but the Romans also watched chariot races and gladiator fights.) *Did both own slaves?* (No, only the Romans did.) *Who were they ruled by?* (The Romans were ruled by an emperor; the Celts had tribal kings and queens.) *How did they fight?* (The Romans were much better organised, with more technological weapons and were therefore more successful in battle; the Celts looked fierce, with their noisy chariots, bleached, spiked hair and so on, but didn't have such effective weapons or military training.)

Lesson objectives

- To know about the Roman Empire and its impact on Britain, including 'Romanisation' of Britain: the impact of technology, culture and beliefs.
- To develop a chronologically secure knowledge and understanding of British, local and world history, establishing clear narratives within and across the periods they study.
- To note connections, contrasts and trends over time and develop the appropriate use of historical terms.
- To regularly address and sometimes devise historically valid questions about change, cause, similarity and difference, and significance.
- To construct informed responses that involve thoughtful selection and organisation of relevant historical information.

Expected outcomes

- All children will identify at least one difference between Celtic and Roman ways of life.
- Most children will describe some differences between Celtic and Roman ways of life.
- Some children will compare Celtic and Roman ways of life, describing both similarities and differences.

Resources

Photocopiable page 203 'Celts and Romans'; internet access or reference books about Romans and Celts (optional)

Lesson objectives
● To know about the Roman Empire and its impact on Britain, including 'Romanisation' of Britain: the impact of technology, culture and beliefs.
● To develop a chronologically secure knowledge and understanding of British, local and world history, establishing clear narratives within and across the periods they study.
● To note connections, contrasts and trends over time and develop the appropriate use of historical terms.
● To regularly address and sometimes devise historically valid questions about change, cause, similarity and difference, and significance.
● To construct informed responses that involve thoughtful selection and organisation of relevant historical information.

Expected outcomes
● All children will identify at least one difference between Celtic warriors and the Roman army.
● Most children will create a movement piece to represent the contrast between Celtic warriors and the Roman army.
● Some children will describe Celtic warriors and the Roman army in terms of advantages and disadvantages against their opponents.

Resources
Sugar paper and marker pen; photocopiable page 203 'Celts and Romans' (completed sheet from previous lesson); suitable space for movement (for example, school hall, playing field)

2: How did Celtic warriors compare with the Roman army?

Introduction
● Ask the children to review and discuss what they know about Celtic and Roman warfare and weaponry, referring to their notes on photocopiable page 203 'Celts and Romans' if necessary.
● Ask the children to come up with adjectives to describe each fighting style (fierce, aggressive, chaotic, organised, efficient, and so on) and write these on sugar paper.

Whole-class work
● Tell the children that they are going to use movement and physical theatre to portray the fighting styles of the Celtic warriors and of the Roman army (they have already had practice forming a testudo as Roman soldiers).
● Remind them of the adjectives they came up with to describe the Celts and Romans. As a warm up, have the children move around the room. Call out the adjectives one by one and ask the children to incorporate them into their movement. (Remind them about working a safe distance apart – they must not touch each other.)

Independent work or Paired work
● Give the children time to practise portraying first Roman soldiers and then Celtic warriors, using freeze frames then travelling forward. Encourage them to use facial expression as well as body language.
● They could work in pairs, helping each other to work on their poses, movements and facial expressions.

Differentiation
● Support: mixed-ability grouping may be beneficial.

Review
● Split the class into four groups. Select two to be Celts and two to be Romans.
● Pair one of the Celtic groups with one of the Roman groups and ask the other children to sit down and observe as the groups perform their movements facing one another – first one at a time, then both together. Ask the 'audience' to comment on the effectiveness of the chosen movements in portraying the Celtic or Roman style. Ask: *Was it obvious which group was which? Why were their movements and postures suitable for their roles? What worked well? What could be improved?*
● Have the groups swap over so the audience becomes the performers and vice versa.
● Ask: *What advantages would the Celtic warriors have over the Romans?* (The Celts would know the area and land they were fighting on, and could use existing hill forts.) *What disadvantages would they encounter?* (They lacked the armour, weapons, skill and training of the Roman soldiers.)

Week 2 lesson plans

This week focuses on when and why the Romans invaded Britain. Children develop their skills in using timelines as they create a timeline of the important events in Roman British history. They then explore what historians believe to be the main reasons the Romans chose to invade Britain.

1: When did the Romans invade Britain?

Introduction

- Remind children of the concept of BC (Before Christ) and AD (Anno Domini – in the year of Our Lord). Write ten different dates (for example, 37BC, AD49, and so on) on sticky notes or scrap paper and hand them to different children. Ask the first child to call out his or her date and to come and stand at the front, facing the class.
- One by one, the others should call out their dates and stand to the first child's right for an earlier date or left for a later date. Eventually the children should be in a line in correct date order.
- Ask the rest of the class to check that they are in the right order, and to correct them as necessary.

Whole-class work

- Give the children five minutes to recall as much as they can about the Roman Empire and its way of life.
- Tell the children that Britain also became part of the Roman Empire for a period of time.
- Talk through photocopiable page 'Roman Britain timeline' from the CD-ROM. Remind children about timelines – what they show and how they are used. Ask: *Why are these events important enough to be included on a timeline? How can we begin to place them in order?*

Paired work or Independent work

- Ask the children to create a timeline in their books or on paper, cutting out the events from the photocopiable sheet and arranging them in the correct order along the timeline.

Differentiation

- Support: children can work with adult support to place a selection of the events on the photocopiable sheet in order.
- Challenge: children can be expected to create more complex timelines, which show the time differences to scale. As they progress through the topic, they may wish to add other important dates to the timeline.

Review

- Tell the children to look at the timelines they have created. Ask: *How does the way the timeline is set out make it easier to understand when important events occurred?*
- Ask them to discuss, in groups, questions that they would like answered about the Roman period in Britain. They should record these either on sticky notes or in their books, before discussing their ideas as a class.

Lesson objectives

- To know about the Roman Empire and its impact on Britain.
- To develop a chronologically secure knowledge and understanding of British, local and world history, establishing clear narratives within and across the periods they study.
- To develop the appropriate use of historical terms.
- To regularly address and sometimes devise historically valid questions about change, cause, similarity and difference, and significance.

Expected outcomes

- All children will discuss what timelines show.
- Most children will order events to create a timeline of Roman Britain.
- Some children will discuss the relationship between different events on a timeline of Roman Britain.

Resources

Sticky notes or scrap paper; photocopiable page 'Roman Britain timeline' from the CD-ROM; scissors; glue

2: Why did the Romans invade Britain?

Lesson objectives
● To know about the Roman Empire and its impact on Britain.
● To develop a chronologically secure knowledge and understanding of British, local and world history, establishing clear narratives within and across the periods they study.
● To develop the appropriate use of historical terms.
● To regularly address and sometimes devise historically valid questions about change, cause, similarity and difference, and significance.

Expected outcomes
● All children will name a reason why the Romans invaded Britain.
● Most children will describe some of the main reasons why Romans invaded Britain.
● Some children will give a more complex analysis of the reasons for the Roman invasion.

Resources
Materials for letter writing

Introduction
● Explain the differences between invaders (forceful) and settlers (peaceful).
● Ask: *Were the Romans invaders or settlers? What makes you think this?* (They were invaders: they wanted to rule over the Celts, rather than live with them peacefully, and were prepared to fight in order to gain control.)

Whole-class work
● Tell the children that the Romans are thought to have had a number of reasons for invading Britain:
   ● Revenge – British tribes were thought to be helping the Gauls (in what is now France) to fight against the Roman invaders there.
   ● Wealth – Britain was believed to have many natural resources, such as iron, gold, silver, copper and lead, as well as land, grain and slaves.
   ● Prestige – A victory in Britain and the expansion of the Roman Empire would bring glory to the conqueror.
● Discuss each reason in terms of why this might motivate the Romans to invade. Ask questions such as: *Why might revenge have been important to the Romans?* (It would have consolidated their position as rulers and discouraged further rebellions.) *What natural resources did Britain have that the Romans wanted? What would they have done with these resources? Why do you think the Roman emperors valued prestige and glory?* (It would have consolidated their position as ruler; they wanted to be remembered as powerful, successful leaders.)

Independent work or Paired work
● Tell the children that Britain was seen to be a dark, mysterious island with poor weather and home to many fierce tribes, so the Romans would have needed some persuading in order to invade.
● Ask the children to imagine that they are advisers to the Roman leaders. They should write a letter convincing them that invading Britain is a good idea, explaining their reasons (including those discussed).
● If necessary, discuss the features of a persuasive letter (powerful adjectives, repetition, counter argument, facts, formal language, and so on) making a list on the board for the children to refer to throughout the lesson.

Differentiation
● Support: children could discuss their ideas in a small group with adult support.
● Challenge: children should provide more detailed analysis of the reasons for invading in their persuasive letters, as well as providing counter arguments for the Roman trepidation.

Review
● Invite some children to share their letters.
● Ask the rest of the class: *Would this letter have persuaded you? Why/Why not? Which is the strongest reason for invasion? Were there any risks involved?* (Invasions were costly in terms of money, resources and lives. If the invasion was unsuccessful this might have brought shame rather than glory; it also might have strengthened the position of the Celts, encouraging them to take further action against the Romans in France.)

Week 3 lesson plans

This week helps children to develop their analytical skills as they learn about the life of Julius Caesar and consider why he was both loved and hated. They then role play members of a Celtic tribe, speculating about the Celts' reaction to the Roman invasion, before finding out what actually happened in 55BC and 54BC.

1: Who was Julius Caesar?

Introduction

- Tell the children that two months of the year are named after Roman leaders. Can they guess which ones? (July and August).
- Remind children of Emperor Julius Caesar, who featured on the Roman timeline they created in the previous week. Ask: *Which month might have been named after Julius – what does it sound like?* Explain that the Romans named July after Julius Caesar. (August was named after Augustus, who succeeded Julius Caesar).
- Tell the children that this lesson, they are going to learn about why Caesar was so important.

Whole-class work

- Show the children an image of a statue of Julius Caesar (source online). Ask them to come up with words to describe how the sculptor has depicted him (for example, determined, powerful).
- Work through interactive activity 'Julius Caesar interview' on the CD-ROM as a class or in groups. This activity allows the children to 'interview' Julius Caesar, by clicking on questions about his life and achievements, to reveal his answers.

Group work

- Split the class into two groups. Write on the board: 'Julius Caesar was a great man'.
- Ask one half of the class to argue in favour of this statement and the other half to argue against it. The children could use only the information from the interactive activity to help them or they could carry out additional research into Caesar's life.

Differentiation
- Support: groups should include a fairly even spread of ability.

Review

- Hold a class debate exploring Julius Caesar's merits and faults.
- Ask: *Julius Caesar died over 2000 years ago; why do you think he is still remembered today? Why might Julius Caesar have been both loved and hated? How did Julius Caesar influence the course of Rome's history? How are today's leaders similar to or different from Caesar?*

Lesson objectives
- To know about the Roman Empire and its impact on Britain, including: the Roman Empire by AD42; Julius Caesar's attempted invasion in 55–54BC.
- To develop a chronologically secure knowledge and understanding of British, local and world history, establishing clear narratives within and across the periods they study.
- To regularly address and sometimes devise historically valid questions about change, cause, similarity and difference, and significance.

Expected outcomes
- All children will know that Julius Caesar was a famous Roman.
- Most children will describe some of the events in Julius Caesar's life.
- Some children will describe how Julius Caesar influenced Rome's history.

Resources
Image of a statue of Julius Caesar (source online); interactive activity 'Julius Caesar interview' on the CD-ROM; internet access (optional)

Lesson objectives
● To know about the Roman Empire and its impact on Britain, including Julius Caesar's attempted invasion in 55-54BC.
● To develop a chronologically secure knowledge and understanding of British, local and world history, establishing clear narratives within and across the periods they study.
● To regularly address and sometimes devise historically valid questions about change, cause, similarity and difference, and significance.

Expected outcomes
● All children will know that the Romans invaded but withdrew from Britain in 55 and 54BC.
● Most children will discuss the Celts' possible reaction to the Roman invaders.
● Some children will analyse the success of Julius Caesar's invasions.

Resources
Completed timelines from photocopiable page 'Roman Britain timeline' from week 2; photocopiable pages 'The Romans are coming' and 'Julius Caesar's invasion of Britain' from the CD-ROM

2: What happened when Julius Caesar attempted to invade Britain?

Introduction
● Tell the children to look again at their timelines from week 2. Ask: *When did Julius Caesar invade Britain?* (55BC and 54BC)

Group work
● Organise the children into groups of seven. Tell them to imagine that it is 55BC and they are members of Celtic tribes. Explain that a tribal member has seen a Roman warship off the coast and it looks as though the Romans are about to invade their lands. They have met together to decide what to do.
● Within each group, give six children a cut-out role card from photocopiable page 'The Romans are coming' from the CD-ROM. The seventh child will take the role of the tribal chief or king. He or she should listen to the arguments and decide whether the tribe will fight the Romans or try to make peace with them. Note: the children with the cards should role play their designated character and not simply read out what is on the card.

Whole-class work
● Ask the 'kings' to share what their group has discussed and the decision reached.
● Now they are going to find out what happened when the Romans did invade in 55BC and 54BC. Read through the information about the first two invasions of Britain by Julius Caesar on photocopiable page 'Julius Caesar's invasion of Britain' from the CD-ROM.
● Ask: *Were these invasions a complete failure for the Romans?* Establish that the Roman withdrawal could indicate a failed full invasion or a moderately successful reconnaissance trip to increase the Roman's knowledge about the Britons' capabilities.

Differentiation
● Support: children could work with adult support to elicit their ideas.

Review
● Hold a quick quiz to check the children's understanding of the events of 55BC and 54BC. Split the class into two teams, with the person who puts their hand up first answering the question (or choose children) and a point for each correct answer. Ask questions such as:
1. How many legions of men did Caesar take in the first invasion (2)
2. How many in the second? (5)
3. How did the soldiers get to shore in the first invasion? (Waded.)
4. What happened the second time? (Caesar took ships that could land on beaches.)
5. Where did the Celts attack in 55BC? (At the coast.)
6. Give one reason why Caesar withdrew in 55BC. (Shortage of food; stormy weather; unpredictable tides nearly destroying the ships.)
7. Where did the Celts attack in 54BC? (By a river, 12 miles inland.)
8. Who led the attack in 54BC? (Cassivellaunus.)
9. Why did Caesar withdraw after the second invasion? (Trouble in Gaul.)
10. How could Caesar's invasion be said to be a success for Caesar? (Useful reconnaissance trips; he chose to withdraw – they weren't actually defeated.)

Week 4 lesson plans

This week focuses on the events of the successful Roman invasion by Claudius in AD43 and the British resistance. Children read about the invasion and answer comprehension questions. They then explore Caratacus' eight-year resistance of the Roman invaders through performance poetry.

I: How did the Roman invasion in AD43 take place?

Lesson objectives
- To know about the Roman Empire and its impact on Britain, including the successful invasion by Claudius and conquest.
- To develop a chronologically secure knowledge and understanding of British, local and world history, establishing clear narratives within and across the periods they study.
- To regularly address and sometimes devise historically valid questions about change, cause, similarity and difference, and significance.

Expected outcomes
- All children will know that Britain was invaded successfully by the Romans in AD43.
- Most children will describe the main events of the Roman invasion of AD43.
- Some children will describe the build-up to and causes and main events of the Roman invasion of AD43.

Resources
Photocopiable page 204 'Roman invasion in AD43'

Introduction
- Give the children an 'answer' (for example, Julius Caesar, the Roman army, or 54) and ask them to provide suggestions for what the question might be (for example: When was the second Roman invasion of Britain?)

Whole-class work
- Read through and discuss the information about the Roman invasion by Claudius on photocopiable page 204 'Roman Invasion in AD43'.
- The photocopiable sheet includes a set of questions for the children to answer. Discuss anything the children are unclear about before they start the questions.

Paired work or Independent work
- Ask the children to work through the comprehension questions on the photocopiable sheet.

> **Differentiation**
> - Support: children should complete the first six questions only.

Review
- Go through the answers to the questions on the photocopiable sheet, as follows:
    1. Claudius was Emperor.
    2. 40,000 soldiers were sent to Britain.
    3. The Medway and the Thames were sites of battles.
    4. Camulodunum (Colchester) was captured.
    5. Aulus Plautius was the first Roman governor of Britain.
    6. Vespasian continued the invasion in AD44.
    7. Claudius invaded Britain because his position was insecure; he needed the glory of a victory to increase his popularity and secure his position.
    8. Some tribes would have surrendered because they realised that the Romans were more successful in battle and that if they were able to live peacefully with the Romans, they could also benefit from their roads, baths, buildings and so on.
    9. This invasion was perhaps more successful because of the knowledge gained from the previous ones. Claudius planned the invasion carefully and took more men than Julius Caesar did.
    10. How the Celts felt about living under Roman rule probably would have depended on how they were treated. Some Celts would have been happy to live under Roman rule if allowed to keep their land, and have access to Roman luxuries and technologies. Others may have been enslaved, or would have resented living in an occupied country.

Lesson objectives
● To know about the Roman Empire and its impact on Britain, including the successful invasion by Claudius and conquest; and British resistance.
● To develop a chronologically secure knowledge and understanding of British, local and world history, establishing clear narratives within and across the periods they study.
● To regularly address and sometimes devise historically valid questions about change, cause, similarity and difference, and significance.

Expected outcomes
● All children will know that Caratacus resisted the Roman invaders.
● Most children will participate in performing a poem about Caratacus' resistance of the Romans.
● Some children will describe why Caratacus was allowed to live.

Resources
Photocopiable page 'Caratacus' from the CD-ROM

2: Who was Caratacus?

Introduction
● Ask the children to recall the differences between the Celtic warriors and Roman soldiers in terms of the advantages and disadvantages for each side (different weapons, dress, battle formations, knowledge of the lie of the land, and so on – see week 1).

Whole-class work
● In this lesson, children will perform a poem about the life of Caratacus, leader of the Catuvellauni tribe. Caratacus fought the Romans for many years but was eventually pushed back into the Welsh mountains. He then fled to the Brigantes tribe in Northern England and was handed over to the Romans by its leader, Queen Cartimandua. He was taken to Rome, where his boldness impressed the emperor, and he was allowed to live there for the rest of his life. He famously remarked, 'And can you, then, who have got such possessions, and so many of them, covet our poor tents?'
● Read through and discuss photocopiable page 'Caratacus' from the CD-ROM, as a class. This contains a poem about Caratacus. Practise reading the poem aloud several times.
● Tell the children that they are going to create a performance around the poem. Talk about different ways to make the performance interesting for an audience. How could they use their voices? Could they incorporate any of the movements they put together when exploring Celt warriors and Roman soldiers in week 1?

Group work
● Split the class into five groups. Depending on ability, and the time available, the groups could perform the whole poem or one stanza each.
● After a rehearsal period, bring the groups together to see what they have put together. Alternatively, this could be developed into a performance for an assembly.

> ### Differentiation
> ● Support: mixed-ability groupings may be beneficial.
> ● Challenge: children could write their own stanzas or full poems on the same theme.

Review
● Tell the groups to perform their poems, or stanzas, to the rest of the class. Invite positive criticism, asking questions such as: *How do their actions support what's being described in the poem? What did you like about this performance?*
● Ask additional questions to elicit the children's understanding of the life and significance of Caratacus, such as: *Why is Caratacus remembered today? What tribe was he from? Why might the queen of the Brigante tribe have turned him over to the Romans?* (She was pro-Roman and a truce existed between the Brigantes and the Romans.) *Why did the Roman emperor let him live?*

Week 5 lesson plans

This week explores where the Romans settled in Britain and introduces the children to Queen Boudica, who is further explored in the following week. Children locate major Roman towns and cities on a map of Roman Britain. They read a Roman description of Boudica and use this to create a portrait of her. They also explore the two societies' differing attitudes towards women.

1: Where did Romans settle in Britain?

Introduction

- Write 'Londinium', 'Lutonium' and 'Mamucium' on the board (or include Roman names for locations near your school).
- Ask the children to guess which modern day cities or towns began as these Roman locations (London, Luton and Manchester).

Whole-class work

- Ask: *How do you think historians know where the Romans settled in Britain?* Talk about the use of written evidence as well as excavations of Roman sites around the country. (Next term, they may visit a Roman archaeological site.)
- Show a picture of the Roman walls around Chester or the Roman baths in Bath as examples of Roman remains (source online). Ask the children to point out any features of Roman architecture that they recognise from previous lessons, such as columns, arches, stone carvings, pediments, and so on.
- Tell the children that many places around the UK today were founded by the Romans, though they now have different names.

Group work or Paired work

- Using atlases and the map on photocopiable page 205 'Map of Roman Britain', ask the children to label the locations with the main Roman cities, as listed on the sheet.

> **Differentiation**
> - Mixed-ability groupings or pairings may be beneficial.
> - Challenge: children may wish to research Roman remains in some of the locations mentioned.

Review

- Ask several children to come and add location labels to the map on the photocopiable sheet displayed on the whiteboard. (Photocopiable page 'Map of Roman Britain (answers)' from the CD-ROM has the map with the labels in place.)
- Ask: *Why might the Romans have settled in these locations?* (Factors such as landscape, food and water supply, and natural resources would need to be considered, as well as how aggressive or welcoming Celtic tribes were in different regions.)

Lesson objectives
- To know about the Roman Empire and its impact on Britain, including 'Romanisation' of Britain.
- To develop a chronologically secure knowledge and understanding of British, local and world history, establishing clear narratives within and across the periods they study.
- To regularly address and sometimes devise historically valid questions about change, cause, similarity and difference, and significance.

Expected outcomes
- All children will know that the Romans settled in many locations across Britain.
- Most children will label some major Roman towns and cities on a map of Roman Britain.
- Some children will compare Roman Britain with Britain today.

Resources
Image of Roman walls around Chester, or Roman baths in Bath (source online); atlases; photocopiable page 205 'Map of Roman Britain'; photocopiable page 'Map of Roman Britain (answers)' from the CD-ROM

Lesson objectives

● To know about the Roman Empire and its impact on Britain, including British resistance, for example, Boudica.
● To develop a chronologically secure knowledge and understanding of British, local and world history, establishing clear narratives within and across the periods they study.
● To understand how our knowledge of the past is constructed from a range of sources.
● To regularly address and sometimes devise historically valid questions about change, cause, similarity and difference, and significance.

Expected outcomes

● All children will describe Boudica's appearance.
● Most children will use a description of Boudica to create a portrait of her.
● Some children will compare the Roman and Celtic attitude towards women.

Resources

Photocopiable page 'Boudica' from the CD-ROM; media resource 'Boudica' on the CD-ROM; art paper; paints or drawing materials

2: Who was Queen Boudica and what was she like?

Introduction

● Ask: *Would it be better to be a Celtic woman or a Roman woman?* Discuss the advantages and disadvantages of being a woman in each society, considering the female role and attitude towards women in each.
● Through the discussion try to cover the following points: although Celtic society was largely dominated by men, Celtic women could nevertheless become warriors, queens (such as Cartimandua), druids, diplomats, poets and healers, and they could conduct business without permission from their husbands. Roman women were not allowed to vote, hold public office or fight in the army but many wealthy girls would have been educated, and women were relatively free socially; wealthy Roman women enjoyed the latest fashions and hairstyles and lived a luxurious lifestyle; pastimes included weaving, sewing, spinning or perhaps managing a household in a husband's absence.

Whole-class work

● Read photocopiable page 'Boudica' from the CD-ROM and listen to media resource 'Boudica' on the CD-ROM.
● Discuss the description of Boudica by Cassius Dio. Explain that Cassius Dio was a Roman historian, and that the text was written over a hundred years after Boudica's rebellion.
● Ask: *What does this text tell us about what Boudica did? What does it tell us about her appearance? How do you think the Romans felt about Boudica? What does the description tell us about the Roman attitude towards women? How might this compare to the Celtic view of women? How reliable is this text as evidence?*

Paired work or Independent work

● Ask the children to listen to the description of Boudica's appearance again. They should imagine that they have been asked to create a portrait of Boudica for the National Gallery. This description is the only evidence they have of what she looked like.
● The children can use the photocopiable sheet to create either their finished portraits or, if preferred, a preliminary sketch before creating their portraits on art paper.

Differentiation

● Support: children could concentrate on one or two features in order to create their portraits; portraits could be drawn using computer software as an alternative.

Review

● Create a class display of the portraits, or show some at the front of the class.
● Ask: *How does this portrait reflect the written evidence? What impression do we get of Boudica from all these portraits? Why do the portraits look different, even though you all used the same written evidence? What was missing from the written evidence – what did you have to imagine when creating your portraits?*

Week 6 lesson plans

This week furthers children's understanding of Queen Boudica and her revolt against the Romans. They consider the main events and outcomes of Boudica's rebellion, creating a storyboard to depict them. They then consider the different viewpoints that the Romans and the Celts might have had towards Boudica.

I: What happened during Boudica's rebellion?

Lesson objectives
● To know about the Roman Empire and its impact on Britain, including British resistance, for example, Boudica.
● To develop a chronologically secure knowledge and understanding of British, local and world history, establishing clear narratives within and across the periods they study.

Expected outcomes
● All children will know that Boudica led a revolt against the Romans in AD61.
● Most children will help to create a storyboard to show the main events of Boudica's rebellion.
● Some children will consider the events and outcomes of Boudica's rebellion in more detail.

Resources
Photocopiable page 'Boudica's rebellion' from the CD-ROM (enlarged to A3 – optional)

Introduction
● Give the children a minute to write down as many adjectives to describe Boudica as they can, before sharing them in class discussion.
● As the children share their ideas, ask: *Why does Boudica make you think of that adjective?*

Whole-class work
● Tell children that they are now going to learn more about Boudica's rebellion against the Romans in AD61.
● Read through and discuss the main events of the revolt on photocopiable page 'Boudica's rebellion' from the CD-ROM.

Group work, Paired work or Independent work
● Tell the children that they are going to create a storyboard of the events of the revolt. This can be organised in a number of ways. Children could work in pairs or as individuals to create an entire storyboard. They could draw directly onto the photocopiable sheet (ideally enlarged to A3).
● Alternatively, create a large storyboard for display around the classroom, using the text on the photocopiable sheet as a guide. Children could work in groups or pairs, taking responsibility for drawing a particular scene. As well as images, they could expand the written text to include dialogue and description.

> **Differentiation**
> ● Support: children could create a simple storyboard, involving a single scene.
> ● Challenge: children could create a complex storyboard, covering all the major events of the rebellion through images and written text.

Review
● If the children have created one large storyboard, jumble up the pieces of paper and ask different children to hold one sheet each at the front of the class. The rest of the children have to put them into the correct order to tell the history of Boudica's rebellion. If the children have created a storyboard each, this activity could be completed by writing key points on sticky notes, or scraps of paper.
● Ask questions to check their understanding of the events, such as: *Why did the Iceni live peacefully with the Romans before Prasutagus died? What happened after he died? Which cities did Boudica attack? Why might you have expected Boudica and her warriors to have defeated the Romans?*

Lesson objectives

● To know about the Roman Empire and its impact on Britain, including British resistance, for example, Boudica.
● To develop a chronologically secure knowledge and understanding of British, local and world history, establishing clear narratives within and across the periods they study.
● To understand how our knowledge of the past is constructed from a range of sources.
● To understand that different versions of past events may exist, giving some reasons for this.

Expected outcomes

● All children will know that the Romans and Celts viewed Boudica differently.
● Most children will write a paragraph to show contrasting viewpoints of Boudica.
● Some children will be able to describe the bias that can be found in written accounts of people and events.

Resources

Media resource 'Boudica' on the CD-ROM

2: Why might opinions about Boudica have differed?

Introduction

● Invite one child to role play Boudica in the 'hot-seat' while other children ask her questions about her rebellion, such as: *Why did you choose to rebel? How did you feel when the Romans broke their agreement with Prasutagus after he died? Why do you think you and your tribe were defeated, despite having far more warriors? Why did you poison yourself?*

Whole-class work

● Ask the children to again listen to Cassius Dio's description of Boudica on media resource 'Boudica' on the CD-ROM, making notes about her appearance.
● Discuss how the Romans might have felt about her (for example, they might have been fearful of her ferocity, and humiliated by the fact that she was a woman).
● Ask: *How might the Romans' opinion of Boudica have differed from the opinion of the Celts? Was Boudica a fierce butcher or a brave heroine? How might each side have felt about the fact that she slaughtered Britons as well as Romans when she attacked the towns?* Write some notes on the board for the children to refer to when completing their writing task later in the lesson.
● Discuss the phrase 'History is written by the winners'. Ask: *What does this mean?* Talk about the fact that written accounts can be biased in favour of the people in charge at the time.

Independent work or Paired work

● Tell the children to divide their page in two and write a paragraph or more on each side describing Boudica. One side should be from the point of view of a Celtic warrior and the other side from the perspective of a Roman soldier.
● Model writing one or two sentences from one perspective, if necessary.

> **Differentiation**
> ● Support: children could discuss their ideas rather than write them down.
> ● Challenge: children could write from the point of view of a Celtic and Roman woman, exploring the gender roles in each group.

Review

● Invite some children to read one of their descriptions to the rest of the class, without telling them from which perspective it has been written. Ask the rest of the class to say whether it's the Celtic or Roman point of view. Ask: *How do you know?*

Lesson objectives
● To know about the Roman Empire and its impact on Britain.
● To develop a chronologically secure knowledge and understanding of British, local and world history, establishing clear narratives within and across the periods they study.

Resources
Sticky notes or cards; interactive activity 'Y4 Summer 1 quiz' on the CD-ROM

Roman Britain quiz (1)

Revise

● Write the following names on sticky notes or cards: Julius Caesar, Emperor Claudius, Caratacus, Boudica.
● Ask four children to come out the front of the class and place a sticky note or card on their forehead. They must guess who they are and can ask the rest of the class up to 20 questions (requiring a 'yes' or 'no' answer) in order to find out.

Assess

● Ask the children to complete interactive activity 'Y4 Summer 1 quiz' on the CD-ROM, in which they answer multiple-choice questions covering the chapter content.
● Give children a set length of time (for example, 15 minutes) to answer the questions. This can be used as part of a formal assessment or as a fun challenge activity, giving children the opportunity to show what they have learned about the topic.
● Less confident readers may need adult support to read the questions aloud.

Further practice

● Ask children to create a board game in which players portray the Roman army trying to conquer Britain. They should use a grid of squares (for example, six by six) and write triumphs in some (for example, 'You capture a hill fort. Move forward three spaces.') and setbacks in others (for example, 'Caratacus and his warriors attack. Move back two spaces.').

Lesson objectives
● To know about the Roman Empire and its impact on Britain, including Julius Caesar's attempted invasion in 55–54BC; and British resistance, for example, Boudica.
● To understand how our knowledge of the past is constructed from a range of sources and that different versions of past events may exist, giving some reasons for this.

Resources
Writing materials

Boudica and Julius Caesar

Revise

● Ask the children to recap the different methods that historians use to find out about the past and think of examples of how these could be used to find out about Roman Britain (for example, the archaeological site of St Albans, Roman artefacts like coins or pottery, Roman eyewitness accounts of Boudica) and what they have told historians about Roman Britain.

Assess

● Talk about the evidence we have for what Boudica and Julius Caesar were like. (Cassius Dio's description of Boudica; Julius Cesar's own writings, descriptions of him by other Romans, busts, coins, and so on) Ask: *Who do we have more evidence about? Can we believe this evidence?*
● Tell the children to write two paragraphs about Boudica and two about Julius Caesar. The first should be from the Roman point of view and the second from the Celt point of view.

Further practice

● Ask children to write a diary from Boudica's viewpoint, covering the course of her rebellion.
● Look back at the questions the children wrote in week 2, which covered what they wanted to know about Roman Britain. Are they able to answer any of these questions now?

Name: _____   Date: _____

Celts and Romans

- Complete this table to show how Iron Age Celtic life compared with Roman life.

	Celts	Romans
Homes		
Clothing and appearance		
What they did for fun		
Who they were ruled by		
Slaves		
Warfare and weapons		
Religion		

- Were there any similarities between the Iron Age Celts and the Romans? Write your answer on the back of this sheet.

I can compare the Celts and Romans.

How did you do?

Roman invasion in AD43

It was nearly a hundred years before the Romans decided to return to Britain. Emperor Claudius was in charge but his position as leader was unstable. A victory in Britain would win him popularity and secure his place as emperor. He planned the invasion carefully, sending around 40,000 soldiers commanded by Aulus Plautius to Britain in early summer, AD43.

The Romans and Celtic Catuvellauni tribe (led by their king, Caratacus, and his brother, Togodumnus) fought a mighty battle over two days by the River Medway and another battle on the River Thames. The Celts were defeated, Togodumnus was killed and Caratacus withdrew. (Eight years later he was defeated and captured.) Emperor Claudius himself arrived in Britain in late summer to oversee the Roman success. The Romans captured the important city of Camulodunum (Colchester) and were now in control of the whole of south-east Britain. Eleven kings from different Celtic tribes surrendered to the Romans and Aulus Plautius was appointed the first Roman governor of Britain.

The invasion continued the following year under the Roman general Vespasian, who captured many hill forts in southern Britain.

Over the next 50 years, the Romans continued to take control and settle in many areas of Britain. Although some Celts organised revolts and were defeated, many surrendered and lived in peace with the Romans. They paid taxes to the Romans for their lands, but also got to enjoy many of the luxuries and technology that the Romans brought with them.

Questions

1. Who was emperor at the time of the invasion?
2. Which two rivers were locations for battles between the Celts and Romans?
3. Who became the first Roman governor of Britain?
4. Which Roman general continued the invasion in AD44?
5. Why did the emperor decide to invade Britain?
6. Why do you think some Celtic tribes surrendered to the Romans?
7. Why do you think this invasion was more successful than the previous ones?
8. How do you think the Celts felt about living under Roman rule?

I can answer questions about the Roman invasion of AD43.

How did you do?

Map of Roman Britain

■ Using an atlas, label these Roman towns and cities on the map of England and Wales.

Aquae Sulis (Bath)	**Camulodunum** (Colchester)	**Deva** (Chester)
Isca (Exeter)	**Glevum** (Gloucester)	**Verulamium** (St Albans)
Lindum (Lincoln)	**Londinium** (London)	**Mamucium** (Manchester)
Ratae (Leicester)	**Dunovernum Cantiacorum** (Canterbury)	

I can label a map of England and Wales with Roman towns and cities.

How did you do?

Roman Britain (2)

This chapter continues the chronological narrative of British history. Having learned about the invasion of Britain by the Romans, children explore what life was like in Roman Britain, for both Romans and Celts. They consider the impact of Roman technology, culture and beliefs and form their own opinions regarding whether this impact was positive or negative. Finally, they are given the opportunity to frame their own historically valid questions as they create an end-of-year project or presentation on a theme of their choice around the topic.

Chapter at a glance

Curriculum objectives

• The Roman Empire and its impact on Britain, including 'Romanisation' of Britain': sites such as Caerwent and the impact of technology, culture and beliefs, including early Christianity; successful invasion by Claudius and conquest, including Hadrian's Wall.

Week	Lesson	Summary of activities	Expected outcomes
1	1	• Children discuss the role of local government in Roman Britain, comparing it to government today.	• Can describe the way Roman Britain was organised.
	2	• Children write a diary entry describing life in a Romano-British town.	• Can describe life in a town in Roman Britain.
2	1	• Children work in groups to build a groma surveying tool and use it to mark straight lines.	• Can describe the construction of Roman roads in Britain.
	2	• Children complete a comprehension exercise about the spread of early Christianity and Saint Alban.	• Can describe the beginnings of early Christianity in Britain.
3	1	• Children write about some of the advantages and disadvantages for the Celts of Roman rule.	• Can describe how life for the Celts changed under Roman rule.
	2	• Children investigate Roman archaeological sites in the UK via the internet.	• Can understand how archaeological sites like Caerwent give us information about the Roman period.
4	1	• Children discuss why Hadrian's Wall was constructed then create their own Hadrian's Wall quiz.	• Can describe why Hadrian's Wall was built.
	2	• Children explore the Vindolanda tablets before writing a letter from the viewpoint of a Roman soldier at Hadrian's Wall.	• Can describe what life might have been like for a soldier on a Hadrian's wall fort.
5	1	• Children visit a local Roman site to make observations.	• Can describe a Roman site in their local area.
	2	• Children select a topic and create a plan for an independent project or presentation on the theme of Roman Britain.	• Can create a presentation about an aspect of Romano-British life.
6	1	• Children continue work on their project or presentation on the theme of Roman Britain.	• Can create a presentation about an aspect of Romano-British life.
	2	• Children complete and share their project or presentation on the theme of Roman Britain.	• Can present their own information about an aspect of Romano-British life.
Assess and review		• To review the half-term's work.	

Expected prior learning

● This chapter is a continuation of the topic of Roman Britain. Children should be familiar with the life of the Iron Age Celts prior to the Roman invasion. They should also be familiar with the main events of the invasion, British resistance and where the Romans settled.
● Children should also have covered the chapter on Rome and its empire, and therefore be familiar with Roman domestic life, customs, religion and military strength.

Overview of progression

● Children will develop their understanding of the themes of cause, consequence and change as they consider the impact of the 'Romanisation' of Britain – both negative and positive consequences.
● They will develop their understanding of the use of archaeological evidence as they examine Roman sites such as Caerwent, the Roman baths at Bath, Hadrian's Wall and Vindolanda fort, and artefacts such as the Vindolanda tablets. Optionally, they pay a visit to a Roman site within their local area to make observations.
● They are also given the opportunity to devise and research their own historically valid questions in an end-of-year project. More confident learners will be able to draw comparisons between Roman and modern times and analyse trends over time, considering the legacy of the Romans today.

Creative context

Cross-curricular opportunities include:
　● building a groma surveying tool, which enabled Romans to build straight or perpendicular roads;
　● a reading comprehension; writing a diary; letter writing; researching a project; speaking and listening.

Background knowledge

● After Boudica's rebellion, the Romans and Celts settled into a largely peaceful coexistence. Many Celtic tribal kings were involved in the local government of their regions and enjoyed the technology and luxurious lifestyle the Romans brought with them.
● The 'Romanisation' of Britain included building a network of roads, facilitating travel and trade and enabling speedy mobilisation of the Roman army. Roman towns brought new culture and technologies such as aqueducts for fresh water supplies, public baths and good sanitation.
● Evidence of the Roman period exists in many archaeological sites around Britain, including Hadrian's Wall. Although the Romans ruled most of Britain, they'd had difficulty keeping the Picts in Caledonia (Scotland) under control. The popular belief is that Hadrian's Wall was built for the purpose of controlling people passing back and forth across the border of the Roman Empire and preventing raids on Roman property.
● At Vindolanda, one of the forts along Hadrian's Wall, a number of handwritten tablets were discovered in 1973. These provide snippets of army life in Roman Britain.
● Today, the legacy of the Romans can be seen in many aspects of British life, including: our language; Christianity; coins (originally featuring the head of the Emperor); local government and taxation; and Britain's network of roads, many of which follow the old Roman routes.

Lesson objectives
● To know about the Roman Empire and its impact on Britain, including 'Romanisation' of Britain: the impact of technology, culture and beliefs.
● To develop a chronologically secure knowledge and understanding of British, local and world history, establishing clear narratives within and across the periods they study.
● To note connections, contrasts and trends over time and develop the appropriate use of historical terms.
● To regularly address and sometimes devise historically valid questions about change, cause, similarity and difference, and significance.

Expected outcomes
● All children will know that the Romans controlled Britain through local government.
● Most children will describe the basic system of local government in Roman Britain.
● Some children will consider the benefits of the Roman system of local government and compare it with government today.

Resources
Interactive activity 'How was Roman Britain organised?' on the CD-ROM

Week 1 lesson plans

This week focuses on when and why the Romans invaded Britain. Children develop their skills in using timelines as they create a timeline of the important events in Romano-British history. They then explore what historians believe to be the main reasons the Romans chose to invade Britain.

1: How was Roman Britain organised?

Introduction
● Discuss the structure of British local government today (for example, explain that the national government is responsible for major decisions affecting the country, such as defence, health and foreign affairs, while local government is responsible for decisions in their area, such as libraries, waste disposal, local roads and schools).

Whole-class work
● Ask: *What do you think were some of the problems the Romans faced when they started their rule in Britain?* (Answers could include: Celtic rebellions; lack of knowledge of the land, language, people; different climate; no infrastructure, compared to what they were used to.)

Group work
● Divide the children into groups and ask them to complete the missing words activity in interactive activity 'How Was Roman Britain organised?' on the CD-ROM. This activity provides some information about how the Romans governed, pacified the Celts, collected taxes and kept law and order.
● Ask the children to discuss these questions:
  ● Why was it a clever idea to involve the wealthy Celts in the governing process?
  ● How might the ordinary Celts have felt about their kings being involved in local Roman government?
  ● What similarities and differences are there between the way the Romans organised Britain and the way it is organised today?

> **Differentiation**
> ● Support: mixed-ability groupings may be beneficial; children could work in a small group, sharing their ideas with adult support.
> ● Challenge: children could be encouraged to consider some of the wider questions, such as the morality of the use of capital punishment versus its potential effectiveness as a deterrent of crime.

Review
● Discuss the answers to the questions as a class. By the end of the discussion the children should be aware that: involving wealthy Celts in the governing process meant that they were less likely to rebel against it and more likely to benefit from the system, and that once the wealthy Celts were on side, they would have brought the rest of the tribe with them; ordinary Celts may have felt suspicious when their kings and queens became involved in government, but this might also have reassured them that they could live peacefully with the Romans and even benefit from the knowledge and technology they brought with them; like the ancient Romans, modern government also uses a system of taxation to pay for public services, with each region having its own local government, but capital punishment is no longer used.
● Ask the following additional questions if time allows: *Why don't you think the governor was put in charge of his area's finances? Do you think the tax system was fair?*

Lesson objectives
● To know about the Roman Empire and its impact on Britain, including 'Romanisation' of Britain: the impact of technology, culture and beliefs.
● To develop a chronologically secure knowledge and understanding of British, local and world history, establishing clear narratives within and across the periods they study.
● To note connections, contrasts and trends over time and develop the appropriate use of historical terms.
● To regularly address and sometimes devise historically valid questions about change, cause, similarity and difference, and significance.

Expected outcomes
● All children will describe some features of towns in Roman Britain.
● Most children will create a diary entry describing a day in a town in Roman Britain.
● Some children will provide detailed description of different features of life in a town in Roman Britain.

Resources
Photocopiable page 'Town life in Roman Britain' from the CD-ROM

2: What was life like in a Romano-British town?

Introduction
● Ask the children to describe some of the features of their local town, suburb or village. Ask: *Where do we do our shopping? What entertainment is there? Where do we socialise? What are our houses like?*

Whole-class work
● Tell the children that the Romans built many towns in Britain and that they brought their own culture, style and technology with them.
● Read through and discuss photocopiable page 'Town life in Roman Britain' from the CD-ROM. This explains the various features of Roman towns (public baths, the basilica, forum, temples, and so on) and describes how they were used.
● Ask the children to share their ideas about what it would be like to visit some of the town's attractions. Ask: *Who might you meet there? What might people be doing? What might you hear, see and smell?*
● Encourage them to draw comparisons between the features of a Roman town and the features of their local area. For example, is there a special council building for government and administration? Are there places of worship? Is there a public swimming pool, gymnasium or another place in which people spend their leisure time?

Paired work or Independent work
● Ask the children to imagine that they are able to go back in time and spend a day in a town in Roman Britain. Ask: *How would you spend your day? What would you do?*
● Ask them to write a diary entry describing their day in Roman Britain. They could use the photocopiable sheet for ideas. They should consider whether they are writing as a wealthy Roman, a tradesperson or someone very poor. How might this dictate how they spend their time and what they can afford to do? How might this affect how people treat them?

Differentiation
● Support: children could write a few sentences only or share ideas verbally with a supporting adult.
● Challenge: children should complete a detailed diary with vivid description, feelings and an exciting narrative.

Review
● Invite some children to share their diary entries. Ask: *Was this written by a wealthy person or a poor person? How do you know? Would you like to spend a day in this way?*
● Ask the following additional questions: *What would be some of the best things about visiting a town in Roman Britain? What wouldn't be so good? How do towns in Roman Britain compare with towns today?*

Week 2 lesson plans

The first lesson this week continues to explore the technology that the Romans introduced to Britain: the building of roads and their impact on travel and trade. Children construct a groma surveying tool in order to understand how straight roads were created. The second lesson explores the spread of early Christianity and Saint Alban, Britain's first martyr, with children completing comprehension questions.

1: How were Roman roads built?

Introduction

● Show the children an image of a modern road. Ask: *What are our roads made from? What are they used for? Who uses them?*

Whole-class work

● Show the children an image of a Roman road (for example, the Appian Way leading to Rome, or the streets of Pompeii – source online). Ask: *What do you notice about it? What is it made from? How is it similar to one of our roads? How does it differ? Who might have used it? How might they be travelling?*
● Read and discuss the first three paragraphs of photocopiable page 221 'Roman roads'. Ask: *How do you think Roman roads benefitted the army? How did they benefit traders?* Encourage their understanding that the roads helped to unite Britain as a nation by creating trade links and joining together places that had been largely isolated.

Group work

● Split the children into small groups and give each a set of materials to build a groma (two straight sticks or rulers, one short pole, some longer poles or markers, four pieces of string, tape for binding and modelling clay to make weights).
● Ask the children to read through the last two paragraphs on the photocopiable sheet, which describe how Roman roads were planned.
● Give them time to discuss and plan, and then construct, their own Roman groma models.
● They should then go into an open space and try using their groma to mark out straight lines with poles or markers.

Differentiation

● Support: mixed-ability groupings may be beneficial; adult support may be needed to help bind the materials together.
● Challenge: children should be encouraged to think about the benefits of the roads in terms of travel and trade, as well as in helping to bring Britain together. They could look at a modern road map to look for roads that follow the Roman routes (for example, the A2 and A5).

Review

● Ask each group to show their 'roads' and discuss how they were made. What worked well? What did they find difficult?
● Explain that their roads are short, so they can probably see if they are straight using their naked eye; Roman roads were very long, and going off-course, which would not have been seen easily over a long distance, would have made a big difference to where the road ended up.

Lesson objectives
● To know about the Roman Empire and its impact on Britain, including 'Romanisation' of Britain: the impact of technology, culture and beliefs.
● To develop a chronologically secure knowledge and understanding of British, local and world history, establishing clear narratives within and across the periods they study.
● To note connections, contrasts and trends over time and develop the appropriate use of historical terms.
● To regularly address and sometimes devise historically valid questions about change, cause, similarity and difference, and significance.

Expected outcomes
● All children will know that the Romans built roads around Britain.
● Most children will describe where and how Roman roads were built.
● Some children will discuss the impact of the Roman roads on travel and trade in Britain.

Resources
Image of a modern road and Roman road (source online); photocopiable page 221 'Roman roads'; straight sticks or rulers; short poles; longer poles or markers; string; tape; modelling clay; open space (such as school hall or playground)

Lesson objectives
● To know about the Roman Empire and its impact on Britain, including 'Romanisation of Britain': the impact of technology, culture and beliefs, including early Christianity.
● To develop a chronologically secure knowledge and understanding of British, local and world history, establishing clear narratives within and across the periods they study.
● To note connections, contrasts and trends over time and develop the appropriate use of historical terms.
● To regularly address and sometimes devise historically valid questions about change, cause, similarity and difference, and significance.

Expected outcomes
● All children will describe at least two facts about early Christianity.
● Most children will answer basic comprehension questions about early Christianity.
● Some children will also be able to retell the story of Saint Alban in their own words.

Resources
Photocopiable page 'Early Christianity' from the CD-ROM

2: How did Christianity begin in Britain?

Introduction
● Talk about the fact that we have many different religions in the UK today. Invite some children to describe briefly their own religious beliefs, if appropriate.
● Explain that in 2011 a government census discovered that there were 33.2 million Christians in the UK – 59 per cent of the population. Remind the children that the Iron Age Celts weren't Christians. Ask: *Who do you think brought Christianity to Britain?* (The children may already be aware that this was the Romans, from discussions in previous lessons.)

Whole-class work
● Tell the children that they are going to learn about how Christianity began and how it spread as a religion all over the world. Explain that Christianity began in Britain during Roman times.
● Ask the children what they already know about Jesus Christ.
● Read through and discuss photocopiable page 'Early Christianity' from the CD-ROM, which gives an overview of how Christianity spread through the Roman Empire.

Independent work or Paired work
● Ask children to complete the comprehension questions on the photocopiable sheet.

Group work
● Organise the children into groups and ask them to create a two-minute play to depict the story of Saint Alban (optional).

Differentiation
● Support: children should answer the first five questions only, which relate to the first two paragraphs.
● Challenge: children should complete all the questions, including the more reflective questions towards the end.

Review
● Invite the groups to perform their plays depicting the story of Saint Alban.
● Check the children's answers to the comprehension questions, as follows:
  1. Jesus lived in Judea.
  2. When Jesus died, his followers travelled the world sharing his teachings.
  3. Alban gave shelter to a priest, who converted him.
  4. Alban wore the priest's cloak and was arrested instead of the priest.
  5. Verulamium is now known as St Albans.
  6. Christianity became the main religion in the Roman Empire when Constantine the Great became Christian, in the fourth century.
  7. A martyr is someone who dies for their beliefs.
  8. Answers will vary.

Week 3 lesson plans

This week, children bring together their knowledge of the changes to Britain made by the Romans in order to consider whether the Celts were better or worse off under Roman rule. They then consolidate their understanding of the use of archaeological evidence in building a picture of the past as they explore Roman ruins around Britain via the internet.

1: How did life for the Celts change under Roman rule?

Lesson objectives
● To know about the Roman Empire and its impact on Britain, including 'Romanisation' of Britain: the impact of technology, culture and beliefs.
● To develop a chronologically secure knowledge and understanding of British, local and world history, establishing clear narratives within and across the periods they study.
● To note connections, contrasts and trends over time.
● To regularly address and sometimes devise historically valid questions about change, cause, similarity and difference, and significance.

Expected outcomes
● All children will know that there were advantages and disadvantages for the Celts under Roman rule.
● Most children will describe some advantages and disadvantages for the Celts under Roman rule.
● Some children will show analysis of the advantages and disadvantages for the Celts under Roman rule.

Resources
Photocopiable page 222 'Life under Roman rule'

Introduction
● Allow the children one minute to recall some of the ways that the Romans changed Britain (building towns and roads; introducing aqueducts, sanitation and public baths; facilitating trade, and so on).

Whole-class work
● Write on the board: *Was life for the Celts better or worse under Roman rule?* Hold a class discussion to gather children's initial ideas.
● Read the ideas on photocopiable page 222 'Life under Roman rule'. Look at one or two more closely, and decide whether they would be points for or against Roman rule.

Paired work or Independent work
● Tell the children to complete the photocopiable sheet in pairs.
● Explain that the speech bubbles represent the opinions of two Celts. They should fill them in, showing the reasons for each Celt's feelings about the Romans, using the arguments at the bottom of the sheet.

Group work
● Split the class in half. Ask one half to prepare points to argue in favour of Roman rule and the other half against, ready for a debate at the end of the lesson. They should try to think of their own ideas, in addition to the ideas on the sheet. (Additional points supporting the Romans could include good roads making travel easier, and aqueducts bringing fresh water; additional points against could include having to obey Roman laws, having to pay taxes in order to keep land they already owned, and having less freedom.)
● Two children could prepare a persuasive speech (one for and one against the motion 'The Celts were better off under Roman rule') to begin the debate. They could consider how the Roman presence might have had different effects depending on whether the Celts were rich or poor.

Differentiation
● Support: children could work in a small group with adult support; they could cut out the ideas from the bottom of the photocopiable sheet and arrange them as either an advantage or disadvantage of Roman rule.
● Challenge: children should be encouraged to reflect on the different effects of Roman rule on rich or poor Celts.

Review
● When the children have had time to prepare their ideas, hold a class debate followed by a vote.
● After the vote, ask any children who haven't contributed to the debate to explain why they voted for or against the motion.

Lesson objectives

● To know about the Roman Empire and its impact on Britain, including sites such as Caerwent and Hadrian's Wall.
● To develop a chronologically secure knowledge and understanding of British, local and world history, establishing clear narratives within and across the periods they study.
● To note connections, contrasts and trends over time.
● To regularly address and sometimes devise historically valid questions about change, cause, similarity and difference, and significance.
● To understand how our knowledge of the past is constructed from a range of sources.

Expected outcomes

● All children will know that archaeological sites from Roman Britain exist in the UK.
● Most children will discuss the importance of archaeological sites in finding out about the past.
● Some children will make their own deductions about the past from archaeological evidence.

Resources

An unusual object; internet access

2: What do Roman sites tell us about Roman Britain?

Introduction

● Pass round an object unfamiliar to the class. Invite volunteers to give a description of what the object is used for (in the style of *Call My Bluff*). Ask the other children to guess which, if any, description is correct.
● Remind the children that archaeologists piece together information about the past in the same way. Reveal the object's true purpose, or keep them guessing – sometimes historians never find out for certain if their assumptions are correct.

Group work or Paired work

● Tell the class that they are going to be looking at some images of Roman ruins in the UK.
● Organise the children into groups or pairs and give them time to explore Roman sites (such as Caerwent in Wales, the Roman baths in Bath, or the Roman city of Wroxeter) online. Useful websites include: www.roman-britain.org, www.romanbaths.co.uk, and www.historvius.com.
● Tell the children to choose an image of one of the sites and either to draw or print it. They could then surround it with different questions an archaeologist might ask (for example: What happened here? Who used this building/ room?) alongside the answer, found online. Encourage the children to write the answers to their questions using their own words; they should not copy sentences directly from the websites.
● Alternatively, they could write bullet points based on the website information.

Differentiation

● Support: mixed-ability groupings or pairings may be beneficial, or children could work with adult support to explore one of the sites.
● Challenge: children can be expected to create more complex questions or facts.

Review

● Divide the class into groups of four and tell the children to present their findings to each other, within the group. Bring the children back together as a whole class. Ask: *What is the most interesting thing you have learnt? How was the site you researched similar to or different from the sites the rest of your group studied?*
● Alternatively, invite one or two children to show the picture of their site to the rest of the class. Then hold a question and answer session – where the other children direct questions to the child at the front about their Roman site.

Week 4 lesson plans

This week focuses on Hadrian's Wall. The children discuss possible reasons to explain why the wall was built and create a Hadrian's Wall quiz. They examine some of the writing tablets found in Vindolanda and then write a letter from the viewpoint of a soldier stationed at the barracks.

1: Why was Hadrian's Wall built?

Introduction
● Write a letter of the alphabet on the board and give the children a minute to come up with as many words related to Roman Britain beginning with that letter as they can.

Whole-class work
● Show a selection of images or footage of Hadrian's Wall (source online). Tell the children that the Romans built a wall to divide northern and southern Britain, which was begun in AD122. Ask: *Why do you think it might be called Hadrian's Wall? Who do you think Hadrian was?*
● Read through photocopiable page 'Hadrian's Wall' from the CD-ROM, as a class, and discuss each of the reasons given for its construction.
● Divide the classroom into four sections (one for each reason) and ask the children to stand in a section according to which they think is the main reason the wall was built.

Group work or Paired work
● Split children into small groups or pairs. They should use the photocopiable sheet and/or research Hadrian's Wall online and produce a Hadrian's Wall quiz, based on facts about the Wall (for example: How long is the wall? When was it built? Who guarded it?)
● As an alternative activity, the children could produce a scale model of the wall.

> **Differentiation**
> ● Support: children could work in a small group with an adult to discuss the different reasons for the wall being built and produce a sheet of facts.

Review
● Invite one group or pair to act as quiz masters/mistresses and divide the rest of the class into teams. The quiz could be organised in various ways, for example: each team could write down their answers and the teams could then mark each other's papers at the end of the quiz; the person who puts up their hand first, at the end of each question, could answer the question and score a point for their team; or each team could be asked two or three questions, with other teams allowed the opportunity to answer any the first team gets wrong.

Lesson objectives
● To know about the Roman Empire and its impact on Britain, including sites such as Caerwent and Hadrian's Wall.
● To develop a chronologically secure knowledge and understanding of British, local and world history, establishing clear narratives within and across the periods they study.
● To note connections, contrasts and trends over time.
● To regularly address and sometimes devise historically valid questions about change, cause, similarity and difference, and significance.
● To understand how our knowledge of the past is constructed from a range of sources.

Expected outcomes
● All children will know that the Vindolanda tablets have helped to tell us about the past.
● Most children will write a letter from the point of view of a Roman soldier at Vindolanda.
● Some children will use written and archaeological evidence to demonstrate understanding of a soldier's life.

Resources
Images of Vindolanda and the tablets (source online); photocopiable page 'Hadrian's Wall' from the CD-ROM

2: What was life like for a soldier at a Hadrian's Wall fort?

Introduction
● Use one of the children's Hadrian's Wall quizzes from the previous lesson to test the class (a different quiz from the one used at the end of the previous lesson).

Whole-class work
● Tell the children that there was an important archaeological find at Vindolanda, one of the forts along Hadrian's Wall – writing tablets – which revealed snippets of information about life in the army barracks.
● Look at some images of the tablets (source online). Explain that the tablets were very thin pieces of wood, on which the Romans wrote in ink, and that they were found in oxygen-free parts of the remains of the fort; they are the oldest surviving handwritten documents in Britain.
● Read or describe some of the inscriptions on the tablets. For example:
  ● 'The Britons are unprotected by armour. There are very many cavalry. The cavalry do not use swords nor do the wretched Britons mount in order to throw javelins.'
  ● 'I have sent you ... pairs of socks from Sattua, two pairs of sandals and two pairs of underpants.'
  ● 'Claudia Severa to her Lepidina greetings. On 11 September, sister, for the day of the celebration of my birthday, I give you a warm invitation to make sure that you come to us, to make the day more enjoyable for me by your arrival... I shall expect you, sister. Farewell, sister, my dearest soul, as I hope to prosper, and hail.'
● More information about the tablets and the messages inscribed on them can be found at http://www.vindolanda.csad.ox.ac.uk.

Group work
● Show the children an image of a reconstruction, or the ruins, of Vindolanda fort (source online). Ask them to imagine that they are soldiers stationed in the barracks there. They should write a letter home to their mother and father describing their life.
● As much as possible, the children should use the letter to demonstrate their knowledge of Roman Britain, the Roman army and Hadrian's Wall. For example, they may describe a Pict attack or talk about the weather in Britain. They should refer to photocopiable page 'Hadrian's Wall' from the CD-ROM, and the quizzes from the previous lesson for ideas.
● It might be helpful to ask the children some questions to get them started, such as: *What might the daily life of the soldier be like? What sort of duties might he perform? How might he feel about life in Britain?*

Differentiation
● Support: children could work in a small group with an adult to look at images of Vindolanda and discuss what a soldier's life there might have been like.
● Challenge: children should use the archaeological and written evidence to form the basis of their letter.

Review
● Invite some children to share their letters with the rest of the class.
● Ask: *Would you have liked to have been a soldier stationed in one of the forts along Hadrian's Wall? Why/Why not?*

Week 5 lesson plans

This week begins to draw the topic of Roman Britain to a climax. If possible, children pay a visit to a Roman site within the local area to make observations. Finally, they are given the opportunity to carry out some independent research on an aspect of Roman Britain that interests them, coming up with their own historically valid question to explore.

1: What can we learn from a local Roman site? (optional)

Introduction

● This lesson is designed for use if there is a Roman site within reach for a school trip.
● Before leaving, ask the children to think of some questions that they would like to investigate at the site (for example: When was it built? Who used it?).

Whole-class work

● Investigate the site before the trip, referring to websites or leaflets. This could be a general exploration, or the children could be given a specific focus (such as the layout of the building/s, the materials used, artwork, and so on).

Paired work or Independent work

● Give children a copy of photocopiable page 223 'Investigating a Roman site', which contains questions to guide their visit.
● It may be useful for children to have extra paper or clipboards, if available, to make notes during their visit.
● Children could also draw objects or sections of the site.

Differentiation
● Support: mixed-ability pairings may be beneficial.

Review

● Back in the classroom, talk through the children's thoughts about the trip and the things they have learned.

Lesson objectives

● To know about the Roman Empire and its impact on Britain, including 'Romanisation' of Britain: the impact of technology, culture and beliefs.
● To develop a chronologically secure knowledge and understanding of British, local and world history, establishing clear narratives within and across the periods they study.
● To note connections, contrasts and trends over time.
● To regularly address and sometimes devise historically valid questions about change, cause, similarity and difference, and significance.
● To understand how our knowledge of the past is constructed from a range of sources.
● To understand that different versions of past events may exist, giving some reasons for this.

Expected outcomes

● All children will make basic observations about a visit to a Roman site.
● Most children will make more complex observations about a visit to a Roman site.
● Some children will demonstrate in-depth reflection on a visit to a Roman site.

Resources

Photocopiable page 223 'Investigating a Roman site'; clipboards (optional)

■ SCHOLASTIC
www.scholastic.co.uk

Lesson objectives
- To know about the Roman Empire and its impact on Britain, including 'Romanisation' of Britain: the impact of technology, culture and beliefs.
- To develop a chronologically secure knowledge and understanding of British, local and world history, establishing clear narratives within and across the periods they study.
- To note connections, contrasts and trends over time.
- To regularly address and sometimes devise historically valid questions about change, cause, similarity and difference, and significance.
- To understand how our knowledge of the past is constructed from a range of sources.

Expected outcomes
- All children will describe an aspect of life in Roman Britain.
- Most children will create a project/presentation about an aspect of life in Roman Britain.
- Some children will create a project/presentation considering the legacy of Roman Britain.

Resources
Internet access or reference books on Roman Britain

2: What was life like in Roman Britain? (1)

Introduction
- Invite each child to say one thing they have learned about Roman Britain.
- Ask: *What have you enjoyed learning about most?*

Whole-class work
- Explain to the children that for the next three lessons they will be working on a project about an aspect of Roman life. Projects allow children the opportunity to carry out some independent research into an area of their choice, answering their own historically valid questions. They will be planned and put together over the next three lessons, though children could also complete some work at home. Children can work on their projects individually or in pairs. It may be beneficial to allow them the freedom to choose the format of their project (for example, booklet, poster, oral presentation, slideshow).
- List suggestions on the board for what the project might cover (for example, Roman leisure activities, aqueducts, Roman clothing, Celtic and Roman gods and goddesses, Boudica, Hadrian's Wall).
- Talk about how to turn their areas of interest into historically valid questions that can be investigated (for example: What did Romans do for fun? Why and how did the Romans build aqueducts?) This may be a good opportunity to refer to the questions for investigation that children raised at the beginning of the Roman Britain topic (see summer 1, week 2).

Paired work or Independent work
- Children create a plan for their projects or presentations. Allow them to begin to research their questions, using the internet or reference books, when ready.

Differentiation
- Support: children could create simple A4 sheets containing bulleted facts and images, or they could present their work orally.
- Challenge: children should be encouraged to choose a more complex topic, such as the legacy of Roman Britain today, or the impact of the Romans on Celtic life.

Review
- Check the children's progress. Make sure that all children have chosen a topic and have a historically valid question to answer.

Week 6 lesson plans

This week, children continue work on their independent projects or presentations, finding information to help answer their historically valid questions. Finally, they have the opportunity to share their work with the rest of the class.

I: What was life like in Roman Britain? (2)

Introduction

- Tell the children to talk about their project work so far, with a partner. Give them the opportunity to ask questions or request assistance if needed. Ask: *What are you finding enjoyable or difficult about independent work?*
- Remind the children of the kinds of criteria that make a good project or presentation (for example: being eye catching and clear – using subheadings and bullet points; including images and interesting information or ideas).

Paired work or Independent work

- Give the children time to work on their projects or presentations; circulate around the class, helping where necessary.

Differentiation

- Support: children could create simple A4 sheets containing bulleted facts and images, or they could present their work orally.
- Challenge: children should be encouraged to choose a more complex topic, such as the legacy of Roman Britain today, or the impact of the Romans on Celtic life.

Review

- Check the children's progress at the end of the lesson. Remind them that they only have a small amount of time in the next lesson in which to complete their projects.

Lesson objectives

- To know about the Roman Empire and its impact on Britain, including 'Romanisation' of Britain: the impact of technology, culture and beliefs.
- To develop a chronologically secure knowledge and understanding of British, local and world history, establishing clear narratives within and across the periods they study.
- To note connections, contrasts and trends over time.
- To regularly address and sometimes devise historically valid questions about change, cause, similarity and difference, and significance.
- To understand how our knowledge of the past is constructed from a range of sources.

Expected outcomes

- All children will describe an aspect of life in Roman Britain.
- Most children will continue work on a project about an aspect of life in Roman Britain.
- Some children will continue work on a project considering the legacy of Roman Britain.

Resources

Internet access or reference books on Roman Britain

Lesson objectives

● To know about the Roman Empire and its impact on Britain, including 'Romanisation' of Britain: the impact of technology, culture and beliefs.
● To develop a chronologically secure knowledge and understanding of British, local and world history, establishing clear narratives within and across the periods they study.
● To note connections, contrasts and trends over time.
● To regularly address and sometimes devise historically valid questions about change, cause, similarity and difference, and significance.
● To understand how our knowledge of the past is constructed from a range of sources.

Expected outcomes

● All children will describe an aspect of life in Roman Britain.
● Most children will complete and share a project about an aspect of life in Roman Britain.
● Some children will complete and share a project considering the legacy of Roman Britain.

Resources

Internet access or suitable books on Roman Britain

2: What was life like in Roman Britain? (3)

Introduction

● Remind children of features of a good project discussed in the previous lesson, this time also emphasising the importance of the presentation being easy to see and hear.

Paired work or Independent work

● Allow the children time to put the finishing touches to their projects or presentations. Circulate around the class, helping where necessary.

Differentiation

● Support: children could create simple A4 sheets containing bulleted facts and images, or they could present their work orally.
● Challenge: children should be encouraged to show in-depth reflection and analysis of a more complex topic, such as the legacy of Roman Britain today, or the impact of the Romans on Celtic life.

Review

● Give each child or pair the opportunity to give their presentation or show and discuss their project in front of the rest of the class.
● Invite children to offer constructive praise to their peers.

Lesson objectives
● To know about the Roman Empire and its impact on Britain.
● To develop a chronologically secure knowledge and understanding of British, local and world history, establishing clear narratives within and across the periods they study.

Resources
Interactive activity 'Y4 Summer 2 quiz' on the CD-ROM

Roman Britain quiz (2)

Revise
● Hold a class debate around the following question: *Overall, was the Roman invasion and settlement a good or bad thing for Britain?*

Assess
● Ask the children to complete interactive activity 'Y4 Summer 2 quiz' on the CD-ROM, in which they answer multiple-choice questions covering the chapter content.
● Give children a set length of time (for example, 15 minutes) to answer the questions. This can be used as part of a formal assessment or as a fun challenge activity, giving children the opportunity to show what they have learned about the topic.
● Less confident readers may need adult support to read the questions aloud.

Further practice
● Ask the children to discuss or write down a list of similarities and differences between the ancient Greek and ancient Roman civilisations.

Lesson objectives
● To know about the Roman Empire and its impact on Britain.
● To construct informed responses that involve thoughtful selection and organisation of relevant historical information.

Resources
Children's Roman Britain projects or presentations

Roman Britain project review

Revise
● As a class, come up with a list of sub-topics the children have covered under the overall topic of Roman Britain (for example: Celt warriors versus Roman soldiers; Julius Caesar's invasion; rebellions of Caratacus and Boudica; Hadrian's Wall; Roman roads; Roman towns).

Assess
● Ask the children to write a review of their own project or presentation, answering the follow questions:
  ● What question did you investigate?
  ● Why did you choose this topic?
  ● How did you research your topic?
  ● How did you organise your information?
  ● What worked well?
  ● How could your work have been improved?
  ● What was most challenging?
  ● What questions about Roman Britain would you now like to investigate?

Further practice
● Ask the children to devise a short drama scene, poem or mini presentation for a Roman Britain assembly.

Name: _____   Date: _____

Roman roads

What were British roads like before the Romans?

Before the Romans arrived, roads in Britain tended to be disorganised mud or timber paths, which connected fields and local villages. There were few major roads designed to help people move great distances.

Why did the Romans build their own roads?

The Romans needed to be able to move their army and transport supplies around Britain quickly and easily.

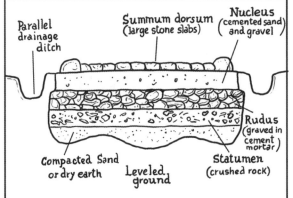

Where were Roman roads built?

Romans built roads to link together their major towns. For example Londinium (London) was linked to Deva (Chester), Dubris (Dover), Lindum (Lincoln), Noviomagus (Chichester) and Camelodunum (Colchester). The roads were built as straight as they could be to make the route as short as possible.

How were Roman roads constructed?

To construct the roads, the Romans dug a trench and added a layer of large stones. The next layer contained sand, broken stones, pebbles and cement. Onto that was poured more cement containing broken tiles. On top were laid flat stones, which were cut to fit together. These were built in a curve so rainwater ran to the sides. Large stones were placed at the sides and trenches built to drain the water away.

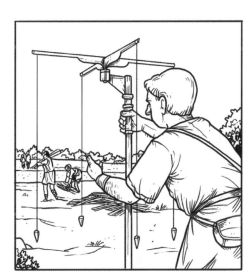

How were Roman roads planned?

Skilled surveyors planned out the route for roads very carefully, using special tools. A groma was used to make sure the roads were straight. It consisted of two straight sticks crossed at right angles on top of a pole. A length of string was attached to each of the four corners of the cross and a weight hung at each end. The surveyor would look along the line of the two strings that followed the direction of the road, to make sure they lined up, and direct his assistant where to place a pole in the ground. The straight line of poles would provide the layout of the roads to be built.

■ Use the text and picture above to help you to build your own groma.
■ You will need: 2 straight sticks or rulers, 1 short pole, some longer poles or markers, 4 pieces of string, tape for binding and modelling clay to make weights.

Life under Roman rule

■ Complete the two speech bubbles with the ideas from the bottom of the page.

I hate life under the Romans because...

Life under the Romans is great because...

We are expected to worship Roman gods.	We have Roman fashion and style.	Celts can join the Roman army.
More goods are available because trade is easier.	We have sewage systems and improved hygiene.	We are expected to speak Latin.
New foods have been introduced.	We have public baths and toilets	Rich Celts want to live in Roman-style villas.

I can consider arguments for and against life under Roman rule in Britain.

How did you do?

Investigating a Roman site

■ Complete the tasks in the boxes as you investigate the Roman site.

Write some words to describe the site.

Why do you think the Romans chose this location?

What was this site or building used for? Who might have used it?

Which materials have been used? Why were these chosen?

What have you learned that you did not know before?

I can carry out research into an archaeological site.

How did you do?

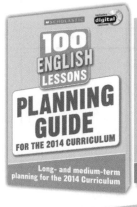 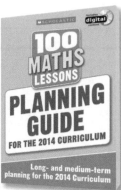 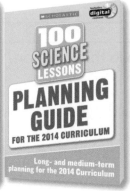  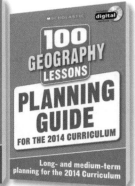
   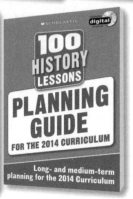